HUNGER IN AMERICA 2006

A project of
America's Second Harvest—
The Nation's Food Bank Network

Full Report

March 2006

Rhoda Cohen
Myoung Kim
Jim Ohls

Submitted to:

America's Second Harvest—The Nation's
  Food Bank Network
35 E. Wacker Drive, Suite 2000
Chicago, IL 60601

Douglas O'Brien
  Vice President of Public Policy and Research
Halley Torres Aldeen
  Director of Research and Analysis

Submitted by:

Mathematica Policy Research, Inc.
P.O. Box 2393
Princeton, NJ 08543-2393
(609) 799-3535

Rhoda Cohen
  Project Director

ACKNOWLEDGMENTS

We would like to acknowledge the strong support and vision of the staff at America's Second Harvest, Doug O'Brien, Halley Aldeen, and Teff Uchima, who provided sound guidance and strong support throughout the research process. The quality of the product was also much improved through the participation of the Technical Advisory Group: John Cook, Beth Osborne Daponte, Steve Carlson, Kirk Johnson, Lynn Parker, Jan Poppendieck, Martha Raske, Ken Rice, Rob Santos, and Tommy Wright.

Also, a number of staff from Mathematica Policy Research, Inc. (MPR) made important contributions, which contributed to the success of the project. Frank Potter, working with Zhanyun Zhao, developed and implemented the sampling plan and developed the analysis weights for the project, with the assistance of Yuhong Zheng and Cathy Lu. MPR internal advisors, including Ronette Briefel, Barbara Carlson, John Hall, Donsig Jang, Dan Kasprzyk, and Stuart Kerachsky made many important suggestions for the analysis and reports.

On the survey side, Daniel Gundersen and Laurie Bach spent long hours obtaining the sample frames from the food banks and providing feedback to them throughout the sampling process. The data they obtained were placed in a comprehensive computer tracking database developed by Shilpa Khambati. Jim Cashion worked tirelessly to update and produce the training video for affiliates to use in training large numbers of field interviewers. He also coordinated the work of our subcontractor, Questar, in processing the completed instruments to generate electronic data files for the analysis team.

Marcia Comly, Loring Funaki, Cheryl Lichtenstein, Michael Smith, Marcia Tobias, and Lawrence Vittoriano provided guidance to the Second Harvest affiliates on an ongoing basis as they implemented the survey work. More than 85 staff at MPR's Survey Operations Center, under the leadership of Susan Golden and Rachel Reed, assisted in reviewing and preparing the completed questionnaires for shipment to Questar.

Jeffrey Holt and Jacob Rugh, with assistance from Amy Zambrowski, provided critical and advanced programming skills on the complex analysis database needed to produce the report. Carlo Cummings-Caci offered extraordinary computer skills in enhancing and implementing a system to expeditiously generate more than 150 local reports from the analysis database. Bill Garrett provided exceptional secretarial support throughout the process. The competency and flexibility demonstrated by all involved were key factors in the success of the project.

CONTENTS

CONTENTS (*continued*)

CONTENTS (*continued*)

CONTENTS (*continued*)

Chapter   **Page**

CONTENTS (*continued*)

Chapter

Page

CONTENTS (*continued*)

CHARTS

CHARTS *(continued)*

CHARTS *(continued)*

Chart   **Page**

TABLES

TABLES *(continued)*

Table		**Page**

TABLES *(continued)*

Table		Page

TABLES *(continued)*

TABLES *(continued)*

Table		Page

TABLES *(continued)*

Table   **Page**

1. HIGHLIGHTS OF FINDINGS

This report presents the result of a study conducted in 2005 for America's Second Harvest—The Nation's Food Bank Network (A2H), the nation's largest network of emergency food providers. The study is based on completed in-person interviews with 52,878 clients served by the A2H National Network, as well as on completed questionnaires from 31,342 A2H agencies. The study summarized below focuses mainly on emergency food providers and their clients who are supplied with food and other services by members of the A2H Network. Here, emergency food providers are defined to include food pantries, soup kitchens, and emergency shelters serving short-term residents. It should be recognized that many other types of provider organizations and programs served by food banks are, for the most part, *not* described in this study. These providers who are not covered included such services as congregate meals for seniors, day care facilities, and after school programs.

Key findings are summarized below:

HOW MANY CLIENTS RECEIVED EMERGENCY FOOD FROM THE A2H NETWORK OF FOOD BANKS?

- The A2H system served an estimated 24 to 27 million unduplicated people annually, with a midpoint of 25.3 million. This includes 22 to 25 million pantry users, 1.2 to 1.4 million kitchen users, and 0.8 million shelter users (Table 4.2.1).

- Approximately 4.5 million different people receive emergency food assistance from the A2H system in any given week (Table 4.2.1).

WHO RECEIVES EMERGENCY FOOD ASSISTANCE?

A2H Network agencies serve a broad cross-section of households in America. Estimates of key characteristics include:

- 36.4% of the members of households served by the A2H National Network are children under 18 years old (Table 5.3.2).

- 8% of the members of households are children age 0 to 5 years (Table 5.3.2).

- 10% of the members of households are elderly ages 65 or older (Table 5.3.2).

- About 40% of clients are non-Hispanic white, 38% are non-Hispanic black, 17% are Hispanic (Table 5.6.1).

- 36% of households include at least one employed adult (Table 5.7.1).

- 68% of households had incomes below the official federal poverty level (Table 5.8.2.1) during the previous month.

- 12% are homeless (Table 5.9.1.1).

MANY A2H CLIENTS ARE FOOD INSECURE OR ARE EXPERIENCING HUNGER

- Among all client households served by emergency food programs of the A2H National Network, 70% are estimated to be food insecure, according to the U.S. government's official food security scale. This includes client households who are food insecure without hunger and those who are food insecure with hunger (Table 6.1.1).

- 33% of the clients have experienced hunger (Table 6.1.1).

- Among households with children, 73% are food insecure and 31% have experienced hunger (Table 6.1.1).

MANY CLIENT HOUSEHOLDS REPORT HAVING TO CHOOSE BETWEEN FOOD AND OTHER NECESSITIES

- 42% of households served by the A2H National Network report having to choose between paying for food and paying for utilities or heating fuel (Table 6.5.1).

- 35% of households had to choose between paying for food and paying their rent or mortgage (Table 6.5.1).

- 32% of households had to choose between paying for food and paying for medicine or medical care (Table 6.5.1).

DO A2H CLIENTS ALSO RECEIVE FOOD ASSISTANCE FROM THE GOVERNMENT?

- 35% of client households served by the A2H National Network are receiving Food Stamp Program benefits (Table 7.1.1); however, it is likely that many more are eligible (Table 7.3.2).

- Among households with children ages 0-3 years, 51% participate in the Supplemental Nutrition Program for Women, Infants, and Children (WIC) (Table 7.4.1).

- Among households with school-age children, 62% and 51%, respectively, participate in the federal school lunch and school breakfast programs (Table 7.4.1).

MANY A2H CLIENTS ARE IN POOR HEALTH

- 29% of households served by the A2H National Network report having at least one household member in poor health (Table 8.1.1)

MOST CLIENTS ARE SATISFIED WITH THE SERVICES THEY RECEIVE FROM THE AGENCIES OF THE A2H NATIONAL NETWORK

- 92% of adult clients said they were either "very satisfied" or "somewhat satisfied" with the amount of food they received from their A2H provider; 93% were satisfied with the quality of the food they received (Table 9.2.1).

HOW LARGE IS THE A2H NATIONAL NETWORK?

- The members of the A2H National Network participating in the study include 43,141 agencies, of which 31,111 provided usable responses to the agency survey. Of the responding agencies, 21,834 had at least one food pantry, soup kitchen, or emergency shelter (Chart 3.5.1).

- The A2H National Network includes approximately 29,700 food pantries, 5,600 soup kitchens and 4,100 emergency shelters.

WHAT KINDS OF ORGANIZATIONS OPERATE EMERGENCY FOOD PROGRAMS OF THE A2H NATIONAL NETWORK?

- 74% of pantries, 65% of kitchens, and 43% of shelters are run by faith-based agencies affiliated with churches, mosques, synagogues, and other religious organizations (Table 10.6.1).

- At the agency level, 69% of agencies with at least one pantry, kitchen, or shelter and 56% of all agencies including those with other types of programs are faith-based (Table 10.6.1).

- Private nonprofit organizations with no religious affiliation make up a large share of other types of agencies (Table 10.6.1).

HAVE AGENCIES BEEN EXPERIENCING CHANGES IN THE NEED FOR THEIR SERVICES?

- 65% of pantries, 61% of kitchens, and 52% of shelters of the A2H National Network reported that there had been an increase since 2001 in the number of clients who come to their emergency food program sites (Table 10.8.1).

WHERE DO THESE AGENCIES OBTAIN THEIR FOOD?

- Food banks are by far the single most important source of food for the agencies, accounting for 74% of the food distributed by pantries, 49% of the food distributed by kitchens, and 42% of the food distributed by shelters (Table 13.1.1).

- Other important sources of food include religious organizations, government, and direct purchases from wholesalers and retailers (Table 13.1.1).

- 69% of pantries, 49% of kitchens, and 46% of shelters receive food from government commodity programs (TEFAP or CSFP) (Table 13.1.1).

VOLUNTEERS ARE EXTREMELY IMPORTANT IN THE A2H NETWORK

- As many as 90% of pantries, 86% of kitchens, and 71% of shelters in the A2H National Network use volunteers (Table 13.2.1).

- Many programs rely *entirely* on volunteers; 66% of pantry programs and 40% of kitchens have no paid staff at all (Table 13.2.1).

2. INTRODUCTION

Recent government data indicate that at least 13.5 million households in the United States (11.9% of all households) were food insecure in 2004, of which 4.4 million (3.9% of all U.S. households) had experienced hunger at some point in that year. The food insecure households contained an estimated 38 million people, of whom almost 14 million were children. The existence of large numbers of people without secure access to adequate nutritious food represents a serious national concern.[1]

An important response to this problem has been the growth of private-sector institutions that have been created to provide food for the needy. In particular, throughout the United States, food pantries, emergency kitchens, and homeless shelters play a critical role in meeting the nutritional needs of America's low-income population. By providing people who need assistance with food for home preparation (pantries) and with prepared food that can be eaten at the agencies (kitchens and shelters), these organizations help meet the needs of people and households that otherwise, in many instances, would lack sufficient food.

America's Second Harvest—The Nation's Food Bank Network (A2H) plays a critical role in helping these organizations accomplish their mission. A2H, a network of about 80% of all food banks in this country, supports the emergency food system by obtaining food for the system from national organizations, such as major food companies, and providing technical

---

[1] Nord, Mark, Margaret Andrews, and Steven Carlson. "Household Food Security in the United States, 2003." U.S. Department of Agriculture, Food and Nutrition Service, 2004. Economic Research Report No. 11 (ERS-11) October 2005.

assistance and other services to the food banks and food rescue organizations.[2] A2H also represents the interests of the emergency food community in the national public policy process.

Beginning in 1993, A2H has every four years studied the workings of its network and the characteristics of the clients the network serves, both to assess the severity of food adequacy problems of the poor in America and to identify ways of increasing the effectiveness of its operations. This report presents the results of the fourth comprehensive study sponsored by A2H. The study provides detailed information about the programs and agencies that operate under A2H Network members and the clients the programs serve.

This chapter of the report provides important background for the findings. Subsequent subsections are as follows:

- Highlight the objectives of the study
- Provide an overview of the America's Second Harvest Network
- Identify the groups of organizations involved in conducting the study
- Provide an overview of the rest of the report

2.1 OBJECTIVES

The Hunger in America 2006 study comprises a national survey of A2H emergency food providers and their clients. The study had the following primary objectives:

- To describe the national demographic characteristics, income levels, food stamp utilization, food security status, and service needs of low-income clients who access emergency food assistance from the A2H Network at the national level;

---

[2] Ohls, James, Fazana Saleem-Ismail, Rhoda Cohen, and Brenda Cox. "Providing Food for the Poor: Findings from the Provider Survey for the Emergency Food Assistance System Study." Report prepared for the Economic Research Service, U.S. Department of Agriculture. Princeton, NJ: Mathematica Policy Research, Inc., February 2001.

- To describe the demographic profiles of clients of local agencies and to examine the ability of local agencies to meet the food security needs of their clients;

- To compare data, where possible, between the 2001 and 2005 A2H research studies, to identify trends in emergency food assistance demands, and to relate observed trends to welfare policies;

- To compare local-level and national-level data on the characteristics of agencies in describing the charitable response to hunger throughout the nation.

The Hunger in America 2006 study was designed to provide a comprehensive profile of the extent and nature of hunger and food insecurity as experienced by people who access A2H's national network of charitable feeding agencies. Information was collected on clients' sociodemographic characteristics, including income and employment, benefits from food stamp and other federal or private programs, frequency of visits to emergency feeding sites, and satisfaction with local access to emergency food assistance. Information obtained from local provider agencies included size of programs, services provided, sources of food, and adequacy of food supplies.

2.2   OVERVIEW OF THE SECOND HARVEST NETWORK

The A2H Network's 210 certified members are regularly monitored by A2H staff and food industry professionals to ensure compliance with acceptable food handling, storage, and distribution standards and practices. A2H Network members distribute food and grocery products to charitable organizations in their specified service areas, as shown in Chart 2.2.1.

Within this system, a number of different types of charitable organizations and programs provide food, directly or indirectly, to needy clients. However, there is no uniform use of terms identifying the essential nature of the organizations. Hunger relief organizations are usually grassroot responses to local needs. As such, they frequently differ throughout the country and use different terminology. For clarity, the terms used in this report are defined as follows:

CHART 2.2.1

SOURCES OF FOOD AND CHANNELS OF FOOD DISTRIBUTION FOR FOOD BANKS

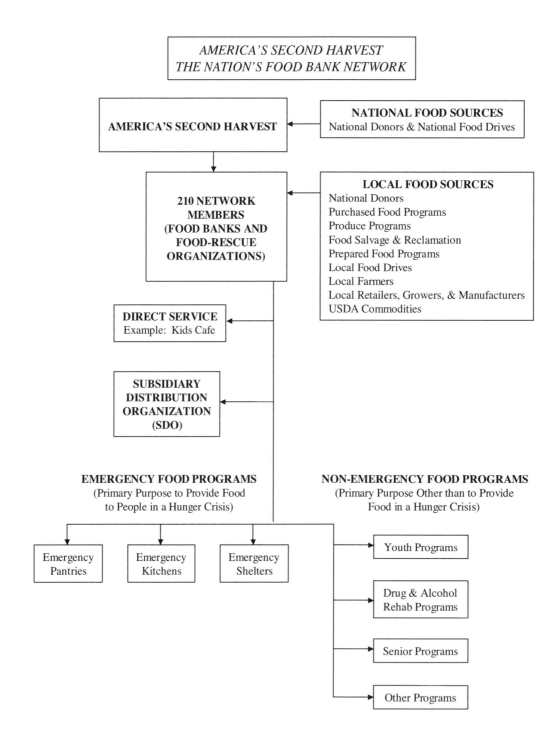

Food Bank. A food bank is a charitable organization that solicits, receives, inventories, stores, and distributes donated food and grocery products to charitable agencies that directly serve needy clients. These agencies include churches and qualifying nonprofit [Internal Revenue Code 501(c)(3)] charitable organizations.

Subsidiary Distribution Organization (SDO). SDOs, smaller food banks or larger agencies allied with affiliated food banks, are private, nonprofit, charitable organizations providing important community services. Although some are agencies, all SDOs distribute part of their food to other charities for direct distribution to clients.

Food Rescue Organization (FRO). FROs are nonprofit organizations that obtain mainly prepared and perishable food products from food service organizations, such as restaurants, hospitals, caterers, and cafeterias, and from distributors of fresh fruits and vegetables and distribute to agencies that serve clients.

Agencies and Food Programs. A2H Network members distribute food to qualifying charitable agencies (agencies are required to be nonprofit-501(c)(3)-organizations or equivalent), most of which provide food directly to needy clients through food programs. Some agencies operate single-type and single-site food programs, while others operate food programs at multiple sites and sometimes operate several types of food programs.

For this research, there are two general categories of food programs that A2H Network members serve: emergency and nonemergency.

Emergency food programs include food pantries, soup kitchens, and shelters. Their clients typically need short-term or emergency assistance.

- *Emergency Food Pantries*, also called "Food Shelves," distribute nonprepared foods and other grocery products to needy clients, who then prepare and use these items where they live. Food is distributed on a short-term or emergency basis until clients are able to meet their food needs. An agency that picks up boxed food from the food bank to distribute to its clients was included as a food pantry. The study excluded from this category any agency that does not directly distribute food to clients or distributes bulk food only on a basis other than emergency need (such as U.S. Department of Agriculture [USDA] commodities to all people over age 60). On the other hand, a food bank distributing food directly to clients, including clients referred from another agency, qualified as a food pantry.

- *Emergency Soup Kitchens* provide prepared meals served at the kitchen to needy clients who do not reside on the premises. In some instances, kitchens may also provide lighter meals or snacks, such as sandwiches, for clients to take with them when the kitchen is closed. This category includes "Kids Cafe" providers.

- *Emergency Shelters* provide shelter and serve one or more meals a day on a short-term basis to low-income clients in need. Shelter may be the primary or secondary purpose of the service. Examples include homeless shelters, shelters with substance abuse programs, and transitional shelters such as those for battered women. The study did not categorize as shelters residential programs that provide services to the same clients for an extended time period. Other excluded programs are mental health/retardation group homes and juvenile probation group homes.

Nonemergency organizations refer to any programs that have a primary purpose other than emergency food distribution but also distribute food. Examples include day care programs, senior congregate-feeding programs, and summer camps.

2.3   GROUPS AND ORGANIZATIONS INVOLVED IN THE STUDY

The study was conceived and coordinated by the national offices of A2H. Data were collected by 163 A2H Network food bank members around the country. A2H's research contractor, Mathematica Policy Research, Inc. (MPR), provided technical advice throughout the study and implemented the sampling and data analysis activities.

Throughout all stages of the study, oversight and advice were provided by a Technical Advisory Group convened by A2H. John Cook of Boston University Medical Center Department of Pediatrics and Beth Osborne Daponte of Yale University were the chair and co-chair, respectively, of the Group. Other members included Steven Carlson of the Food and

Nutrition Service, U.S. Department of Agriculture, Kirk Johnson of The Heritage Foundation, Lynn Parker of the Food Research and Action Center, Janet Poppendieck of Hunter College, Martha Raske of the University of Southern Indiana, Ken Rice of Leo J. Shapiro and Associates, Rob Santos of NuStats, and Tommy Wright of the Census Bureau.

Also, the Affiliate Advisory Committee (AAC) consisting of selected members of the A2H National Network, provided valuable input during the research process. AAC includes: John Krakowski of City Harvest, Jayne Wright of Food Bank of Central Louisiana, Erica Hanson of Rhode Island Community Food Bank, Michelle Pierceall of Harvesters—The Community Food Network, Ellen Stroud of San Francisco Food Bank, Marian Blanchard of God's Pantry Food Bank, Inc., and Natasha Thompson of Food Bank of the Southern Tier.

2.4   OVERVIEW OF THE REST OF REPORT

Chapter 3 provides an overview of the methodologies used in the study and shows the proportion of agencies that participated among all eligible agencies of the A2H National Network. Chapter 4 estimates the numbers of clients served by the A2H National Network. Chapters 5 through 9 present detailed findings from the client survey, including information about characteristics of A2H clients, their levels of need, and their experiences with the program. Chapters 10 through 14 present findings from the agency survey, including data on characteristics and program operations of A2H agencies. Chapter 15 presents selected preliminary cross-tabulations designed to illustrate the potential of the data for additional research. Finally, Chapter 16 highlights general trends in the data over the period covered by the four A2H reports: 1993, 1997, 2001, and 2005.

3. METHODS

This study had two components: (1) an agency survey that collected information about the food programs operating in the A2H Network, and (2) a client survey that would characterize the people using food pantries, emergency kitchens, and shelters and provide a better understanding of their needs. Each of the participating food banks helped MPR with the development of the sampling frame and with the data collection. MPR provided technical assistance with the implementation of the agency and client surveys.

This section provides an overview of the methods used in the survey and analysis work. (Detailed information is contained in the technical volume of the report.) We first discuss two key activities common to both surveys: (1) instrument development, and (2) the training of food bank staff on survey procedures. We then describe each of the two surveys.

3.1   INSTRUMENT DEVELOPMENT

The data collection instruments for this study were based on the questionnaires used in the 2001 study, revised to reflect the 2001 data collection experience and the needs of A2H. MPR worked closely with A2H and the Technical Advisory Group to revise the questionnaires so that they would provide high-quality data.

3.2   TRAINING

To ensure that each food bank study coordinator had the proper knowledge to administer the surveys, MPR conducted three regional, two-day, in-depth training sessions. Most of the training dealt with showing the study coordinators how to prepare local interviewers to randomly sample clients and to conduct the client survey. Each study coordinator also received a training video demonstrating the client interview process and a manual containing sample materials and an outline of the A2H Network members' responsibilities.

3.3   AGENCY SURVEY

MPR developed the sampling frame for the agency survey by first obtaining, from participating A2H Network members, lists of all active agencies each member served and then entering the names into a database. The agency survey sample consisted of a census of the agencies provided by the participating members.

After entering the data, MPR staff printed bar-coded mailing labels to identify the agencies and their addresses and then shipped the proper number of questionnaires, labels, and mailing envelopes to each participating member. Some members mailed advance letters informing agencies of the planned survey. Study coordinators were instructed, at the training and in the manual, how to assemble and mail the questionnaires. Each envelope included a personalized cover letter.

The cover letter, as well as the instructions on the questionnaire, directed the agency to complete the questionnaire and mail it back to MPR. In most instances, agencies did so, but some members collected the instruments from their agencies and mailed them to MPR in bulk. When MPR received a questionnaire, staff logged it into a database by scanning the bar code on the mailing label. Each Monday morning, MPR sent an e-mail to the members listing all the questionnaires received the previous week. These e-mails served as the basis for the mailing of reminder postcards to those agencies that did not return the questionnaire within two weeks of the initial mailing, and a second mailing, this time of questionnaires, to agencies that did not return the first one within two weeks after the mailing of reminder postcards. The weekly e-mails also helped the member study coordinators schedule reminder calls to agencies that did not return the questionnaire within three weeks after the second mailing. Occasionally, in areas where response to the mailings of questionnaires was particularly low, member coordinators completed the questionnaires with nonresponding agencies over the phone. Members were also asked to apprise MPR of agencies that no longer provided food services so that they could be identified as ineligible in the database.

After MPR received, logged into the database, and reviewed the questionnaires, they were shipped to a subcontractor for data capture and imaging. The subcontractor optically scanned all questionnaires and produced data files and CD-ROMs with images of each completed questionnaire for MPR. Chart 3.3.1 summarizes the sequence of activities of the agency survey.

CHART 3.3.1

AGENCY SURVEY ACTIVITIES

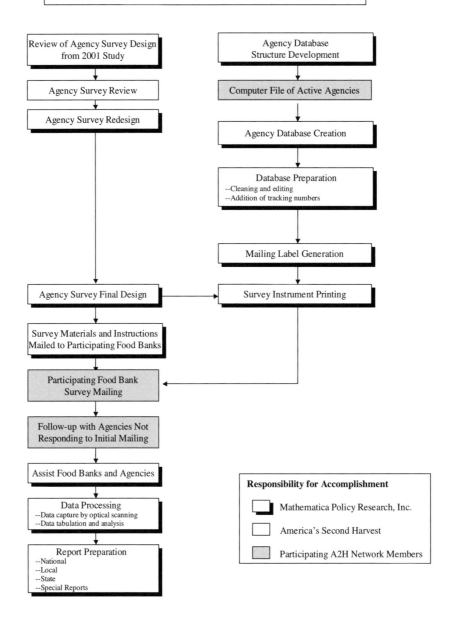

3.4   CLIENT SURVEY

Preparation for the client survey began with the selection of the A2H providers where interviewing was to take place. As previous A2H surveys had done, the client survey in the 2005 study focused on obtaining data on emergency food providers in the A2H system and on the people those providers serve. The three types of providers whose clients were included in the 2005 survey (and previous A2H surveys) were food pantries, emergency kitchens, and shelters. Many food banks also provide food to *other types* of agencies, such as those serving congregate meals to seniors and agencies operating day care centers or after-school programs. These other types of agencies perform important roles, but they were defined to be outside the purview of the study because they do not focus on supplying *emergency* food to low-income clients.

At the outset of the 2005 study, we asked the A2H food banks that chose to participate to provide MPR with lists of all the agencies they served, indicating whether each agency was involved in emergency food provision and, if so, what type of agency it was (pantry, kitchen, shelter, or multitype). MPR sampling statisticians then drew initial samples of the agencies where interviews were to take place. These selections were made with probabilities proportional to a measure of size based on reported poundage distributions as the measure of size; that is, large agencies had greater probabilities of selection.

After the initial sampling, MPR asked the food banks to provide detailed information for the providers or programs in the sample of agencies. The information sought included when they were open and the average number of clients they served per day. For small food banks (as classified by A2H), the sample of agencies for this detailed information was about 47. For larger food banks, the sample of agencies could be as high as 79. MPR then used the detailed information from the sample of agencies to form three pools of providers, and we drew samples of providers for the client interviewing. At this time, we also selected a reserve sample to account for possible refusal or ineligibility of a provider selected in the primary sample.

For each sampled provider or program, MPR selected a specific day and time when the interviewing was to occur, based on the detailed information the food bank had sent to MPR. We also provided a range of acceptable dates and times if our selection was not workable for the data collectors. The food banks were responsible for sending staff or volunteers to each selected program at the specified date and time to conduct the interviews. The data collectors were to use (1) the client selection forms developed by MPR and approved by A2H, and (2) an interview questionnaire that MPR and A2H had designed jointly. Clients at the facilities were selected for the interviews through locally implemented randomization procedures designed by MPR.[3] In total, more than 50,000 clients were interviewed. MPR had another firm (a subcontractor) optically scan the completed questionnaires into an electronic database, and the resulting data files provided the basis for the client analysis.

During the fielding, we used randomly selected site replacements only when an agency, provider, or program refused to participate in the client interview effort or if, after conferring with the food bank and agency, we determined the provider to be ineligible for the study. In cases where food banks did not have reserve sample, we drew a supplemental first-stage sample and requested additional information or assigned an additional visit to a program among the programs already sampled. In some instances, we discovered while obtaining additional information that an agency (or provider) was no longer operating or did not run a pantry, kitchen, or shelter. In such instances, we dropped the agency (or provider) from the sample.

---

[3] These procedures involve enumerating the client being served at the time of data collection (for example, by when they came to the facility or their place in a line), then taking a "1 in n" sample with a random starting point.

MPR prepared bar-coded labels with identification numbers for the client questionnaires. We also developed and printed, for use by interviewers, client selection forms designed to allow the interviewer to randomly select program participants and to enumerate the number of completed interviews, refusals, and ineligible sample members during on-site data collection. We shipped these materials and client questionnaires to food bank for distribution to the individual data collectors.

After data collection at a provider was completed, the food bank study coordinators shipped questionnaires and client selection forms back to MPR. MPR staff then logged each questionnaire into a database by scanning the bar-coded label on the cover page. As with the agency survey, each Monday morning MPR sent an e-mail to the members listing the agencies where client questionnaires were completed the previous week. The e-mails allowed the member study coordinators to monitor their progress in completing the client survey portion of the study.

After MPR received the questionnaires and MPR staff logged them into the database, the questionnaires were shipped to the subcontractor for data capture and imaging. The subcontractor optically scanned the questionnaires and produced data files for MPR. As with the agency survey, MPR received data files and electronic images of all completed client questionnaires on CD-ROMs. Chart 3.4.1 summarizes the sequence of activities in the client survey.

CHART 3.4.1

CLIENT SURVEY ACTIVITIES

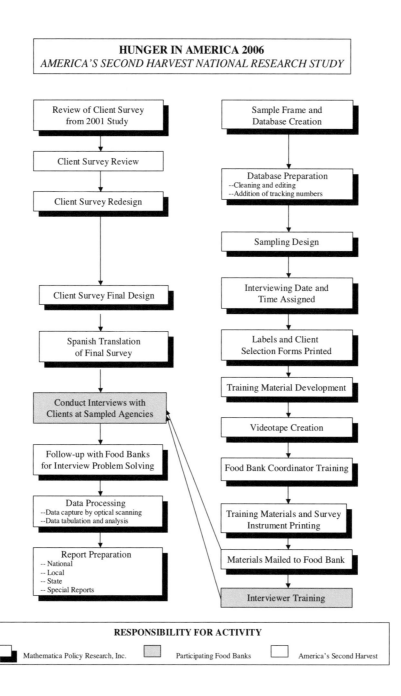

3.5 RESPONSE RATES

As Chart 3.5.1 shows, of the A2H National Network of 210 members, 163 individual members covering all or part of 45 states and the District of Columbia participated in the agency survey. Of those members, 156 participated in the client survey.[4]

Client Survey. A total of 156 individual members contacted 10,076 agencies to gain access for on-site client data collection. Of those agencies, 9,874 provided detailed information about their programs and 4,593 were sampled for and participated in client data collection.

A2H Network members' staff and volunteers sampled 72,399 clients at the eligible agencies; of those 1,439 were determined to be ineligible for age or other reasons. Client interviews were completed with 52,878, or 74.5%, of the eligible respondents.[5]

Agency Survey. A total of 163 participating A2H Network members sent out questionnaires to 43,141 eligible agencies.[6] MPR received completed questionnaires from 31,342 (72.7%) agencies.

A2H Research Involvement. Chart 3.5.2 shows the organizations and individuals involved in the national study. It also identifies the completed numbers of responses from the client interviews and the agency survey, by program type. For the service area of the A2H National Network, see Chart 3.5.3.

---

[4] The national report represents client data collected from 155 members and agency data from 162 members due to delayed data collection from one member.

[5] Interviews were conducted only with respondents age 18 or older.

[6] Some additional questionnaires were mailed out to agencies who were later found to be no longer operating or to be otherwise ineligible.

CHART 3.5.1

STUDY OVERVIEW

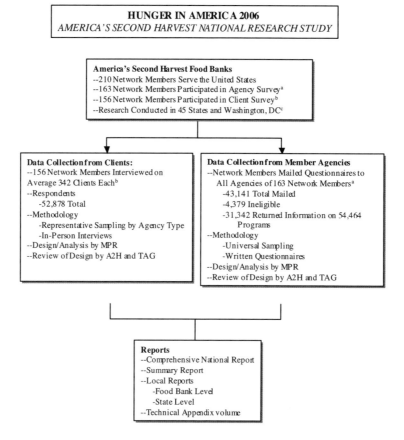

[a]Information from 162 Network members reflected in the national report due to delays in data collection in some Network members.

[b]Information from 155 Network members reflected in the national report due to delays in data collection in some Network members.

[c]Client survey conducted in 44 states and Washington, DC.

CHART 3.5.2

ORGANIZATIONS AND INDIVIDUALS INVOLVED IN THE RESEARCH PROCESS

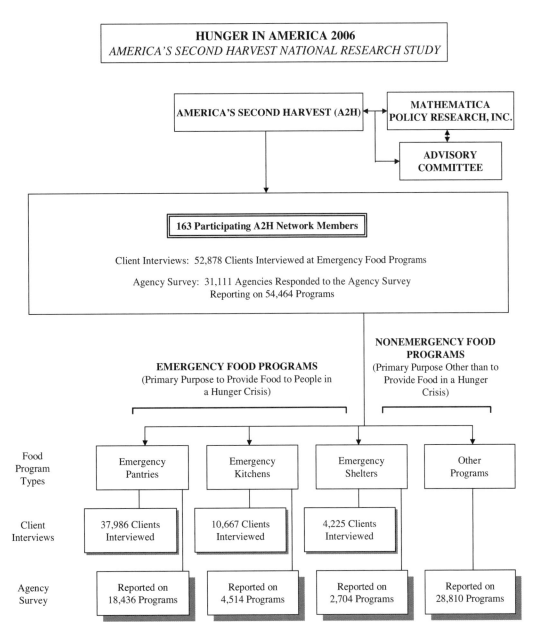

CHART 3.5.3

THE A2H NATIONAL NETWORK SERVICE AREA

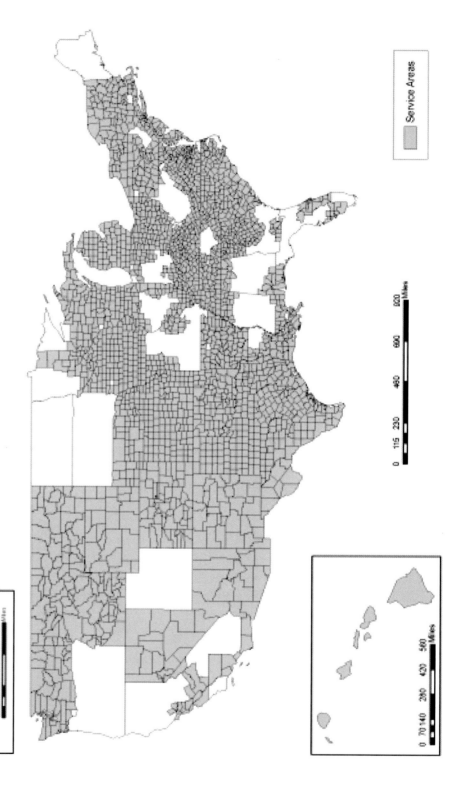

Service Areas

3.6   ANALYSIS METHODS

Most of the findings presented in this report are based on tabulations of the survey data. In this section, we describe the methods used in this work.

3.6.1   Tables

In the descriptive tabulations of clients presented in chapters 5 through 9, the percentage figures in the tables are based on the total weighted number of usable responses to the client survey, unless specified otherwise. Responses are weighted to represent clients or households of all emergency food programs in the A2H Network. In general, weights are based on the inverse probabilities of selection in the sampling and also account for survey nonresponse.[7] Weights were scaled so that the final weights represent a month-level count of different clients, as derived in Chapter 4 of the national report.[8]

Similarly, all tables containing information obtained from the agency survey, as presented in chapters 10 through 14, are based on the weighted total number of usable responses to the agency survey, unless specified otherwise. The descriptive tabulations in these chapters represent all A2H emergency food programs. The weights, calculated based on the sampling frame, also account for survey nonresponse.

Percentage distributions in the client tables are presented by the type of the programs where clients were interviewed (pantries, kitchens, or shelters). When appropriate, the

---

[7] To reduce variances in the analysis, we truncated weights with extremely large values. However, to keep the sum of weights unchanged, we then adjusted the weights by an adjustment factor, which is the ratio of the sum of the original weights to the sum of the truncated weights.

[8] Originally, we computed weights to make the sample representative at the weekly level. We later converted them to a monthly scale to take into account the fact that, compared with kitchen and shelter users, most pantry users do not visit the program in any given week.

percentage distribution for "all clients" is shown in the last column. Most tabulations of the agency data are presented by the type of programs operated by the agencies.

The percentages in the tables are rounded to one decimal place and are based only on the valid responses. They exclude missing, "don't know," refusal, and other responses deemed incomplete for the question.

The sample sizes presented at the bottom of single-panel tables (or at the bottom of each panel of multipanel tables) reflect the total number of responses to the question (unweighted). Where the question relates to a subset of the respondents, the appropriate sample size is presented. In general, these sample sizes include missing responses, as well as "don't know" and refusal responses. We report the percentages of item nonresponse in notes to each table.

The main reason for including only valid responses is to present appropriately the weighted percentage distribution among the main response categories of interest. Our preliminary analysis of item nonresponse revealed little evidence of any systematic biases, and excluding missing data also has the advantage of being consistent with the convention used for previous studies commissioned by A2H.

Some tables also present the average (mean) or the median values associated with the variable of interest. The average, a measure of central tendency for continuous variables, is calculated as the weighted sum of all valid values in a distribution, divided by the weighted number of valid responses. The median is another measure of central tendency. It is the value that exactly divides an ordered frequency distribution into equal halves. Therefore, 50% of the weighted number of valid responses have values smaller than the median, and the other 50% have values larger. The median is suitable only for describing central tendency in distributions where the categories of the variable can be ordered, as from lowest to highest.

3.6.2   Other Methodological Considerations

Certain other conventions should be noted in interpreting the findings of the study and how they are presented. Below we discuss the distinction between clients and respondents and describe the structure of reports available from the project.

Clients Versus Respondents. *Clients* are defined differently by program type. The kitchen and shelter programs are viewed as serving only those who are present at the program site. (Thus, in general for these providers, the survey respondents are representative of all clients.)[9] However, pantry programs are regarded as serving all members of respondents' households.

At the kitchen and shelter providers, the sampling unit was the individual. That is, the interviewers were instructed to treat members of a single household as separate respondents if they were selected by our random sampling process and met other eligibility criteria (such as being at least 18 years of age). At the pantry programs, on the other hand, the sampling unit was the household, and only one interview was completed for each randomly selected household, even when two or more members of the household were present at the program.

Ideally, the survey would have obtained all relevant information about every member of the household, especially among pantry users. However, so as not to overburden respondents, the survey was designed to acquire information about at most 10 members of the household, including the respondent. Also, this series of questions was limited to a set of variables of interest, such as sex, age, relationship to the respondent, citizenship, and employment status.

---

[9] One exception was children at the kitchens and shelters. They were clients, but they were not respondents, because only clients age 18 or older were interviewed for this study. However, the children were taken into account in estimating the total number of clients.

Because households with more than 10 members are uncommon, we do not believe that this has significantly affected our estimates.

National and Local Reports. Hunger in America 2006 has produced a set of reports to serve both national and local interests and to be useful to a wide range of audiences with varying needs. This national report consists of information gathered through 155 participating members for the client survey and 162 members for the agency survey. In addition, in most cases, a local report was generated containing information on clients and agencies served by a particular member. There are roughly 155 member-level local reports. In addition, state-level reports were produced when all A2H Network members in a particular state participated in this study. About 20 states achieved full participation of their members.

In addition to the comprehensive national and local reports, A2H will disseminate *Hunger in America 2006: An Extended Executive Summary,* which contains key findings from the comprehensive national report. A Technical Appendix, which describes in detail the methodologies of the current study, will be available separately for technical audiences.

Tables in the local and national reports are numbered comparably to facilitate comparisons between the local and national findings. Not all tables from the national report are reproduced in the local documents.

Statistical Sampling Variation and Measurement Error. As with all estimates relying on statistical samples, the client survey estimates in this report are subject to "sampling error," resulting from the fact that they are based on *samples* of clients rather than information about *all* clients. The margins of error due to this factor vary among individual estimates, depending on factors such as:

- Sample sizes
- The nature of the client characteristics being estimated

- The number of different providers within a food bank at which the client data collection took place

In addition to the sampling error, error also exists in the estimates from the operational components of the survey (non-sampling error), such as nonresponse, reporting error, and measurement error. While the sampling design and sample sizes can impose some control on the sampling error (and while this error can be quantified), the non-sampling error reflects the degree of success in designing the questionnaire and data collection procedures and in conducting the data collection activities at all stages. Unfortunately, the non-sampling error cannot be quantified. The exact amount of variation (both sampling error and non-sampling error) will be different for different data items, and the relative contribution of sampling error and non-sampling error to the total survey error will also vary by survey estimate.

The client survey information is derived from a cluster-based sample, giving the local estimates potentially large sampling error. For most percentage estimates based on the full sample size for a food bank, this sampling variation can lead to "confidence intervals" extending approximately plus or minus 1.5 percentage points around the estimate.[10] For instance, if a certain client characteristic percentage is estimated to be 60% within a given food bank, and the "margin of error" is 1.5 percentage points, we can be reasonably certain it is someplace in the range of 58.5 to 61.5 percentage points. In many instances, particularly when the sample is divided into subgroups, the width of the confidence interval can be greater. Confidence intervals are discussed in more detail in Appendix A.

---

[10] The confidence interval for most tables in this report is 95% unless noted otherwise.

Confidence intervals for pantry clients, who make up most of the overall sample, are similar to that described above. For kitchens or shelters, with their smaller sample sizes, confidence intervals tend to be in the range of plus or minus 2.5 percentage points.

The ranges of precision highlighted above focus only on sampling variation due to statistical sampling and the number of completed interviews. As noted previously, other forms of survey error (the non-sampling error) will increase overall survey error. These other forms of error include

- *Nonresponse.* When completed interviews is obtained from only a portion of the clients selected for the survey

- *Response Error.* When the client interviewed does not provide an accurate answer to a question because the client either misunderstands the question or chooses not to provide an accurate answer

- *Reporting Error.* When counts or other information used in the sampling and other data collection activities are in error or missing

- *Measurement Error.* When the question in the questionnaire is not worded effectively to obtain the desired information from the client

These forms of error exist in all surveys, but the size of the non-sampling error (relative to the sampling error) depends on the design of the data collection activities and implementation of these by all persons involved. In this survey, most of the interviewers did not have extensive experience in data collection work, and while MPR supplied general training guidelines and materials, there was undoubtedly considerable variation between food banks as to how the training was implemented. Inevitably, as in any survey, some interviewers may have read questions incorrectly, clients may have understood questions incorrectly, and even correct answers may sometimes have been incorrectly recorded on the survey instrument. All these factors may have led to "non-sampling error" *that is in addition to the sampling error discussed above.*

3.7   REPORTING CONVENTIONS IN MEMBER REPORTS

In some instances, there were certain client-based tabular analyses for which fewer than 30 observations were available. (This happened mostly with shelters and, to a lesser extent, kitchens.) In these instances, the relevant tabulations have not been included in the tables, because there are too few client observations for the results to be statistically reliable.[11]

When client tabulations have been suppressed because of small sample sizes, the entry *n.p.* ("not presented) is made in the relevant columns of the tables. In these cases, the client observations *are* included in computing the "total" column, which is aggregated across the three types of programs.[12]

In some instances, there may be no observations available at all for a column of a table. In those cases, we have entered *N.A.* ("not available").

3.8   DEGREE OF COMPARABILITY BETWEEN 2001 AND 2005 STUDIES

Most aspects of the 2001 and 2005 studies were similar. Both surveys (1) were based on the two-stage provider sampling approach described above, (2) used essentially the same client sampling techniques, (3) used similar questionnaires, and (4) were data-entered and analyzed using similar methods.

---

[11] On the other hand, when presenting agency findings, we have reported tabulations with fewer than 30 programs, in part because some of the smaller members do not have as many as 30 kitchens or shelters.

[12] Because of a limitation of the computer system used to generate the member-level reports, in some instances a chart corresponding to a table with the n.p. or N.A. conventions may actually have a graphic corresponding to the suppressed column in the table.

Nevertheless, some significant changes were made between the two study years. Most were designed to improve the study, by (1) increasing the accuracy of the data collection and analysis, or (2) reducing the considerable burden that falls on the food banks in implementing the study.

The Technical Appendix volume provides a complete description of the survey and analysis methodologies. Here, however, we highlight the main salient methodological considerations:

- Developing improved estimates of client turnover in the A2H Network

- Imputing numbers of clients served by small providers that were not interviewed

- Increasing screening of the provider sample for eligibility

- Improving the treatment of more than one interviewing visit to the same provider on the data file and in the analysis

- Incorporating more detailed information on provider operating hours

- Increasing the number of participating food banks

- Taking into account the possibility of providers being open less than once a week

- Estimating numbers of clients served by small providers

3.8.1   Estimating Client Turnover Rates Within the A2H System

An important goal of the periodic A2H surveys has been to develop *annual* estimates of the number of different clients served. However, this raises substantial methodological issues, as discussed below.

Importance of "Newcomer" Rates and Key Resulting Estimation Issues. An important factor that influences the annual number of clients participating in the A2H emergency food assistance system is the amount of client turnover during the year. It is much more straightforward to estimate the number of clients *at a given point in time* than to estimate the number over a year. This is because the *annual* number depends on turnover in the system. As an example, consider a pantry that serves 100 clients per month. If mostly the *same* clients go to the pantry month after month, then the *annual* number of clients for the pantry will be at least 100, or a small number more to account for a few clients leaving and others replacing them. If mostly *different* clients come each month, however, the pantry could serve 1,000 clients, or even more, in a year. Furthermore, even much more modest rates of turnover could increase the annual total from about 100 to perhaps 300 or 400. Thus, taking into account the amount of client turnover can have major implications for overall client estimates.

The study depends on information obtained during the client interviews to draw inferences about client usage of the system over a 12-month period. Survey recall problems pose formidable challenges to interpreting the data, however, because many clients may not accurately recall and report their past usage patterns for an entire year. Typically, clients are able to supply accurate information about their usage of the emergency food system during a recent period, such as a week (or even perhaps a month), but as the period gets longer, recall usually becomes less reliable. While long recall periods are a problem for many surveys, they may be particularly problematic for the A2H client population, because many of them are elderly, have disabilities, or are in low-income households where they are concentrating on how to meet day-to-day household needs with low resources, rather than thinking about the past year.

The 2001 Survey Questions Related to Client Turnover. In the 2001 and 2005 surveys, we tried to examine client turnover based on the self-reports of survey respondents about their patterns of using the A2H system. The research strategy focuses on what the 2001 report called the "newcomer rate," defined as the percentage of clients at a given point in time who have started using A2H providers within the past month but had not used the A2H system in the previous 12 months. If we can estimate "newcomers" defined in this way for 12 months in a

row, the sum yields a measure of all the people who entered the system during the past year.[13]

The questions used to obtain this information have evolved between the 2001 and 2005

surveys. In 2001, we used the following two questions:

P66.   For how many months in a row have you been using this food pantry or other pantries like this
        one?

        |___|___| NUMBER OF . . .

            1 ☐ WEEKS
            2 ☐ MONTHS
            3 ☐ YEARS
            N ☐ TODAY WAS FIRST TIME
            D ☐ DON T KNOW
            R ☐ REFUSED

P69.   Not counting the last four weeks, when was the last time you or another member of your
        household received groceries from this or any other food pantry?

              |___|___| NUMBER OF . . .

            1 ☐ WEEKS AGO
            2 ☐ MONTHS AGO
            3 ☐ YEARS AGO
            4 ☐ NEVER
            D ☐ DON T KNOW
            R ☐ REFUSED

---

[13] Key to the approach outlined in the text is that a "newcomer" is defined as a person
who starts using the A2H system *and has not previously used it for at least a year.* Of course,
some people may enter and exit the system several times during the year; however, in making
annual unduplicated estimates, we want to count these people only once a year.

(These were the questions for pantries; similar questions were asked of kitchen and shelter users, except that the second question started with "Not counting the past seven days.")

In principle, answers to these questions are sufficient for estimating the number of clients who were "newcomers" as defined by the study. Many respondents did provide usable responses. However, we encountered two problems with these questions. First, during the survey fielding period, many interviewers and respondents said they found these two questions confusing. Second, in analyzing the results of that study, we found that many respondents had given inconsistent answers to these and related questions.

Because of these findings, in the 2001 analysis, we used a conservative definition of "newcomer" (in the sense of not overestimating the relevant population), with clients being treated as "newcomers" only if they gave consistent answers to both the questions reproduced above, indicating that they had just recently entered the A2H system for the first time in at least a year.[14] In addition, because of the uncertainty associated with the information available, the analysis of annual participation was undertaken for a *range* of possible estimates, rather than a single point estimate.

2005 Questions. At the outset of the 2005 study, to improve accuracy, we tried to develop alternative ways of obtaining these data on newcomer rates,. The result was that another question was added to the questionnaire:

---

[14] The issues related to the 2001 analysis approach are discussed on page 38 of *Hunger in America, 2001,* the national report of the 2001 study (October 2001).

P61b　　Now, thinking about the past year, did you or anyone in your household use a pantry

      1 ☐ Every month, (12 MONTHS)

      2 ☐ Almost every month, (10-11 MONTHS)

      3 ☐ Most months, (6-9 MONTHS)

      4 ☐ Some months, (4-5 MONTHS)

      5 ☐ Just a few months, (2-3 MONTHS)

      6 ☐ Just this month?

      D ☐ DON T KNOW

      R ☐ REFUSED

It was felt that this question was more straightforward and understandable and that it could perhaps elicit more accurate information. We kept the two questions used in the 2001 survey to provide backup if the new question did not work as hoped.

Findings. During fielding of the 2005 survey, examination of the answer patterns for the three 2005 questions and the two 2001 questions suggests that (1) the response patterns to the two previous questions are broadly consistent for 2001 and 2005, and (2) the responses to the *new* question were largely consistent with a "higher-estimate" interpretation of the old questions (compared to the more conservative, or lower-bound, interpretation used in the 2001 analysis).

2005 Analysis of Newcomers. Because of these findings, we have based the 2005 newcomer estimates on the responses to the new question. The result of this decision is that the newcomer estimates are significantly higher than in 2001. In particular, for pantries—by far the most important component in the total estimates—the point estimate of the percentage of clients that are newcomers in the previous month is 13%, compared with about 5% in the 2001 analysis.

This 2005 estimate was higher than expected, based on the 2001 analysis. It implies that, at the typical pantry on a given day, 13% of clients have started using the pantry that day or at some other time in the previous month and have not previously used the system for at least a year (or ever). However, several factors suggest that this estimate may be likely. First, as noted above, responses to both the two old questions and the new question seem to point to a newcomer rate higher than that used in the 2001 analysis. Second, many clients may use the A2H system just once or twice and then stop, either because their short-term food insecurity problem is resolved or other reasons.

Third, poverty rates and food insecurity rates have been rising in recent years,[15,16] which has probably increased the need for emergency food. It is likely that as the low-income population and food insecure population has increased, more newcomers use safety net systems such as the emergency food system.

Fourth, evidence for Survey of Income and Program Participation (SIPP) data collected in the late 1990s suggests that there are quite high rates of transition into and out of poverty over time. For example, the available data suggest that 51.1% of poverty spells in the United States between 1996 and 1999 lasted only two to four months. This SIPP-based analysis concludes, "A little over half of the poverty spells, measured by using monthly income and poverty thresholds, were completed after 4 months. Another 19.3% of spells were over after 8 months."[17] The income volatility represented by these high rates of transition into and out of poverty provides

---

[15] Between 2001 and 2004, the overall rate of persons in poverty in the United States rose from 11.7 to 12.7. See [www.census.gov/hhes/www/poverty/histpov/hstpov2.html], accessed on January 10, 2006.

[16] See also Nord, Mark, Margaret Andrews, and Steven Carlson. *Household Food Security in the United States, 2004*. U.S. Department of Agriculture, Economic Research Service, Report Number 11, October 2005.

[17] While now a little dated, the SIPP data are the most recent available to address the issue. See John Iceland, "Dynamics of Economic Well-Being: Poverty 1996-1999," U.S. Census Bureau, Current Population Reports, #P70-91, July 2003. We are indebted to Kirk Johnson for making this point to us.

further evidence that rates of transition into and out of the A2H system might be higher than were estimated in 2001.

Because of these considerations, the 2005 participation analysis has been based on responses to the new question. To exercise caution, however, we have kept the more conservative practice used in the 2001 study of conducting analysis for a range of assumptions around the 2005 point estimate.

3.8.2   Increased Provider Screening

Screening to ensure provider eligibility for the survey was done more intensively in 2005 than in 2001. During the 2001 survey, it had become evident that many food banks had trouble distinguishing between providers that met the eligibility criteria for the survey (by being emergency food providers) and those that did not. For instance, congregate meal programs for seniors were often confused with emergency kitchens. Similarly, long-term group living facilities were sometimes confused with emergency shelters. In 2005, therefore, MPR staff spent more time training food bank personnel on the relevant distinctions than they had in 2001. MPR also did more screening of information on the sample, which lowered participant estimates somewhat. We believe that the result was a sample better focused on the target population, that is, those households accessing "emergency food assistance."

3.8.3   Keeping More Information on Interviewing That Involved More than One Visit to Providers

To achieve interview targets for both surveys (particularly in 2001), it was sometimes necessary to make more than one visit, on different days, to a provider. In 2001, summary information on these visits was combined and placed in a single data record on the analysis file.

In 2005, we kept detailed data on each visit in separate data records. This allowed more complete and precise analysis of the sampling done at the sites.

3.8.4 Taking into Account the Fact That Some Providers Are Open More than Four Hours a Day

In the 2001 data collection and analysis, we assumed that the observation period (including observations of number of clients) was the same as the period that providers were open. By the time of the 2005 survey, we had realized that this is not always true, and we built into the weighting algorithm an expansion factor to allow for clients who may have come on the day of sampling but not while the observers were there. This expansion factor is defined in Equation B-25 of Technical Appendix B.

3.8.5 Number of Participating Food Banks

The 2005 survey had considerably more coverage than the 2001 survey. In 2001, there were 104 food banks participating in the client survey (about half the food banks in the network). After adjusting for size, the 104 food banks were estimated to account for about two-thirds of all A2H operations. In the 2005 study, 156 food banks participated, and they are estimated to account for about 81% of all operations.

3.8.6 Allowing for the Possibility of Food Providers Being Open Less than Once a Week

The 2001 data collection and analysis procedures assumed that all providers were open at least once a week, but it became apparent that this was not always true. Therefore, in 2005, the approach was made more general to allow for the fact that some providers were open less often.

3.8.7 Numbers of Clients Served by Small Providers

During the 2001 survey, some food banks, especially those in rural areas or with agencies in remote areas, were burdened with sending teams of interviewers to very small providers that might have as few as two or three clients in a day. In 2005, we reduced the burden on food banks by excluding very small providers from the survey work and imputing values for them in the data. Our rationale was that it would reduce data collection burden and increase cooperation, and because, by definition, these providers were small and could be accounted for by an adjustment factor in computing the sampling weights, the analysis would not be significantly affected. In general, the criterion chosen was not to send interviewers to providers that served fewer than 10 clients a day.

During the analysis, we considered several methods for accounting for small providers in the estimates. One was to incorporate a design-consistent ratio adjustment factor directly into the weighting process. In this adjustment, the number of clients at small providers would have been accounted for by using the ratio of the projected number of clients at all providers to the projected count of clients at large providers (with the ratio developed by provider type within food bank using 2005 sampling data from the individual food banks). Other methods considered involved imputing the estimates for clients at small providers based on data collected in 2001, when interviewing *was* done at small providers. We performed estimates using both approaches and made judgments about the likely accuracy of the methods in discussions with the Technical Advisory Group for the project and with the MPR analysis team and sampling advisors. Based on these discussions, the method used was based on a variant of the imputation approach. This approach was decided by the Technical Advisory Group and the MPR analysis team to be the most accurate. This final approach was then implemented technically by including a ratio adjustment in the weighting process (by provider type), with the ratio set to achieve the estimate determined in the analysis described above.

3.8.8 Summary

Because of the changes described above between the 2001 and 2005 surveys, and the implementation of improved methodologies and analytical techniques in 2005, the results of the two surveys cannot be directly compared at a formal level. In particular, several changes in the survey and analysis procedures were made to improve accuracy and reduce the burden that the survey imposed on food banks. These changes could have shifted the survey findings, independent of the true underlying changes in the system.

On the other hand, overall, the underlying estimation objectives of the two surveys were essentially the same. Each survey represents the best attempt possible, given the methods available at the time, to estimate the number of A2H clients and their characteristics. Therefore, we believe it is useful to examine the results of the two surveys together to some degree. We do so at the end of the next chapter, after first presenting key findings from the 2005 analysis. However, the conclusions reached by comparing the results across years should be taken as *indicative,* rather than as the results of formal statistical tests.

4. NUMBER OF A2H CLIENTS SERVED

A key factor in assessing the size and contribution of the America's Second Harvest Network is to estimate the number of people the network's emergency food providers serve. Estimates of the numbers of different types of providers in the network are also of great interest. Such estimates are derived in this chapter.

We present both weekly and annual estimates of the number of different people served. In both types of estimates, our objective is to gauge the number of people served food at any time in the period covered. That is, we wish to estimate the number of people *ever served* at least once in a typical week and the number served at least once in the past year. Our weekly estimates are based largely on the analysis weights calculated using the survey sampling design and accounting for nonresponse or non-cooperation at each survey stage (agencies, programs and clients). For the annual results, additional extrapolation across the year is needed, as described below.

4.1   BACKGROUND AND LIMITATIONS

The estimation process draws on several data sources to derive estimates of the size of the A2H system:

- Information from the survey sample frame of providers, which was compiled from food bank records

- Information from the sampling and data collection operations on the observed numbers of clients served by providers, the providers' days of operation, and similar factors

- Information from the client survey on respondents' length and frequency of use of the emergency food system

- Information from A2H administrative files on the sizes of the food banks that participated in the study compared with those that did not participate

Given these rich data sources, several approaches can be taken in the estimation work. In much of the work below, we draw primarily on an approach, rooted in standard statistical estimation theory, where we (1) compute the probabilities of various providers and clients being in our survey sample, (2) compute analysis weights based on these probabilities, and (3) estimate the underlying population totals by summing the relevant analysis weights. In some instances, however, we use alternative approaches to develop certain estimates, compensate for limited information availability, add intuition to the estimation process, and test the robustness of our conclusions. We describe these approaches later in this chapter.

Our estimates unavoidably contain some uncertainty, which comes from several factors:

- ***Statistical Sampling Error.*** Sampling error results from the fact that many of the estimation parameters are based on *statistical samples,* rather than on surveys of all the relevant providers and clients.

- ***Reporting Error.*** Some of the interview questions on which our estimates are based were unavoidably complex. As a result, some error undoubtedly exists because respondents did not always understand the questions and did not always report accurately.

- ***Nonresponse Bias.*** As with any survey, it must be assumed that there is at least some error *due to nonresponse.* In this survey, it would be caused by the agencies and clients who did not respond to our surveys being different from those that did.

- ***Coverage Bias.*** Only about three-fourths of the A2H food banks participated in the study, which may lead to coverage bias. While we have adjusted for this, we cannot determine for sure exactly how accurate our adjustments are.

- ***Alternative Estimation Methods.*** As the subsequent discussion makes clear, several methods could be used in deriving the results presented below. Our discussion explains the reasons for the choices we make, but some judgment is involved in this and may influence the final results.

- ***Seasonality.*** Because of logistical requirements, most of the data were collected during winter and spring 2005. Therefore, it is not possible with this data set to fully examine and correct for fluctuations in the A2H system and clients over the entire year.

Despite these possible sources of error, the MPR research team for the study and A2H believe that the estimates derived below are based on the best survey methods and estimation procedures available, given the resources.

The next section provides an overview of our findings. After that we describe additional details of our calculations. We begin with pantries, since they are the largest component of the A2H Network.

4.2   OVERVIEW OF FINDINGS

Our basic approach to deriving annual estimates of clients served annually is to start with survey-based estimates of clients served per week, then apply several extrapolation factors to get an annual figure. As we discuss in detail, however, we believe that considerable margins of error are unavoidable in extrapolating from weekly estimates to annual estimates of clients served. Therefore, we present ranges of annual estimates, based on different assumptions concerning degrees of client turnover in the system.[18]

Overall, we estimate that A2H pantries, kitchens, and shelters serve between 23.7 and 27.0 million different people annually (Table 4.2.1). Of these, an estimated 4.5 million are served in a typical week.

---

[18] The ranges given are based on uncertainty associated with measuring one of the annual extrapolation factors. They do not reflect statistical sampling error, which adds additional uncertainty. We discuss this later in this chapter.

TABLE 4.2.1

ESTIMATES OF NUMBERS OF DIFFERENT CLIENTS SERVED BY THE A2H NETWORK
(WEEKLY AND ANNUAL ESTIMATES)

	Each Agency Type Considered Separately	After Correcting for Overlap of Clients Across Agencies[a]
Weekly Estimates		
Pantries (Persons)	4.1 million	4.1 million
(Households)	1.5 million	1.5 million
Kitchens (Persons)	0.5 million	0.3 million
Shelters (Persons)	0.2 million	0.1 million
Total (Persons)		**4.5 million**
Annual Estimates		
Pantries (Persons)	21.7 to 24.7 million	21.7 to 24.7 million
(Households)	8.0 to 9.1 million	8.0 to 9.1 million
Kitchens (Persons)	1.8 to 2.0 million	1.2 to 1.4 million
Shelters (Persons)	1.3 to 1.4 million	0.8 to 0.8 million
Total (Persons)		**23.7 to 27.0 million**

[a]Any client using a pantry is counted under pantries. Clients using just kitchens and shelters are counted under kitchens.

By far, the largest client group is that served by pantries, which account for more than 90% of the annual total. Kitchens are the next most commonly used provider.

4.3   ESTIMATES OF NUMBER OF PANTRIES IN THE SYSTEM

To estimate the number of pantries in the A2H Network, we begin by estimating the number of pantries served by the *food banks participating in the data collection*. We then extrapolate to the nonparticipating food banks.

As described in Chapter 3, we began the data collection by asking the participating food banks for lists of all the agencies they served, classified by types of programs the agencies run. A total of 44,332 agencies were listed by the 155 food banks participating in the client survey

(Table 4.3.1).[19,20] However, the food banks listed some of these agencies as running food programs other than pantries, kitchens, or shelters, such as those for day care centers and halfway houses, which were not included in the detailed survey work. As Line 3 of the table shows, after subtracting the agencies without pantries, kitchens, or shelters, 29,547 agencies remained.

To plan the sampling and field operations for the client survey, we obtained detailed operating information for a random sample of these 29,547 agencies. In conducting this work, we found that 16.3% of the agencies that had originally appeared eligible for the survey either were not still operating or were operating types of programs not directly germane to the survey. This left an estimated 24,731 agencies operating types of providers that were to be included in the survey. As Line 6 shows, 83.0% of these 24,731 agencies operated pantries (the others operated kitchens or shelters). An additional step in the derivation accounts for the fact that some agencies operated more than one pantry (Line 8).

Based on these calculations, the estimated final number of pantries served by food banks participating in the client survey is 24,125. The final step in the derivation is to extrapolate from the participating food banks to the entire A2H system. The 155 food banks that participated in the client survey represent about 74% of all A2H food banks. However, the participating food banks are larger, on average, than the typical food bank. In particular, based on food bank reports to A2H, they account for about 81% of all the total food distributed by food banks in the A2H system. Based on this information, we use an extrapolation factor of 1.23 to extend the estimates based just on participating food banks to the system as a whole. With this adjustment, the estimate of total pantries in Table 4.3.1 becomes 29,674.

---

[19] Much of the estimation work focuses on the subset of food banks that participated in the client survey, because we have more complete information on the sample frames for them.

[20] See the Technical Appendix volume under separate cover.

TABLE 4.3.1

ESTIMATED NUMBER OF PANTRIES IN THE A2H NETWORK

1.	Total operating agencies listed in the files of the participating food banks	44,332
2.	Percentage of agencies listed as operating at least one pantry, kitchen, or shelter[a]	66.6
3.	Subtotal	29,547
4.	Percentage of agencies in Line 3 that were found prior to survey operations (during detailed sampling work) no longer to be operating or to be operating only types of agencies other than pantries, kitchens, or shelters	16.3
5.	Revised subtotal	24,731
6.	Percentage of agencies in Line 5 that operate pantries[b]	83.0
7.	Agencies operating pantries	20,529
8.	Average pantry providers per agency operating pantries	1.18
9.	Final estimate of pantries in participating food banks	24,125
10.	Adjustment factor for nonparticipating food banks[c]	1.23
11.	Final estimate of pantries	29,674

SOURCE: Lines 1-7 are based on client survey records; Line 8 is based on tabulations of agency survey data.

[a]Remaining agencies were listed in an "other" category, as operating some other type of provider with food service operations, such as a day care center or a halfway house program.

[b]Some additional ineligible agencies were found during the survey work.

[c]On this table, nonparticipating food banks also include those that participated in the agency survey only.

4.4   ESTIMATE OF NUMBER OF PANTRY CLIENTS

Here we present an estimate of the number of clients served by A2H pantries, based on microlevel information about the design-based analysis weights assigned to individual observations in the sampling work.

For interviewing at pantries, the sampling unit was the household. As discussed in Chapter 3 and detailed in the Technical Appendix volume, we have computed weights for each of the observations in the client survey sample, based on their probabilities of being selected into the sample in a typical week. These weights are based on several factors, including:

- The probability of selecting the client's agency into the subset of agencies used for the client survey and the probability of selecting the client's program. (This reflects the probabilities of the agency being selected at several different stages of the sampling process, the number of days per week the programs are open, and program-level participation rates, in terms of the agencies agreeing to allow the on-site data collection work.)

- The probability of selecting the client into the sample during the on-site work at the agency during the day of client interviewing. (This reflects the number of clients at the agency that day and the number actually selected for interviewing.)

- Client responses to interview questions concerning how many times they had been at any pantry during the week the interviewing took place.

These factors have allowed us to compute probabilities of each of the selected clients (1) being at a pantry *in a typical week,* (2) being selected into the data collection sample, and (3) responding to the survey. The initial set of weekly client weights is calculated based on the inverses of these probabilities. These weights make the sample representative of the universe of households receiving food at least once from a pantry served by a participating food bank *in a typical week.* The sum of these weights, 1.2 million, presented in Line 1 of Table 4.4.1, can be interpreted as an estimate of the number of *different* households obtaining food from pantries served by the participating food banks in a typical week. This estimate is still in terms of

TABLE 4.4.1

DERIVATION OF ESTIMATE OF DIFFERENT PEOPLE
USING PANTRIES ANNUALLY

1.	Estimated number of pantry household visits in a week by different households in areas covered by participating food banks	1.2 million
2.	Weeks in a month	4.0
3.	Pantry household visits in a month	4.9 million
4.	Estimated average household visits per month (per household)	1.8
5.	Different household visits in a month	2.7 million
6.	Estimated average monthly percentage of all client households that start using pantries each month	12.5 to 15.5
7.	Estimated total entrants in months 2 through 12 (Line 6 × Line 5 × 11 months)	3.8 to 4.7 million
8.	Estimated total different households in months 1 through 12 (Line 5 + Line 7)	6.5 to 7.4 million
9.	Average household size (persons per household)	2.7
10.	Different people served in months 1 through 12 in areas covered by participating food banks (Line 8 × Line 9)	17.6 to 20.0 million
11.	Adjustment for nonparticipating food banks	1.23
12.	Different people served annually by pantries in the network (Line 11 × Line 10)	21.7 to 24.7 million

NOTE: The technique used in the table of adjusting totals by average should be viewed as an approximation of the exact relevant numbers, if the relevant variables, including sample weights, are correlated with one another. For instance, if two variables are correlated, the product of the averages for two variables might not be exactly the same as the average of their products.

households, not *persons.* The conversion to persons will be done later in the estimation process below. In addition, the estimate applies only to clients in pantries that the participating food banks cover.

The weekly estimate in Line 1 of the table provides the basis of the annual estimates that we are about to derive. However, weekly estimates are also of considerable interest in themselves as a measure of the size of the system. This is true especially because this weekly estimate is probably somewhat more accurate than the annual estimates derived below. In particular, as our methodological discussion in Chapter 3 indicates, computing *annual* estimates unavoidably required asking survey respondents to report on their use of the emergency food system over a significant amount of time—a year in some instances. This long reporting span undoubtedly increases reporting error. In contrast, the weekly estimate requires only that respondents be able to report on their use of the system *during the week of the survey*—a considerably less exacting requirement.

The estimation process continues by drawing on various survey findings to obtain, ultimately, an *annual* estimate of different clients. The next step is to convert the weekly estimate in Line 1 to pantry visits in a month by multiplying by a factor of four weeks per month.[21] We then divide by a survey-based estimate that shows that, on average, households that use pantries visit them 1.8 times per month. Based on these factors, Line 5 indicates that the number of different client household visits in a month at all A2H pantries that the participating Network members cover is estimated to be 2.7 million.

The next step in the derivation is to go from the estimated monthly number of unique pantry clients to develop an *annual* estimate. As noted above, in all likelihood, this step is subject to more error than the earlier ones, because many of the pantry clients might have had difficulty responding accurately to questions that cover a period as long as a full year.

During the interview, respondents were asked how many months in the past year they had received food from pantries (Question P61b). The response categories to this question, which

---

[21] We considered using a factor of 4.3 weeks per month but elected to use the 4.0 factor because 4.0 may reflect more accurately how survey respondents converted between weeks and months in answering the survey questions. The appropriate choice is not fully clear, but it makes a significant difference. Using 4.3 would increase the pantry estimates by about 7%. The 7% is calculated as: [4.3 ÷ 4]).

interviewers read to respondents, were denominated in months, with the key category being "just this month." We used information from this question to estimate the number of clients who are new to the system, in that they reported not having used a pantry in the 12 months before the current month. About 14% of clients fell into this category, but this figure should be viewed only as an approximation of the new entrants into the pantry system in a given month. To account for uncertainty, we present a range of estimates for the number of new entrants to the pantry system in a month. In particular, to derive the estimate of unique households using the system, we have examined the sensitivity of the results to a range of 12.5% to 15.5% for this critical factor. While considerable judgment is involved in exactly how this range is set, we believe this interval is wide enough to reflect a reasonable range of uncertainty. Further, it is similar to the comparable margin of error considered in the 2001 report.

As Table 4.4.1 indicates, these different assumptions lead to a considerable range in the estimated number of different households in the study areas using pantries. In particular, this number extends from 3.8 to 4.7 million new-entrant households in the past year.

The next step in deriving an estimate of different users annually is to draw on the survey data to estimate the number of people per household. Based on the survey data, there are about 2.7 people per household in the population using pantries. A subsequent adjustment extrapolates the estimates from the areas covered by participating food banks to the entire set of A2H food banks. After making these adjustments, the final estimates of people the A2H Network pantries served in a year range from 21.7 to 24.7 million.

CH 4. NUMBER OF A2H CLIENTS SERVED

4.5   NUMBER OF A2H KITCHENS

Our analysis of the number of emergency kitchens served by A2H food banks uses the same analytical steps as the analysis of pantries. There were 3,335 agencies that, based on the information developed in compiling the sample frame, appeared to be operating kitchens (Table 4.5.1, Line 7). After taking into account that some agencies were operating more than one kitchen program, we estimate that 4,554 kitchens are being served by A2H food banks participating in the study. An adjustment for nonparticipating food banks raises the total estimate of kitchens to 5,601.

TABLE 4.5.1

ESTIMATED NUMBER OF KITCHENS IN THE A2H NETWORK

1.	Total operating agencies listed in the files of the participating food banks	44,332
2.	Percentage of agencies listed as operating at least one pantry, kitchen, or shelter[a]	66.6
3.	Subtotal	29,547
4.	Percentage of agencies in Line 3 that were found no longer to be operating or to be operating only types of agencies other than pantries, kitchens, or shelters	16.3
5.	Subtotal	24,731
6.	Percentage of agencies in Line 5 that operate kitchens[b]	13.5
7.	Agencies operating kitchens	3,335
8.	Average kitchen providers per agency operating kitchens	1.37
9.	Final estimate of kitchens in participating food banks	4,554
10.	Adjustment factor for nonparticipating food banks	1.23
11.	Final estimate of kitchens	5,601

SOURCE: Lines 1-7 are based on client survey records; Line 8 is based on tabulations of agency survey data.

[a]Remaining agencies were listed in an "other" category as operating some other type of provider with food service operations, such as a day care center or a halfway house program.

[b]Some additional ineligible agencies were found during the survey work.

4.6   NUMBER OF DIFFERENT CLIENTS SERVED BY A2H KITCHENS ANNUALLY

Our approach to estimating the number of kitchen clients served in a year also closely parallels that used for pantries. It begins with an estimate of the number of different clients served in a week. We then use data on clients' patterns of use to extrapolate up to an annual estimate. One different factor taken into account is that the sampling unit at the kitchens was adults age 18 and older, rather than households. Therefore, to get a complete measure of clients served, we must use survey data on minors accompanying the adults. As Table 4.6.1 shows, based on the survey weights, an estimated 0.5 million adults used kitchens in a week. Furthermore, there were about 0.3 children per adult. These estimates imply an estimated 0.6 million people using kitchens in a given week.

The next step is to extend this weekly estimate to the month and the year levels. The technique used with pantries—of multiplying the weekly estimates by four weeks per month and then dividing by the average number of times clients use the facility in a month—cannot reasonably be applied to kitchens. This is because kitchen clients tend to use these facilities much more often per week and per month.

An alternative version of the pantry approach is possible, however. Unlike with pantries, the number of people present at kitchens in a given week can be viewed as a reasonable approximation of the clients who are *currently using* the facility at a given point in time. This allows us to use the week as the unit of observation in parts of the accounting. (More formally, most people who can be viewed as "ongoing," or current, clients of a kitchen are likely to use the kitchen at least once during a weekly sampling period and thus have a non-zero probability of selection into the survey on a given week. This is not true of ongoing pantry users, most of whom use pantries only once or twice a month.)

TABLE 4.6.1

DERIVATION OF ESTIMATE OF DIFFERENT PEOPLE
USING KITCHENS ANNUALLY

1.	Estimated number of different adults visiting kitchens in a week in areas covered by participating food banks	0.5 million
2.	Average number of children accompanying adults	0.3 children per adult
3.	Estimated different adults and children visiting kitchens in a week	0.6 million
4.	Estimated average monthly percentage of clients who start using kitchens each month[a]	13.5 to 16.5
5.	Estimated new entrants in a year[b]	0.9 to 1.1 million
6.	Estimated different adults and children using kitchens in a year	1.5 to 1.7 million
7.	Adjustment for nonparticipating food banks	1.23
8.	Different people served annually by kitchens in the A2H Network (Line 6 × Line 7)	1.8 to 2.0 million

SOURCE: See the Technical Appendix volume for details on the derivation of the table entries.

[a]Estimated percentage is percentage entering in a month. The base of the estimates is the estimated clients at a given point in time, as approximated by a week.

[b]Calculated as follows: (11months) × (percentage entering per month from Line 4) × (base estimate of clients at a point in time from Line 3).

The survey question used to identify "newcomer" kitchen clients is essentially the same as that used for the same purpose for pantry clients (Question K70, "Now thinking about the past year, did you or anyone in your household use a soup kitchen . . .). As with pantries, the answer categories are denominated in months of use. Our approach to estimating the percentage of kitchen clients newly receiving services in a given month is based on the percentage of clients responding to the above turnover question by saying that the current month is the only month in the past year that they have been to a kitchen.[22]

---

[22] Even though the weighted survey *base* is, analytically, "clients in a week," the question effectively covers a period extending for the entire previous month, because the answer categories read to the respondents are denominated in months.

About 16% of survey respondents at kitchens said that the current month was the first time in at least a 12-month period that they had used an emergency kitchen. As with pantries, there could be considerable margin of error. Therefore, for the estimates, we assumed a range around the 15% estimate: between 13.5% and 16.5%. Beginning with the weekly estimate of 0.6 million clients in Table 4.6.1, then applying this 13.5%-to-16.5% range of possible newcomers each month, yields a range in the estimated number of new clients during the year between 0.9 and 1.1 million. This leads to an annual estimated number of people using kitchens in the areas covered by participating food banks in the range of 1.5 to 1.7 million. Finally, as shown at the bottom of the table, extrapolating this to the entire A2H Network leads to an estimated range of 1.8 to 2.0 million different kitchen clients per year.

4.7 ESTIMATES OF EMERGENCY SHELTERS AND THE NUMBER OF EMERGENCY SHELTER CLIENTS IN A YEAR

We have derived estimates of the number of emergency shelters and clients attending them using methods exactly the same as those used for kitchens (Table 4.7.1 and Table 4.7.2). Overall, we estimate that the number of emergency shelters served by all A2H food banks is 4,143 and that the number of different clients served meals annually by the shelters is 1.3 to 1.4 million.

TABLE 4.7.1

ESTIMATED NUMBER OF SHELTERS IN THE A2H NETWORK

1.	Total operating agencies listed in the files of the participating food banks	44,332
2.	Percentage of agencies listed as operating at least one pantry, kitchen, or shelter[a]	66.6
3.	Subtotal	29,547
4.	Percentage of agencies in Line 3 that were found no longer to be operating or to be operating only types of agencies other than pantries, kitchens, or shelters	16.3
5.	Subtotal	24,731
6.	Percentage of agencies in Line 5 that operate shelters[b]	7.5
7.	Agencies operating shelters	1,854
8.	Average shelter providers per agency operating shelters	1.92
9.	Final estimate of shelters in participating food banks	3,568
10.	Adjustment factor for nonparticipating food banks	1.23
11.	Final estimate of shelters	4,143

SOURCE: Lines 1-7 are based on client survey records; Line 8 is based on tabulations of agency survey data.

[a]Remaining agencies were listed in an "other" category, as operating some other type of provider with food service operations, such as a day care center or a halfway house program.

[b]Some additional ineligible agencies were found during the survey work.

TABLE 4.7.2

DERIVATION OF ESTIMATE OF DIFFERENT PEOPLE USING SHELTERS ANNUALLY

1.	Estimated number of different people visiting shelters in a week	181,000
2.	Average number of children accompanying adults	0.2
3.	Estimated different adults and children visiting shelters in a week	217,200
4.	Estimated average monthly percentage of all clients who start using shelters each month[a]	34.5 to 37.5
5.	Estimated new entrants in a year[b]	1.0 to 1.1 million
6.	Estimated different adults and children using shelters in a year[c]	1.2 million
7.	Adjustment for nonparticipating food banks	1.23
8.	Different people served annually by shelters in the A2H Network (Line 6 × 7)	1.3 to 1.4 million

SOURCE: See the Technical Appendix volume for details of the derivation of the table entries.

[a]Estimated percentage is percentage entering in a month. The base of the estimates is the estimated clients at a given point in time, as approximated by a week.

[b]Calculated as follows: (11 months) × (percentage entering per month from Line 4) × (base estimate of clients at a point in time from Line 3).

4.8   ESTIMATES OF DIFFERENT CLIENTS ACROSS THE WHOLE A2H SYSTEM

The estimates derived so far, along with additional data collected in the survey, make it possible to derive an estimate of the total number of different clients served by all three types of A2H emergency food providers, taken together. Survey questions asked respondents whether they had used other types of providers (besides the one at which they were interviewed) during the week of the survey. About 31% of kitchen users said they had also used a pantry, and about 31% of shelter users had used a kitchen or a pantry.[23] Using these data, together with the

---

[23] Because we have data on cross-agency use only in a single week (the period before the survey), the figures on multiple-agency use reported in the text may somewhat underestimate the full degree of this type of use when used to estimate different clients in the *annual* estimates.

estimates of provider use derived earlier, we have calculated estimates of system-level clients (displayed in Table 4.8.1). As shown, we estimate that between 23.7 and 27.0 million people used these providers in 2005.

TABLE 4.8.1

ESTIMATED ANNUAL CLIENTS, UNDUPLICATED ACROSS AGENCIES
(PERSONS)

		Each Agency Type Considered Separately	After Correcting for Overlap of Clients Across Agencies[a]
1.	Estimated number of different pantry clients in a year	21.7 to 24.7 million	21.7 to 24.7 million
2.	Estimated number of different kitchen clients in a year	1.8 to 2.0 million	1.2 to 1.4 million
3.	Estimated number of different shelter clients in a year	1.3 to 1.4 million	0.8 to 0.8 million
4.	Total different clients in system	n.a.	23.7 to 27.0 million

[a]Any client using a pantry is counted under pantries. Clients using only kitchens and shelters are counted under kitchens.

n.a. = not applicable.

(continued)
This is true because clients could have used other types of agencies in weeks other than the one asked about. However, because most of the annual counts are based on a single agency type—pantries—we do not believe that the underestimation is substantial. For instance, to establish a probable upper bound on the possible error, suppose the multiple-use factors reported in the text were doubled. The resulting change in the overall annual estimate of different clients would then be less than 5%.

4.9 DISCUSSION OF PARTICIPATION ESTIMATES FROM 2001 AND 2005 SURVEYS

As noted in Chapter 3, a number of significant refinements and improvements were made to the study procedures for the 2005 study, compared with the one undertaken in 2001. Therefore, the two surveys are not directly comparable in a formal statistical sense. However, both surveys focused on the same substantive issues, and the approaches taken in the two studies were similar. Therefore, when examining and interpreting the 2005 survey findings, it is useful to draw on information from both surveys. Next, we highlight several key factors relevant to such comparisons.

4.9.1 How Large Is the A2H Network?

Both the 2001 and the 2005 findings suggest that the A2H system serves a very large number of unduplicated clients in 2001 and 2005. The two surveys show similar participation ranges, and each suggests that the number is well over 22 million. Furthermore, the findings suggest that the system provides comprehensive services that are widely available. A2H facilities include more than 29,900 food pantries, more than 5,500 emergency kitchens, and about 4,100 shelters, and each participating food bank provides supplies to all these types of providers.

4.9.2 Have There Been Changes in the Number of A2H Clients Between 2001 and 2005?

Another obvious question to pose in relation to the 2001 and 2005 estimates is whether there appear to have been changes in the number of A2H participants. Unfortunately, however, we cannot answer this question definitively. As discussed earlier, because of measurement issues, we have developed participation rate estimates in the form of ranges, and the ranges for the two years overlap substantially. Given our analysis, we believe that it is quite possible for the "true" figure for each year to be anywhere within that year's range. Thus, the survey cannot reliably detect changes within the overlapping areas of the intervals. That is, within the overlapping areas of the intervals, we cannot rule out the possibility that differences between years are due to measurement error.[24] For instance, consistent with the estimates from the two studies, it is possible that the "true" number could have been 24 million in 2001 and then risen to, say, 27 million in 2005. It is also possible, however (though we doubt it for reasons discussed below), that the true rate could have stood at 28 million in 2001 and then dropped to 25 million in 2005. Each of these scenarios and many similar ones are consistent with the interval estimates presented above.

Evidence *external* to the current survey does suggest, however, that it is very likely that there has been at least some rise in the number of participants in the A2H systems. One important indicator is changes in the U.S. poverty rate. As noted in Chapter 3, the U.S. poverty rate for persons increased from 11.7 to 12.7 in the 2001 to 2004 period, which suggests need for more emergency food services. Similarly, government estimates based on annual Census Bureau, Current Population Survey (CPS) data indicate that the number of people in the United States experiencing food insecurity rose in a reasonably steady pattern from 12.2 to 13.2 during this same period.[25]

---

[24] Of course, it *is* possible to rule out the likelihood of *very large shifts* in participation between 2001 and 2005. However, such shifts would have to be large enough at least to eliminate the overlap in the intervals discussed in the text. Even then (as discussed later), additional margin would be needed to account for sampling error.

[25] See Nord, Mark, Margaret Andrews, and Steven Carlson. *Household Food Security in the United States, 2004.* U.S. Department of Agriculture, Economic Research Service, Report Number 11, October 2005.

The CPS also provides direct estimates that the use of emergency food has risen. The data show that the percentage of households that reported having received assistance from pantries rose from 3.0% in 2002 to 3.5% in 2004, providing direct evidence of an overall increase in the use of emergency food.[26] Since A2H providers make up a very large share of the overall emergency food system,[27] this provides strong indirect evidence of an upward trend in A2H participation.

(Additional discussion pertinent to possible changes in participants over time is presented in Subsection 5 below, where we discuss simulation analysis relevant to the issue.)

4.9.3 The Two Surveys Paint Somewhat Different Pictures of the Number of New Clients in the System During a Year Relative to Longer-term Clients

Substantial differences exist between the 2001 and 2005 survey estimates in the relative proportions of *longer-term clients* compared with *new entrants* in the composition of the overall A2H client base. This has implications for understanding estimated participation levels.

For a given amount of food distributed in the system, the number of different people who are participants during a year depends both on (1) the number receiving the benefits *at any given*

---

[26] Our focus here is on *trends* in the CPS-based estimates. As discussed in the 2001 report and noted elsewhere in the relevant research literature, the *absolute number* of emergency food clients estimated in the CPS has consistently been substantially lower than the number estimated in the A2H surveys. Possible reasons for the undercount include the known tendency of the CPS to undercount use of assistance programs and, relatedly, the role of embarrassment factors in determining respondents' answers. In particular, in the CPS it is easy for a respondent to decide not to report participation in emergency food if it is embarrassing to do so, while in the A2H survey, this is not possible, since the interview takes place at the emergency food provider. However, these factors notwithstanding, the size of the difference in the estimates should be noted, if not fully understood.

[27] See Ohls, James, Fazana Saleem-Ismail, Rhoda Cohen, and Brenda Cox. "The Emergency Food Assistance Study, Findings from the Providers Survey." Report prepared by Mathematica Policy Research for the U.S. Department of Agriculture, Economic Research Service, 2002.

point in time, and (2) the *rate at which clients leave the system and are replaced by new entrants.* The greater the turnover rate, the more different clients there will be annually, relative to the number of clients at a given point in time.

While the overall annual estimated A2H participation numbers from the 2001 and 2005 surveys are similar, the composition of the participants in this turnover dimension varies somewhat. Below, we describe these differences and their potential causes. We conclude that the apparent differences across the two years are probably mostly a measurement phenomenon attributable to improved methods used in the 2005 study.

Changing Participation Patterns. Our estimate of the number of A2H clients in a *given week* (as opposed to *annually*) is down noticeably, from 7 million in 2001 to 4.5 million in 2005, with decreases estimated for each of the three provider types. This difference is probably due at least in large part to some of the changes in survey methodology described in Chapter 3.

One key change is better screening of providers for survey eligibility. As discussed earlier, the screening changes were implemented for 2005 because in 2001 there was evidence that many food banks had difficulty distinguishing between agencies that met the definition of "emergency" food providers and other agencies that, while important in the overall A2H system, are not considered to be supplying emergency food. (Examples of these other agencies include day care centers and suppliers of congregate meals for the elderly.) As a result, some misclassification of providers probably occurred in 2001. To avoid similar issues in 2005, significant additional effort was devoted in the 2005 study to (1) training food banks on the relevant definitions, and (2) having MPR staff manually check sampling information after the food banks submitted it. This may have lowered the estimates of participation at any given point in time, by reducing the likelihood that misclassification would happen in the first place and by more successfully screening out the ineligible agencies that remained in the sample frame.

A second set of survey changes could also have affected the estimates. At the sampling stages of the 2005 survey, more detailed information was obtained than in 2001 about how often agencies were open during the month and about hours of operation on days they were open. This information, which was used in the sampling and weighting processes, may have reduced participation estimates compared with what they would otherwise have been, by better distinguishing between when agencies were operating and when they were closed.

On the other hand, another set of methodological changes has partially or fully offset the two described above. In particular, significantly higher client turnover rates were estimated in the 2005 data. This is at least partly the effect of the improved survey instrumentation discussed earlier. As described in Chapter 3, interviewers reported that many respondents found the questions designed to obtain information on client turnover in 2001 confusing. In addition, data patterns resulting from those questions were often inconsistent with other survey questions. In the 2001 analysis, as a result, we were very conservative, in the sense of making analysis choices about such issues as appropriate extrapolation factors for the annual estimates, to minimize the risk of inflating estimated participation (see pp. 38–39 of the 2001 Report, *Hunger in America 2001,* dated October 2002).

Because of the reported problems with the 2001 turnover questions, a new question was developed in 2005 and included in the survey. This question was intended to be clearer and less ambiguous in eliciting information about turnover rates.[28] Based on reports from the fielding of

---

[28] The wording of the new question is provided in Chapter 3. The old questions were kept in the survey as a backup.

the survey (and the lack of significant complaints), it appears that the new question worked much better. It also yielded responses that were more consistent with related survey questions.

Somewhat unexpectedly, in the analysis phase of the study, we found that the answers to this new question yielded higher estimates of turnover rates than had been implied in our earlier conservative analysis of the 2001 data. For example, the tabulations suggest that, even for pantries (which tend to have the lowest turnover), about 14% of the clients at a given point in time have begun using them only in the previous month and did not use them previously for at least a year. This has had two related, but distinct, effects on the 2005 estimates. First, we have used the responses to this new question as the basis of our turnover rates, thus directly increasing the estimates of turnover above those used in 2001. Second, the findings from the new question have, more generally, provided new evidence that turnover rates may be higher than previously believed, which has led us to be less conservative in our overall analysis.

In summary, improved survey methodology has resulted in significantly higher estimates of turnover. This has largely offset the drop in the estimated weekly participation number—a drop that itself was due, at least in part, to changed methodology.[29]

4.9.4   Standard Errors of Participation Estimates

As noted earlier, the use of ranges to define the participation estimates presented in this chapter reflects potential *measurement error* in the survey data. These ranges do *not* directly reflect *statistical sampling variation,* which is another potential source of error in the

---

[29] Interestingly, answers to the two questions used in 2001 (and to the same questions included in 2005 as backup) also suggest the possibility of substantially higher turnover rates than used in the 2001 estimates. As noted in the text, however, we chose to interpret the earlier data conservatively until we could obtain more reliable support for estimates of higher rates. The responses to the new question in 2005 provide that support.

participation estimates. To assess the approximate sampling error associated with our estimates, we have calculated standard errors for the weekly client estimates presented earlier, taking into account sample sizes, survey clustering, and other survey design features. The results indicate that for 2005 the standard errors associated with estimated numbers of participants tend to be about 3% of the estimated participation totals.[30] Thus, 95% confidence intervals extend plus or minus about 6 points around the weekly participation estimates. For instance, for participating food banks, the 2005 estimate of the number of people using A2H pantries in a week is 3.24 million.[31] A 95% confidence interval is then estimated to extend plus or minus 6% of the 3.24 estimate, or between 2.9 and 3.4 million.

In the deriving of annual estimates, additional potential statistical error is added, because several of the extrapolation factors are themselves survey-based and thus measured with error. If, however, as an approximation, this added sampling error is ignored, then the plus-or-minus-6% factor for confidence intervals can reasonably be applied to the annual estimates as well. For instance, suppose that one of the endpoints of the ranges in the annual estimates is 25.0 million. The 95% confidence interval would then extend from about 23.5 to 26.5 million. This should be viewed as a low estimate of the range of sampling error, since the use of several survey-based factors in developing the annual estimates undoubtedly increases the overall error.

---

[30] The comparable standard errors for the 2001 estimates are somewhat higher.

[31] Table 4.4.1 reports the number of *households* as 1.2 million. We have multiplied that figure by our estimate of 2.7 persons per household. (Sampling error associated with the 2.7 is ignored here for ease of exposition. The figure also excludes the estimates imputed for small providers where interviewing was not conducted.)

4.9.5 Simulation-Based Analysis of Changes

To examine further the effects of the methodological changes on the 2005 estimates, we have conducted a simulation analysis of the effects of *applying the improved 2005 survey estimation methods to the 2001 data.* This analysis, described more fully in Appendix A, focused on examining weekly estimates of participation, and it simulated as fully as possible the effects of applying the 2005 methods to the earlier data. A limitation of the analysis is that in some instances there was insufficient detail in the 2001 dataset to fully replicate the improved methods. Nevertheless, we were able to examine the approximate effects of four changes:

1. Increased screening of providers for survey eligibility (for example, for whether they were supplying "emergency food" as defined by the study)

2. Consideration of the fact that some providers in 2001 were open less than once per week

3. Adjustment of the assumed hours of operation when, during a day, providers were open longer than the observation period

4. Improved analytic treatment of instances when interviewing at a provider required more than one visit by the interviewing staff.

The results of the simulations, presented in Appendix A, show that most (though not all) of the differences between the 2001 and 2005 weekly-level results can be explained in terms of the four changes in methods that were simulated. Furthermore, after controlling for the simulation results, none of the observed differences between 2001 and 2005 is statistically significant.

4.9.6 Summary

Our "bottom line" estimate is that overall the range of participation estimates for 2005 is similar to that in 2001. Two salient facts should be noted in interpreting this result.

First, the similarity in the estimated participation ranges does not necessarily mean that there have been no changes. Since the estimates for both years have been expressed as ranges, the actual "true" level of participation could have gone up; alternatively, it could have gone down, though we think such a result is very unlikely, for reasons discussed earlier.

Second, in interpreting the estimates, it is important to understand that their apparent overall stability in participation levels hides the effects of two countervailing themes. On the one hand, the estimates of the number of people receiving services in a given week have gone down. However, this is approximately offset by an increase in estimated rates of client turnover in the system, which leads to *annual* estimates that are higher than they would otherwise be.

5.   CLIENTS: DEMOGRAPHIC PROFILE

One of the most important purposes of the study has been to develop a description of the people and households served by the A2H National Network. Key findings are presented in this section. Results reported in Chapters 5 through 9 represent all clients served by the A2H National Network.

We begin by describing the client sample on which the analysis is based. Section 5.2 then provides an overall profile of clients served by the A2H National Network. Subsequent sections then provide additional details about clients' demographic characteristics, citizenship, education levels, household income levels, and other resources.

5.1   NUMBER OF CLIENT RESPONDENTS

A total of 52,878 clients were interviewed at selected program sites of the A2H National Network. The clients interviewed at the pantry programs (37,986 clients) account for 71.8% of all client respondents. Those interviewed at the kitchen programs (10,667 clients) make up 20.2% of the total, and those interviewed at the shelter programs (4,225 clients) account for the remaining 8.0%. See Table 5.1.1 and Chart 5.1.1 which also show the percentage distribution after the weights described earlier were applied to each observation.

TABLE 5.1.1

NUMBER OF CLIENT RESPONDENTS

Site of Interview	Client Respondents		
	Number	Unweighted Percentage	Weighted Percentage
Pantry	37,986	71.8%	76.3%
Kitchen	10,667	20.2%	16.8%
Shelter	4,225	8.0%	6.9%
TOTAL	52,878	100.0%	100.0%

69

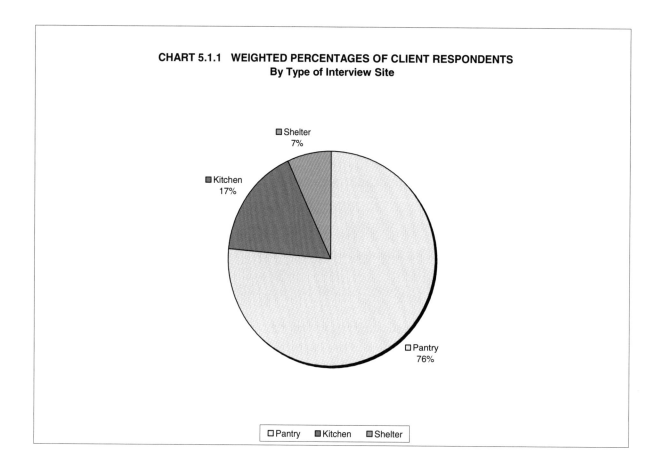

CHART 5.1.1   WEIGHTED PERCENTAGES OF CLIENT RESPONDENTS
By Type of Interview Site

CH 5. CLIENTS: DEMOGRAPHIC PROFILE

5.2   SUMMARY DEMOGRAPHIC PROFILE

Client respondents provided information about various demographic characteristics of themselves and their households. Table 5.2.1 summarizes the demographic profile of the client households of the A2H National Network. It also contains statistics about adult clients who visit A2H emergency food programs.

TABLE 5.2.1

SUMMARY DEMOGRAPHIC PROFILE OF A2H CLIENTS
(Client Households of A2H Emergency Food Providers)

	Pantry	Kitchen	Shelter	All
Client Households				
Size of household[a]				
Households with 1 member	32.8%	60.2%	81.7%	40.7%
Households with 2-3 members	38.8%	28.1%	13.4%	35.3%
Households with 4-6 members	24.4%	10.1%	3.4%	20.6%
Households with more than 6 members	4.0%	1.7%	1.5%	3.4%
Average household size	2.7	1.9	1.4	2.5
Median household size	2	1	1	2
Households with nonfamily members	5.1%	5.9%	1.9%	5.0%
Households with one or more adults employed	37.3%	35.1%	24.3%	36.0%
Households with single parents	17.3%	6.5%	6.7%	14.8%
Households with single parents among households with children younger than age 18[b]	43.0%	39.7%	68.9%	43.3%
Elderly and children in household				
Households with children younger than age 18	40.7%	16.8%	10.7%	34.6%
Households with children ages 0-5 years	18.5%	7.4%	6.4%	15.8%
Households with children ages 0-3 years	12.3%	4.6%	4.0%	10.4%
Households with any member 65 years or older	24.8%	14.1%	2.9%	21.5%
Adult Clients at Program Sites				
Adult Clients at Program Sites				
Male	31.5%	60.7%	71.5%	39.2%

CH 5. CLIENTS: DEMOGRAPHIC PROFILE

TABLE 5.2.1 *(continued)*

	Pantry	Kitchen	Shelter	All
Female	68.5%	39.3%	28.5%	60.8%
U.S. citizens	92.4%	94.6%	94.7%	93.0%
Registered voters[c]	70.3%	66.9%	53.3%	68.5%
Married or living as married	33.7%	21.5%	9.3%	30.0%
High school graduate	60.4%	69.4%	68.0%	62.5%
Currently employed	21.9%	25.2%	22.9%	22.5%
Clients in suburban/rural areas	47.9%	24.9%	27.2%	42.6%
SAMPLE SIZE (N)	**37,986**	**10,667**	**4,225**	**52,878**

SOURCE: This table was constructed based on usable responses to questions 2, 3, 4, 5, 6, 7, 9, 10, 11, 11a, 12, 81a, and 82 of the client survey.

NOTES: The percentages presented in this table are based only on usable responses, excluding missing, don't know, and refusal responses, except for the percentage of employed clients (See Table 5.7.2). All usable responses were weighted as described in Chapter 3 and in the Technical Appendix volume to represent all emergency food clients of the A2H National Network. The sample sizes (N) also include missing data.

[a]For all programs, responses greater than 24 people in a household were recoded as 24 people. Additional data are available for at most 10 members of each household. See Chapter 3 for details.

[b]The sample size is 15,756 for the pantry, 1,518 for the kitchen 745 for the shelter, and 18,019 for all.

[c]For registered voters, missing, don't know, and refusal responses combined are 2.6% for pantry clients, 4.2% for kitchen clients, 2.9% for shelter clients, and 2.9% for all clients.

The upper part of Table 5.2.1 shows the compositions of A2H client households. The mean household size is 2.5, and 36.0% of the households have an employed adult. In addition:

- 40.7% of the client households are single-person households.

- 3.4% of the client households have more than six members.

- Among client households with children younger than age 18, 43.3% are single-parent households.

- 34.6% of the client households have at least one member younger than age 18.

- 15.8% of the client households have one or more children ages 0 to 5 years.

- 21.5% of the households have at least one member age 65 years or older.

The lower part of Table 5.2.1 shows that 39.2% of the adult clients visiting emergency food programs are men, while 60.8% are women. (Table 5.3.1 contains detailed age, gender, and citizenship information.) Among adults at emergency providers, 93.0% are U.S. citizens, 62.5% are high school graduates, and 22.5% are currently working. These statistics, however, take into account only the client population who come to the program sites. Since the pantries' client base is not limited to the individual members who come to pick up food, but includes all members of such clients' households, it is also of interest to examine similar tabulations based on all individual members of client households. Table 5.3.2 in the next section presents age, gender, and citizenship composition of all members of client households.

.

CH 5. CLIENTS: DEMOGRAPHIC PROFILE

5.3   AGE, GENDER, AND CITIZENSHIP COMPOSITION

Clients interviewed were asked to provide information on age, gender, and U.S. citizenship for themselves and for at most nine members of their households. Table 5.3.1 shows the distribution of each variable only among the population represented by clients interviewed at program sites while Chart 5.3.1 shows the gender composition of clients. Table 5.3.2 shows the distribution among all members of client households.

TABLE 5.3.1

AGE, GENDER, AND CITIZENSHIP COMPOSITION
(Adult Clients at A2H Program Sites)

	Adult Clients Who Pick Up Food at a Pantry	Adult Clients at a Kitchen	Adult Clients at a Shelter	Adult Clients at All Program Sites
Age				
18-29	10.6%	11.3%	17.0%	11.1%
30-49	43.2%	52.3%	58.1%	45.7%
50-64	26.2%	25.4%	22.6%	25.8%
65 and over	20.1%	11.0%	2.3%	17.3%
TOTAL	100.0%	100.0%	100.0%	100.0%
Gender				
Male	31.5%	60.7%	71.5%	39.2%
Female	68.5%	39.3%	28.5%	60.8%
TOTAL	100.0%	100.0%	100.0%	100.0%
U.S. Citizen				
Yes	92.4%	94.6%	94.7%	93.0%
No	7.6%	5.4%	5.3%	7.0%
TOTAL	100.0%	100.0%	100.0%	100.0%
SAMPLE SIZE (N)	**37,986**	**10,667**	**4,225**	**52,878**

SOURCE: This table was constructed based on usable responses to questions 2, 3, and 5 of the client survey.

NOTES: The percentages presented in this table are based only on usable responses, excluding missing, don't know, and refusal responses. All usable responses were weighted as described in Chapter 3 and in the Technical Appendix volume to represent all emergency food clients of the A2H National Network. The sample sizes (N) also include missing data.

For age, missing, don't know, and refusal responses combined are 1.4% for pantry clients, 1.1% for kitchen clients, 2.3% for shelter clients, and 1.4% for all clients.

For gender, missing, don't know, and refusal responses combined are 1.1% for pantry clients, 0.8% for kitchen clients, 1.4% for shelter clients, and 1.1% for all clients.

For citizenship, missing, don't know, and refusal responses combined are 0.6% for pantry clients, 0.5% for kitchen clients, 1.1% for shelter clients, and 0.6% for all clients.

CH 5. CLIENTS: DEMOGRAPHIC PROFILE

Among the adult clients who come to program sites, 11.1% are ages 18 to 29; 45.7% ages

30 to 49; 25.8% ages 50 to 64; and 17.3% ages 65 and older. In addition:

- Among the adult pantry clients who were represented at the interview sites (not including all members of their households), 10.6% are ages 18 to 29; 43.2% ages 30 to 49; 26.2% ages 50 to 64; and 20.1% ages 65 and older.

- 31.5% of adult pantry clients at program sites are male.

- 92.4% of adult pantry clients at program sites are U.S. citizens.

- Among the adult kitchen clients, 11.3% are ages 18 to 29, 52.3% ages 30 to 49, 25.4% ages 50 to 64, and 11.0% ages 65 and older.

- 60.7% of adult kitchen clients at program sites are male.

- 94.6% of adult kitchen clients at program sites are U.S. citizens.

- Among the adult shelter clients, 17.0% are ages 18 to 29, 58.1% ages 30 to 49, 22.6% ages 50 to 64, and 2.3% ages 65 and older.

- 71.5% of adult shelter clients at program sites are male.

- 94.7% of adult shelter clients at program sites are U.S. citizens.

CH 5. CLIENTS: DEMOGRAPHIC PROFILE

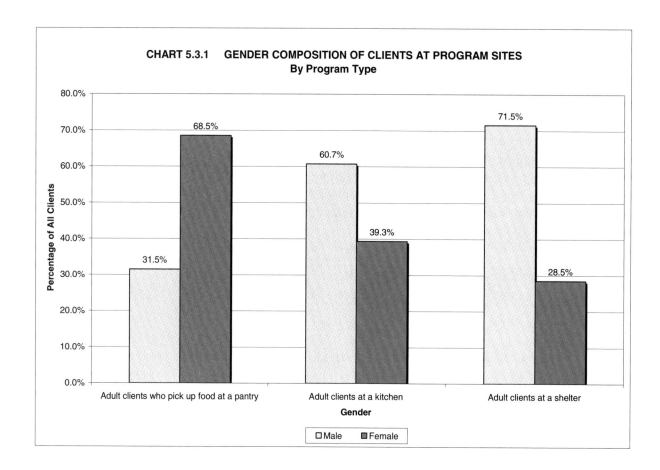

CH 5. CLIENTS: DEMOGRAPHIC PROFILE

TABLE 5.3.2

AGE, GENDER, AND CITIZENSHIP COMPOSITION
(All Members of Households)[a,b]

	All Members of Household, Pantry	All Members of Household, Kitchen	All Members of Household, Shelter	All Members of Household, All Programs
Age				
0-3	5.5%	3.2%	3.3%	5.1%
4-5	3.3%	1.9%	1.9%	3.1%
6-17	30.4%	18.4%	11.3%	28.2%
CHILDREN SUBTOTAL	39.2%	23.5%	16.5%	36.4%
18-29	11.8%	11.7%	15.1%	11.9%
30-49	24.8%	37.6%	48.4%	27.2%
50-64	13.8%	18.3%	17.5%	14.5%
65 and over	10.5%	9.0%	2.4%	10.0%
TOTAL	100.0%	100.0%	100.0%	100.0%
SAMPLE SIZE (N)[c]	**104,415**	**18,755**	**6,652**	**129,822**
Gender				
Male	45.6%	56.9%	67.9%	47.9%
Female	54.4%	43.1%	32.1%	52.1%
TOTAL	100.0%	100.0%	100.0%	100.0%
U.S. Citizen				
Yes	91.9%	94.7%	94.5%	92.4%
No	8.1%	5.3%	5.5%	7.6%
TOTAL	100.0%	100.0%	100.0%	100.0%
SAMPLE SIZE (N)	**100,773**	**18,139**	**6,117**	**125,029**

SOURCE: This table was constructed based on usable responses to questions 2, 3, 5, 6a, and 6b of the client survey.

NOTES: The percentages presented in this table are based only on usable responses, excluding missing, don't know, and refusal responses. All usable responses were weighted as described in Chapter 3 and in the Technical Appendix volume to represent all emergency food clients of the A2H National Network. The sample sizes (N) also include missing data.

For age, missing, don't know, and refusal responses combined are 1.8% for pantry clients, 2.8% for kitchen clients, 2.9% for shelter clients, and 2.0% for all clients.

For gender, missing, don't know, and refusal responses combined are 1.1% for pantry clients, 0.9% for kitchen clients, 2.0% for shelter clients, and 1.1% for all clients.

For citizenship, missing, don't know, and refusal responses combined are 0.9% for pantry clients, 0.8% for kitchen clients, 2.0% for shelter clients, and 0.9% for all clients.

[a]Data available for at most 10 members of household. See the Technical Appendix volume for details.

CH 5. CLIENTS: DEMOGRAPHIC PROFILE

TABLE 5.3.2 *(continued)*

_____

[b]In early tabulations of the 2005 "client age" data, we found that the estimated percentages changed somewhat when we made changes in how we dealth with inconsistent data and how we applied algorithms for imputing missing data for households with numbers of members exceeding the size of the grid. In the end, however, because of A2H's need for as much comparability as possible between years, essentially the 2001 data cleaning procedures were used in the estimates presented in this table.

[c]The sample sizes for age variables may be larger than those for the other two variables in this table. This is because the client questionnaire had additional questions to identify household members who are younger than age 18 and whether the household has any children between ages 0 and 5.

When we consider all members of client households, 8.2% are ages 0 to 5, 28.2% ages 6 to 17, 11.9% ages 18 to 29, 27.2% ages 30 to 49, 14.5% ages 50 to 64, and 10.0% ages 65 and older. Information on age distribution, as well as gender and citizenship distributions, by program type follows:

- Among all members of pantry client households, 8.8% are ages 0 to 5; 30.4% ages 6 to 17; 11.8% ages 18 to 29; 24.8% ages 30 to 49, 13.8% ages 50 to 64, and 10.5% ages 65 and older.

- 45.6% of all members of pantry client households are male.

- 91.9% of all members of pantry client households are U.S. citizens.

- Among all members of kitchen client households, 5.1% are ages 0 to 5; 18.4% ages 6 to 17; 11.7% ages 18 to 29; 37.6% 30 to 49; 18.3% ages 50 to 64, and 9.0% ages 65 and older.

- 56.9% of all members of kitchen client households are male.

- 94.7% of all members of kitchen client households are U.S. citizens.

- Among all members of shelter client households, 5.2% are ages 0 and 5; 11.3% ages 6 and 17; 15.1% ages 18 to 29; 48.4% ages 30 to 49; 17.5% ages 50 to 64; and 2.4% ages 65 and older.

- 67.9% of all members of shelter client households are male.

- 94.5% of all members of shelter client households are U.S. citizens.

CH 5. CLIENTS: DEMOGRAPHIC PROFILE

Table 5.3.2N translates the percentage distribution in the previous table (Table 5.3.2) into estimates of the numbers of members of A2H client households by age bracket and by type of provider. The numbers in this table (and similar tables) are based on the midpoints of the estimated ranges of annual client counts presented in Chapter 4 (see Appendix B for details). In reviewing this table, it is important to note that for kitchens and shelters, it include all members of the households; not just the members present at the A2H providers.

TABLE 5.3.2N

AGE COMPOSITION (ESTIMATED NUMBER OF CLIENTS)
(ALL MEMBERS OF HOUSEHOLDS)

	All Members of Household, Pantry	All Members of Household, Kitchen	All Members of Household, Shelter	All Members of Household, All Programs
Age				
0-3	1,275,000	60,700	31,100	1,336,200
4-5	763,100	36,400	17,500	798,700
6-17	7,051,200	349,000	106,400	7,345,800
18-29	2,732,500	221,600	141,900	3,094,800
30-49	5,755,000	713,500	455,300	7,094,700
50-64	3,192,200	347,000	164,900	3,763,900
65 and over	2,431,000	171,800	23,000	2,605,800
TOTAL ESTIMATED NUMBER OF PEOPLE IN CLIENT HOUSEHOLDS	**23,200,000**	**1,900,000**	**940,000**	**26,040,000**

NOTES: See Appendix B for the estimated number of people served in subgroups of A2H clients.

Columns in this table do not exactly add up to the column total. This discrepancy occurs because tables showing percentage distributions are weighted with the monthly weight, while the number of clients presented in this table is estimated at the annual level. Because the relationship between the monthly and annual weights varies across individuals depending on the frequency of visits to program sites, applying annual estimates to a monthly snapshot of percentage distributions results in small discrepancies in column totals.

CH 5. CLIENTS: DEMOGRAPHIC PROFILE

As shown in the table, pantries are estimated to serve annually more than 2 million young children and more than 9 million children under 18, overall. Pantries also serve more than 2.4 million elderly clients per year. In addition:

- Members of households of clients at A2H kitchens include more than 0.4 million children under 18; the comparable number for shelters is 0.1 million.

- Members of the households of clients at A2H kitchens include 0.2 million people 65 and older; the comparable number for shelters is much smaller, reflecting not only the smaller numbers at shelters but also their different clientele.

CH 5. CLIENTS: DEMOGRAPHIC PROFILE

5.4   MARITAL STATUS

Clients were also asked about their marital status. Table 5.4.1 presents the findings.

TABLE 5.4.1

MARITAL STATUS
(Adults Interviewed at A2H Emergency Food Providers)

Clients' Marital Status	Adult Clients Who Pick Up Food at a Pantry	Adult Clients at a Kitchen	Adult Clients at a Shelter	Adult Clients at All Program Sites
Married	27.6%	15.6%	7.0%	24.2%
Living as married	6.2%	5.9%	2.3%	5.9%
Widowed	14.3%	9.4%	6.0%	12.9%
Divorced	18.3%	20.7%	28.0%	19.3%
Separated	9.6%	9.9%	12.5%	9.9%
Never been married	24.1%	38.4%	44.1%	27.9%
TOTAL	100.0%	100.0%	100.0%	100.0%
SAMPLE SIZE (N)	**37,986**	**10,667**	**4,225**	**52,878**

SOURCE: This table was constructed based on usable responses to Question 9 of the client survey.

NOTES: The percentages presented in this table are based only on usable responses, excluding missing, don't know, and refusal responses. All usable responses were weighted as described in Chapter 3 and in the Technical Appendix volume to represent all emergency food clients of the A2H National Network. The sample sizes (N) also include missing data.

Missing, don't know, and refusal responses combined are 1.3% for pantry clients, 1.8% for kitchen clients, 2.5% for shelter clients, and 1.4% for all clients.

Key findings include:

- Overall, 24.2% of the clients at all program sites are married.

    - The percentage of married clients at pantry programs is 27.6%.

    - The percentage of married clients at kitchen programs is 15.6%.

    - The percentage of married clients at shelter programs is 7.0%.

- 5.9% of the clients at all program sites are living as married.

- 12.9% of the clients at all program sites are widowed.

- 9.9% of the clients at all program sites are separated.

- 27.9% of the clients at all program sites have never been married.

5.5   HIGHEST EDUCATION LEVEL ATTAINED

Clients were asked the highest education level they had attained. Education levels of

clients based on their responses are provided in Table 5.5.1.

TABLE 5.5.1

HIGHEST EDUCATION LEVEL ATTAINED
(Adults Interviewed at A2H Emergency Food Providers)

Clients' Education Level	Adult Clients Who Pick Up Food at a Pantry	Adult Clients at a Kitchen	Adult Clients at a Shelter	All Adult Clients
Less than high school	39.6%	30.6%	32.0%	37.5%
Completed high school or equivalent degree	36.6%	37.6%	38.0%	36.9%
Completed noncollege business/trade/ technical school	3.4%	4.0%	4.0%	3.6%
Some college/two-year degree	15.4%	21.5%	19.8%	16.8%
Completed college or higher	5.0%	6.3%	6.1%	5.3%
TOTAL	100.0%	100.0%	100.0%	100.0%
SAMPLE SIZE (N)	**37,986**	**10,667**	**4,225**	**52,878**

SOURCE: This table was constructed based on usable responses to Question 10 of the client survey.

NOTES: The percentages presented in this table are based only on usable responses, excluding missing, don't know, and refusal responses. All usable responses were weighted as described in Chapter 3 and in the Technical Appendix volume to represent all emergency food clients of the A2H National Network. The sample sizes (N) also include missing data.

At Missing, don't know, and refusal responses combined are 1.6% for pantry clients, 1.2% for kitchen clients, 2.6% for shelter clients, and 1.6% for all clients.

As Table 5.5.1 shows, 37.5% of the clients at emergency food programs have not

completed high school. The comparable percentage for the entire U.S. adult population is

15.4%.[32] More details follow:

---

[32] *Statistical Abstract of the United States, 2004-2005.* Table No. 212.

- 36.9% of all clients finished high school but no further education beyond high school.

- 16.8% of all clients have some college education or completed a two-year degree.

- 5.3% of all clients have completed college or beyond.

CH 5. CLIENTS: DEMOGRAPHIC PROFILE

5.6   RACIAL AND ETHNIC BACKGROUND

Clients were asked about their racial and ethnic background. Table 5.6.1 and Chart 5.6.1 summarize the results.

TABLE 5.6.1

RACIAL AND ETHNIC BACKGROUND
(Adults Interviewed at A2H Emergency Food Providers)

Clients' Racial[a] and Ethnic Background	Adult Clients Who Pick Up Food at a Pantry	Adult Clients at a Kitchen	Adult Clients at a Shelter	All Adult Clients
Non-Hispanic White[b]	40.0%	37.5%	42.4%	39.8%
Non-Hispanic Black	37.1%	42.0%	36.0%	37.9%
American Indian or Alaskan Native	4.1%	6.2%	5.3%	4.5%
Native Hawaiian or other Pacific Islander	0.5%	0.3%	1.3%	0.5%
Asian	1.2%	0.5%	0.4%	1.0%
Latino or Hispanic				
Mexican, Mexican American, Chicano	9.6%	6.4%	9.2%	9.0%
Puerto Rican	2.2%	3.2%	1.9%	2.3%
Cuban	0.1%	0.1%	0.0%	0.1%
Other Latino or Hispanic	6.0%	6.1%	4.4%	5.9%
SUBTOTAL	17.9%	15.8%	15.5%	17.4%
Other[c]	2.0%	2.3%	3.8%	2.2%
SAMPLE SIZE (N)	**37,986**	**10,667**	**4,225**	**52,878**

SOURCE: This table was constructed based on usable responses to questions 11, 11a, and 12 of the client survey.

NOTES: The percentages presented in this table are based only on usable responses, excluding missing, don't know, and refusal responses. All usable responses were weighted as described in Chapter 3 and in the Technical Appendix volume to represent all emergency food clients of the A2H National Network. The sample sizes (N) also include missing data.

For race, missing, don't know, and refusal responses combined are 0.7% for pantry clients, 0.8% for kitchen clients, 1.2% for shelter clients, and 0.7% for all clients.

For ethnicity, missing, don't know, and refusal responses combined are 2.7% for pantry clients, 3.3% for kitchen clients, 2.8% for shelter clients, and 2.8% for all clients.

[a]Multiple responses were accepted for races.

[b]Note that Table 5.6.1 of *Hunger in America 2001* showed racial distribution of all respondents regardless of their ethnicity. In the current table, race categories (including "Other") reflect racial distribution of non-Hispanic respondents only.

[c]Most respondents who marked "Other" as their choice did not provide further information. Those who provided an answer sometimes indicated their nationality, but because the number of usable responses was small, recoding of those responses based on this information was not performed.

Racial or ethnic background of the clients at emergency food program sites follows:

- Among the clients who come to all program sites, 39.8% are non-Hispanic white; 37.9% non-Hispanic black; and 4.5% American Indian or Alaskan Native.

- 0.5% are native Hawaiian or other Pacific Islander, and 1.0% are Asian.

- A total of 17.4% of the clients at all program sites indicate they are Spanish, Latino, or of Hispanic descent or origin.

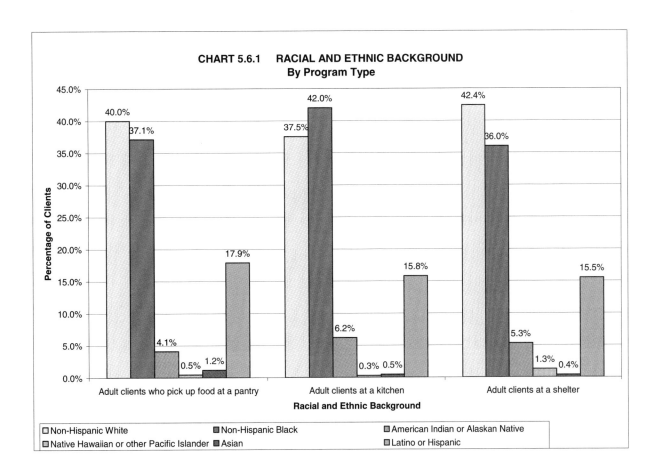

CH 5. CLIENTS: DEMOGRAPHIC PROFILE

5.7   EMPLOYMENT OF ADULTS IN HOUSEHOLD

Client respondents provided information on their households' current employment status.

Tables 5.7.1 and 5.7.2 present the findings regarding all adults in the households[33] while Chart

5.7.1 presents households with at least one working adult.

TABLE 5.7.1

EMPLOYMENT STATUS OF ADULTS IN HOUSEHOLD

	Pantry	Kitchen	Shelter	All
Percentage of employed adults among all adults in client households	27.9%	28.7%	23.3%	27.8%
SAMPLE SIZE (N)	**65,773**	**14,882**	**4,647**	**85,302**
Percentage of employed adults among adults younger than age 65 in client household	34.1%	32.8%	24.5%	33.3%
SAMPLE SIZE (N)	**54,086**	**12,319**	**4,507**	**70,912**
Percentage of client households with one or more adults employed	37.3%	35.1%	24.3%	36.0%
SAMPLE SIZE (N)	**37,986**	**10,667**	**4,225**	**52,878**

SOURCE: This table was constructed based on all responses to questions 3 and 6 of the client survey.

NOTES: The percentages in this table, unlike those in most other tables, were calculated without leaving out item nonresponses. Because this table was constructed combining responses to several questions, excluding item nonresponses could have caused confusion.

For all adults in the household, missing, don't know, and refusal responses combined are 0.6% for pantry clients, 0.8% for kitchen clients, 1.3% for shelter clients, and 0.6% for all clients.

For adults younger than age 65 in the household, missing, don't know, and refusal responses combined are 0.7% for pantry clients, 0.9% for kitchen clients, 1.3% for shelter clients, and 0.7% for all clients.

For client households, missing, don't know, and refusal responses combined are 0.1% for pantry clients, 0.1% for kitchen clients, 0.3% for shelter clients, and 0.1% for all clients.

[33] Data are available for at most 10 members of the household. See Technical Appendix volume for details.

Among all adults in client households, 27.8% are employed. When we consider adults younger than age 65, 33.3% are currently working. At the household level, 36.0% have one or more adults employed. Results by program type show:

- 37.3% of the pantry client households have one or more adults currently employed.

- 35.1% of the kitchen client households have one or more adults currently employed.

- 24.3% of the shelter client households have one or more adults currently employed.

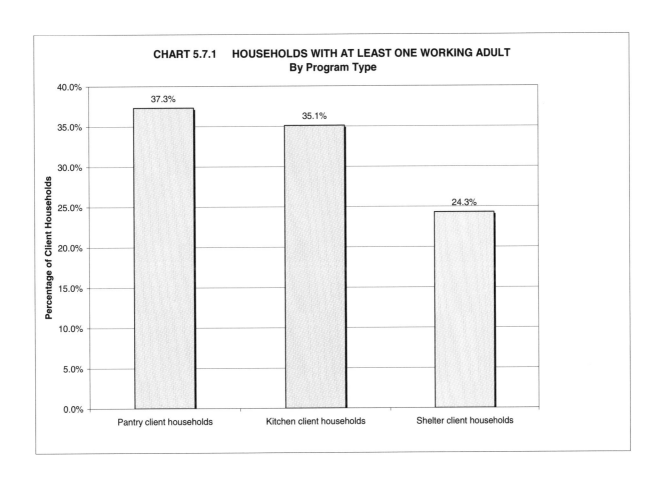

CH 5. CLIENTS: DEMOGRAPHIC PROFILE

TABLE 5.7.2

DETAILED EMPLOYMENT STATUS OF ADULTS IN HOUSEHOLD

	Pantry	Kitchen	Shelter	All
Current employment status of all adults in client households				
Full-time	14.5%	15.9%	12.9%	14.6%
Part-time	13.4%	12.8%	10.4%	13.2%
Unemployed	72.1%	71.3%	76.7%	72.2%
SAMPLE SIZE (N)	**65,773**	**14,882**	**4,647**	**85,302**
Current employment status of all adults in client households younger than age 65[a]				
Full-time	17.4%	18.0%	13.3%	17.3%
Part-time	15.6%	14.0%	10.9%	15.1%
Unemployed	67.0%	68.0%	75.8%	67.6%
SAMPLE SIZE (N)	**54,086**	**12,319**	**4,507**	**70,912**
Employment status of adult clients interviewed at program sites				
Currently working				
Full-time	9.1%	11.9%	11.3%	9.7%
Part-time	12.9%	13.4%	11.5%	12.9%
Unknown	0.1%	0.1%	0.3%	0.1%
SUBTOTAL	21.9%	25.2%	22.9%	22.5%
Currently not working	78.1%	74.8%	77.1%	77.5%
Have not worked for				
Less than 3 months	5.8%	12.5%	21.3%	8.0%
3-5 months	4.6%	5.1%	6.9%	4.8%
6-8 months	4.0%	3.7%	6.2%	4.1%
9-11 months	1.7%	1.8%	3.2%	1.8%
1-2 years	11.6%	11.0%	13.6%	11.6%
More than 2 years	44.4%	35.4%	23.9%	41.5%
Unknown	2.7%	3.9%	3.0%	3.0%
SUBTOTAL	74.7%	73.4%	78.0%	74.7%
Never worked	4.0%	2.0%	1.0%	3.4%
Unknown	0.3%	0.7%	0.4%	0.4%
TOTAL	100.0%	100.0%	100.0%	100.0%
SAMPLE SIZE (N)	**37,986**	**10,667**	**4,225**	**52,878**

TABLE 5.7.2 *(continued)*

	Pantry	Kitchen	Shelter	All
Clients with managerial or professional jobs among those who have worked before or are currently working	15.8%	15.8%	14.5%	15.7%
SAMPLE SIZE (N) – Clients at program sites who have worked before or are currently working	**35,132**	**9,997**	**4,025**	**49,154**
Clients participating in government-sponsored job training or work experience programs among those who have never worked	n.p.	n.p.	n.p.	n.p.
SAMPLE SIZE (N) – Clients who have never worked	**0**	**0**	**0**	**0**

SOURCE: This table was constructed based on all responses to questions 3, 6, 12a, 13, 14a, and 15 of the client survey.

NOTE: The percentages in this table, unlike those in most other tables, were calculated without leaving out item nonresponses (labeled "unknown"). Because this table was constructed combining responses to several questions, excluding item nonresponses could have caused confusion. All responses were weighted as described in Chapter 3 and in the Technical Appendix volume to represent all emergency food clients or households of the A2H National Network.

[a]Includes only households with at least one adult younger than age 65.

As shown in Table 5.7.2, when we consider the employment status of all adults in client households, 14.6% are employed full-time, 13.2% are employed part-time, and the remaining 72.2% are currently unemployed. Details of the employment status of adult clients who come to program sites follow:

- Overall, 9.7% of the adult clients at program sites are currently employed full-time; 12.9% employed part-time.

- 8.0% of the clients have recently lost their job, having been unemployed for three months or less.

- 11.6% of all clients have been unemployed for one to two years.

- 41.5% of all clients have not worked for more than two years.

- Among those who have worked before or are currently working, 15.7% either had or currently have managerial or professional jobs.

- 3.4% of the clients had never worked; of these, n.p. are participating in government-sponsored job training or work experience programs.

As shown in Table 5.7.2N, the above percentages translate to estimates of very substantial numbers of employed people in the A2H client households.

TABLE 5.7.2N

ESTIMATED NUMBER OF EMPLOYED ADULTS, FULL-TIME AND PART TIME

	Pantry	Kitchen	Shelter	All
Employment status of all known adults in client households				
Full-time	2,218,700	238,300	105,400	2,577,500
Part-time	2,054,700	192,000	85,600	2,324,400
Unemployed	11,026,600	1,069,800	629,000	12,718,100
ESTIMATED TOTAL NUMBER OF ALL ADULTS IN CLIENT HOUSEHOLDS	**15,300,000**	**1,500,000**	**820,000**	**17,620,000**
Employment status of adult clients at program sites				
Full-time	777,700	118,600	75,700	993,200
Part-time	1,106,100	133,600	76,700	1,319,700
Unknown	5,800	1,100	1,900	9,200
Unemployed	6,710,400	746,700	515,600	7,947,900
ESTIMATED TOTAL NUMBER OF ADULT CLIENTS AT PROGRAM SITES	**8,600,000**	**1,000,000**	**670,000**	**10,270,000**

NOTES: See Appendix B for the estimated number of people in subgroups of A2H clients.

Columns in this table do not exactly add up to the column total. This discrepancy occurs because tables showing percentage distributions are weighted with the monthly weight, while the number of clients presented in this table is estimated at the annual level. Because the relationship between the monthly and annual weights varies across individuals depending on the frequency of visits to program sites, applying annual estimates to a monthly snapshot of percentage distributions results in small discrepancies in column totals.

Overall, households with members served by A2H include almost 2.6 million adults with full-time jobs and another 2.3 million adults with part time jobs.

- The working adults include 4.2 million in households served by pantries, 0.4 million in households served by kitchens, and 0.2 million in households served by shelters.

- When only adults visiting the program sites are considered, the numbers of employed adults (counting both full- and part-time) are 1.8 million for pantries 0.3 million for kitchens, and 0.1 million for shelters.

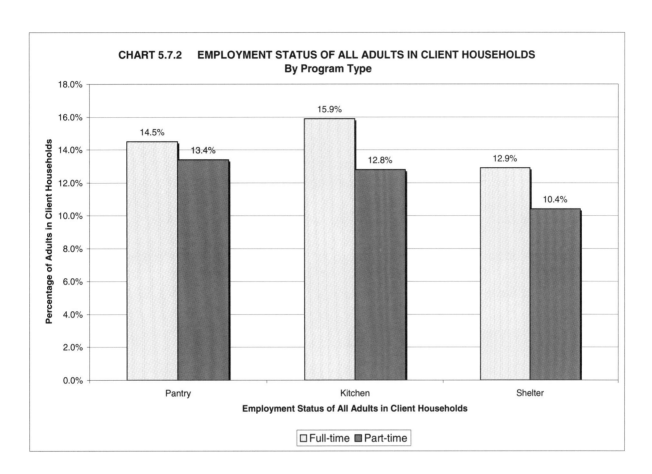

CHART 5.7.2   EMPLOYMENT STATUS OF ALL ADULTS IN CLIENT HOUSEHOLDS
By Program Type

CH 5. CLIENTS: DEMOGRAPHIC PROFILE

5.8   HOUSEHOLD INCOME

Lack of sufficient income usually plays a major role in forcing a person or a family to seek assistance from an A2H emergency food provider. In this section, we examine patterns of income receipt, for both monthly and annual income.

5.8.1   Federal Poverty Level

The U.S. government periodically establishes poverty guidelines to provide an indication of the levels of income below which households of various sizes would be considered impoverished. In parts of the analysis in this section, it will be useful to refer to these guidelines as a tool in understanding the meaning of various income levels. For reference, Table 5.8.1.1 presents 100% of these federal poverty levels.

TABLE 5.8.1.1

THE 2005 FEDERAL POVERTY LEVEL—MONTHLY INCOME

Household Size	48 Contiguous States and DC	Alaska	Hawaii
1	$798	$996	$918
2	$1,069	$1,336	$1,230
3	$1,341	$1,676	$1,543
4	$1,613	$2,016	$1,855
5	$1,884	$2,356	$2,168
6	$2,156	$2,696	$2,480
7	$2,428	$3,036	$2,793
8	$2,699	$3,376	$3,105
Each additional member	+$272	+$340	+$313

SOURCE: Federal Register, Vol. 70, No. 33, February 18, 2005, pp. 8373-8375.

NOTE: The 2005 federal poverty guidelines (also known as the federal poverty level) reflect price changes through calendar year 2004; accordingly they are approximately equal to the Census Bureau poverty thresholds for calendar year 2004.

5.8.2   Household Income for the Previous Month

Clients were asked to report their total household income for the previous month or to choose from a set of predefined income brackets.   The results are in Table 5.8.2.1 while Chart 5.8.2.1 presents monthly incomes as a percentage of the federal poverty level.

TABLE 5.8.2.1

HOUSEHOLD INCOME FOR THE PREVIOUS MONTH

Income for the Previous Month	Pantry Client Households	Kitchen Client Households	Shelter Client Households	All Client Households
Total monthly income				
No income	6.7%	15.9%	32.6%	10.0%
$1-$499	13.3%	16.6%	20.4%	14.3%
$500-$999	38.6%	31.4%	22.2%	36.3%
$1,000-$1,499	17.6%	11.7%	6.2%	15.8%
$1,500-$1,999	6.7%	5.2%	4.2%	6.2%
$2,000-$2,499	3.1%	4.6%	1.8%	3.3%
$2,500-$2,999	1.0%	1.1%	0.2%	1.0%
$3,000 or more	1.6%	3.0%	2.4%	1.9%
Unknown	11.4%	10.7%	9.8%	11.2%
TOTAL	100.0%	100.0%	100.0%	100.0%
Average monthly income among valid responses (in dollars)[a]	890	820	550	860
Median monthly income among valid responses (in dollars)	750	640	250	750
Income as a percentage of the federal poverty level[b]				
0% (no income)	6.7%	15.9%	32.6%	10.0%
1%-50%	23.3%	19.7%	21.7%	22.6%
51%-75%	23.2%	17.5%	10.0%	21.4%
76%-100%	15.1%	13.7%	9.6%	14.5%
101%-130%	10.5%	7.8%	5.3%	9.6%
131%-150%	4.1%	4.2%	2.1%	4.0%
151%-185%	2.6%	1.8%	1.8%	2.4%
186% or higher	3.0%	8.8%	7.1%	4.2%
Unknown	11.5%	10.7%	9.8%	11.2%
TOTAL	100.0%	100.0%	100.0%	100.0%
Average monthly income as percentage of the poverty level among valid responses	74.8%	81.2%	61.8%	75.0%

TABLE 5.8.2.1 *(continued)*

Income for the Previous Month	Pantry Client Households	Kitchen Client Households	Shelter Client Households	All Client Households
Median monthly income as percentage of the poverty level among valid responses	70.1%	69.0%	31.3%	68.2%
SAMPLE SIZE (N)	**37,986**	**10,667**	**4,225**	**52,878**

SOURCE: This table was constructed based on all responses to questions 29 and 29a of the client survey.

NOTES: The percentages presented in this table, unlike those in most other tables, were calculated without leaving out item nonresponses (labeled "unknown"). To ensure that key percentages, such as that for no income, appear consistent within this table and across related tables, a constant denominator, which includes item nonresponses, was used. All responses were weighted as described in Chapter 3 and in the Technical Appendix volume to represent all emergency food clients or households of the A2H National Network.

For total monthly income, missing, don't know, and refusal responses combined are 11.4% for pantry clients, 10.7% for kitchen clients, 9.8% for shelter clients, and 11.2% for all clients. The missing rates we report here were obtained after we cross-imputed missing responses for monthly and yearly income variables.

For income as percentage of federal poverty level, missing, don't know, and refusal responses combined are 11.5% for pantry clients, 10.7% for kitchen clients, 9.8% for shelter clients, and 11.2% for all clients.

[a]For the calculation of the average and the median, responses given as a range were recoded to be the midpoint of the range.

[b]The percentages in this panel may not be equal to those in the corresponding row of the upper panel of this table because the two panels of data may have different item nonresponse rates. The calculation in the lower panel required information about household size as well as household income.

Table 5.8.2.1 shows that 10.0% of all client households had no income at all for the month prior to the interview. More details on income follow:

- 6.7% of the pantry client households had no monthly income.
- 15.9% of the kitchen client households had no monthly income.
- 32.6% of the shelter client households had no monthly income.
- 60.6% of all client households had monthly household income less than $1,000.
- Average household income among all clients during the previous month was $860 (median: $750). By contrast, the mean for the U.S. population as a whole in 2004 was $5,006 (median: $3,724).[34]

---

[34] U.S. Census Bureau. Income, Poverty, and Health Insurance Coverage in the United States: 2004. August 2005, pp. 60-229.

- Average monthly household income among the pantry clients was $890 (median: $750).

- Average monthly household income among the kitchen clients was $820 (median: $640).

- Average monthly household income among the shelter clients was $550 (median: $250).

- 78.1% of client households had an income of 130% or below the federal poverty level during the previous month.

- Average monthly household income among all client households as a percentage of the federal poverty level was 75.0% (median: 68.2%).

- Average monthly household income among pantry client households was 74.8% (median: 70.1%) of the federal poverty level.

- Average monthly household income among kitchen client households was 81.2% (median: 69.0%) of the federal poverty level.

- Average monthly household income among shelter client households was 61.8% (median: 31.3%) of the federal poverty level.

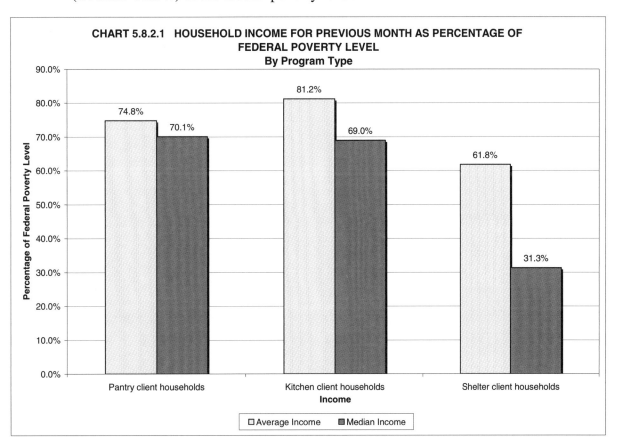

CH 5. CLIENTS: DEMOGRAPHIC PROFILE

5.8.3   Sources of Household Income for the Previous Month

Clients were asked to indicate the major source of their household income for the previous month. They were then asked to name all sources of their household income. Table 5.8.3.1 and Table 5.8.3.2 summarize the findings. Chart 5.8.3.1 presents the main sources of income among all clients while Chart 5.8.3.2 presents all sources of household income.

TABLE 5.8.3.1

MAIN SOURCE OF HOUSEHOLD INCOME FOR THE PREVIOUS MONTH

Main Source of Household Income for Previous Month	Pantry Client Households	Kitchen Client Households	Shelter Client Households	All Client Households
Job	25.0%	26.8%	26.8%	25.5%
Government welfare assistance				
Temporary Assistance for Needy Families (TANF)	1.8%	1.1%	1.1%	1.7%
General Assistance (GA)[a]	2.0%	3.4%	4.6%	2.4%
SUBTOTAL	3.9%	4.5%	5.6%	4.1%
Other government sources				
Social Security	22.1%	13.5%	5.1%	19.5%
Unemployment compensation	1.5%	1.2%	1.0%	1.4%
Disability (SSDI)/Workers' Compensation	7.2%	6.4%	4.3%	6.9%
Supplemental Security Income (SSI)	10.1%	9.5%	5.5%	9.7%
SUBTOTAL	40.9%	30.5%	15.8%	37.4%
Nongovernment, nonjob sources				
Pension	2.6%	2.4%	0.6%	2.4%
Child support	1.2%	0.6%	0.5%	1.1%
Churches	0.0%	0.1%	0.3%	0.1%
Alimony	0.0%	0.0%	0.1%	0.0%
Relatives	1.3%	1.3%	1.4%	1.3%
SUBTOTAL	5.3%	4.3%	2.8%	4.9%
Other[b]	2.4%	4.1%	4.0%	2.8%
No income	6.7%	15.9%	32.6%	10.0%
Unknown	15.8%	13.8%	12.3%	15.2%
TOTAL	100.0%	100.0%	100.0%	100.0%
SAMPLE SIZE (N)	**37,986**	**10,667**	**4,225**	**52,878**

CH 5. CLIENTS: DEMOGRAPHIC PROFILE

TABLE 5.8.3.1 *(continued)*

_____

SOURCE: This table was constructed based on all responses to questions 29 and 30 of the client survey.

NOTES: The percentages presented in this table, unlike those in most other tables, were calculated without leaving out item nonresponses (labeled "unknown"). To ensure that key percentages, such as that for no income, appear consistent within this table and across related tables, a constant denominator, which includes item nonresponses, was used. All responses were weighted as described in Chapter 3 and in the Technical Appendix volume to represent all emergency food clients or households of the A2H National Network.

Missing, don't know, and refusal responses combined are 15.8% for pantry clients, 13.8% for kitchen clients, 12.3% for shelter clients, and 15.2% for all clients.

[a]Estimates for GA and TANF should be used with caution, since some respondents may not have understood the names of the programs under which they were receiving benefits. Indeed, in some states, the regular GA program is not offered, although other sources of assistance are sometimes available and could have been confused with GA. States where GA is not available include but are not limited to Georgia, Michigan, and Oklahoma.

[b]This includes some form of limited savings.

Overall, 25.5% of the clients indicated that a job was the main source of income for their households for the previous month. Other sources of income are as follows:

- For 4.1% of all clients, welfare assistance from the government such as TANF and GA was the main source of household income.

- For 37.4% of all clients, other government assistance such as social security or unemployment compensation was the main source of household income.

- For 4.9% of all clients, income came mainly from nongovernment, nonjob sources, such as pension and child support.

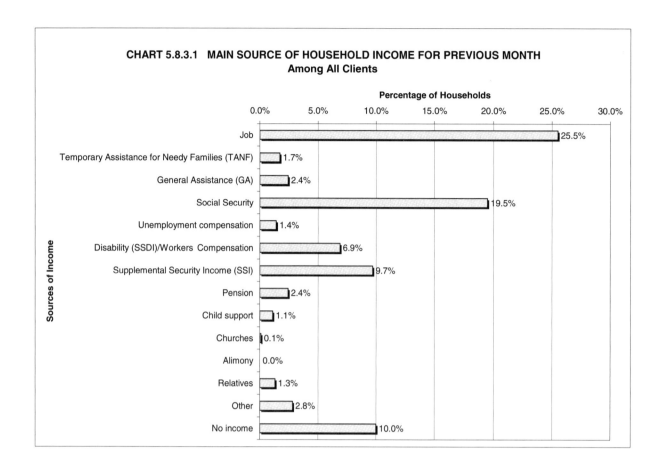

CHART 5.8.3.1   MAIN SOURCE OF HOUSEHOLD INCOME FOR PREVIOUS MONTH
Among All Clients

CH 5. CLIENTS: DEMOGRAPHIC PROFILE

TABLE 5.8.3.2

ALL SOURCES OF HOUSEHOLD INCOME FOR PREVIOUS MONTH

All Sources of Household Income for Previous Month[a]	Pantry Client Households	Kitchen Client Households	Shelter Client Households	All Client Households
Job	37.3%	35.1%	24.3%	36.0%
Government welfare assistance				
Temporary Assistance for Needy Families (TANF)	5.5%	3.8%	3.3%	5.1%
General Assistance (GA)[b]	6.6%	9.2%	11.3%	7.4%
Other government sources				
Social Security	36.4%	25.1%	12.5%	32.8%
Unemployment compensation	3.4%	2.7%	1.9%	3.2%
Disability (SSDI)/Workers' Compensation	14.3%	13.0%	7.6%	13.6%
Supplemental Security Income (SSI)	22.1%	20.8%	11.1%	21.1%
Government assistance with child care costs	2.5%	1.6%	0.9%	2.3%
Nongovernment, nonjob sources				
Pension	10.0%	8.5%	2.8%	9.2%
Child support	6.0%	2.4%	1.8%	5.1%
Alimony	0.3%	0.2%	0.5%	0.3%
Relatives	10.7%	10.6%	14.1%	10.9%
No income	6.7%	15.9%	32.6%	10.0%
SAMPLE SIZE (N)	**37,986**	**10,667**	**4,225**	**52,878**

SOURCE: This table was constructed based on all responses to questions 6, 25, and 29 of the client survey.

NOTES: The percentages presented in this table, unlike those in most other tables, were calculated without leaving out item nonresponses (labeled "unknown"). To ensure that key percentages, such as that for no income, appear consistent within this table and across related tables, a constant denominator, which includes item nonresponses, was used. All responses were weighted as described in Chapter 3 and in the Technical Appendix volume to represent all emergency food clients or households of the A2H National Network.

Missing, don't know, and refusal responses combined are 1.7% for pantry clients, 1.3% for kitchen clients, 1.5% for shelter clients, and 1.6% for all clients.

[a]Multiple responses were accepted.

[b]Estimates for GA and TANF should be used with caution, since some respondents may not have understood the names of the programs under which they were receiving benefits. Indeed, in some states, the regular GA program is not offered, although other sources of assistance are sometimes available and could have been confused with GA. States where GA is not available include but are not limited to Georgia, Michigan, and Oklahoma.

When clients were asked about *all* sources of their household income for the previous month, 36.0% included a job as a source.

- For 5.1% of all clients, TANF was a source of household income during the previous month.

- For 7.4%, GA was a source of household income.

- 32.8% of all clients said they received social security benefits

- 13.6% chose SSDI or workers' compensation as a source of household income.

- 21.1% mentioned SSI as a source.

- In addition, 9.2%, 5.1%, and 10.9% of the clients indicate pension, child support, and their relatives, respectively, as a source of income.

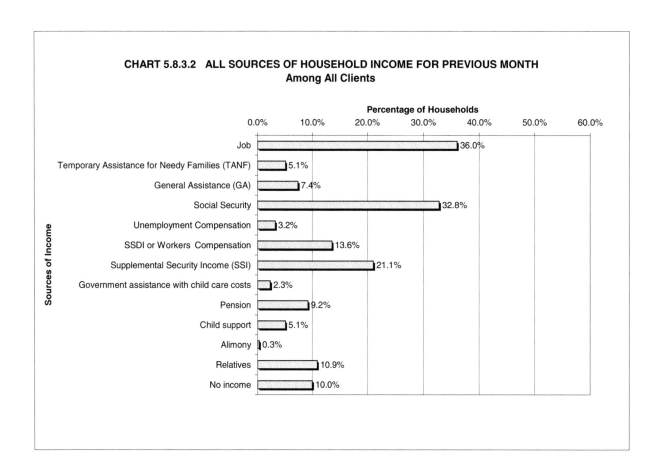

CHART 5.8.3.2   ALL SOURCES OF HOUSEHOLD INCOME FOR PREVIOUS MONTH
Among All Clients

100

5.8.4 Annual Household Income in 2004

Clients also provided estimates of their total household income in the year 2004. Table 5.8.4.1 shows their annual income in dollars and as a percentage of the federal poverty level. Chart 5.8.4.1 presents annual income by program type as a percentage of the federal poverty level.

TABLE 5.8.4.1

HOUSEHOLD INCOME FOR 2004

	Pantry Client Households	Kitchen Client Households	Shelter Client Households	All Client Households
Total annual income				
No income	4.8%	11.5%	20.6%	7.0%
$1-$4,999	13.0%	18.3%	24.6%	14.7%
$5,000-$9,999	31.2%	27.6%	19.8%	29.8%
$10,000-$14,999	17.1%	12.5%	9.9%	15.8%
$15,000-$19,999	10.8%	7.5%	4.9%	9.8%
$20,000-$24,999	5.5%	4.7%	4.0%	5.3%
$25,000-$29,999	2.5%	2.8%	1.5%	2.5%
$30,000-$34,999	1.6%	1.2%	1.8%	1.5%
$35,000-$39,999	1.0%	1.1%	1.0%	1.0%
$40,000-$44,999	0.5%	0.8%	0.4%	0.6%
$45,000-$49,999	0.3%	0.8%	1.1%	0.4%
$50,000 and over	1.0%	2.0%	1.6%	1.2%
Unknown	10.8%	9.2%	8.6%	10.4%
TOTAL	100.0%	100.0%	100.0%	100.0%
Average annual income among valid responses (in dollars)[a]	11,560	10,790	8,460	11,210
Median annual income among valid responses (in dollars)	9,000	7,990	5,000	9,000
Income as a percentage of the federal poverty level[b]				
0% (no income)[c]	4.8%	11.5%	20.6%	7.0%
1%-50%	24.4%	23.0%	26.8%	24.3%
51%-75%	22.0%	17.9%	12.4%	20.7%
76%-100%	14.6%	12.5%	7.2%	13.8%
101%-130%	10.7%	8.1%	7.0%	10.0%
131%-150%	4.2%	3.6%	3.1%	4.0%
151%-185%	3.6%	3.5%	3.2%	3.5%

CH 5. CLIENTS: DEMOGRAPHIC PROFILE

TABLE 5.8.4.1 *(continued)*

	Pantry Client Households	Kitchen Client Households	Shelter Client Households	All Client Households
186% or higher	4.8%	10.7%	10.7%	6.2%
Unknown	10.9%	9.2%	9.0%	10.5%
TOTAL	100.0%	100.0%	100.0%	100.0%
Average annual income as percentage of the poverty level among valid responses	80%	90%	80%	82%
Median annual income as percentage of the poverty level among valid responses	70%	70%	42%	70%
SAMPLE SIZE (N)	**37,986**	**10,667**	**4,225**	**52,878**

SOURCE: This table was constructed based on all responses to questions 29 and 31 of the client survey.

NOTES: The percentages presented in this table, unlike those in most other tables, were calculated without leaving out item nonresponses (labeled "unknown"). To ensure that key percentages, such as that for no income, appear consistent within this table, a constant denominator, which includes item nonresponses, was used. All responses were weighted as described in Chapter 3 and in the Technical Appendix volume to represent all emergency food clients or households of the A2H National Network.

For total annual income, missing, don't know, and refusal responses combined are 10.8% for pantry clients, 9.2% for kitchen clients, 8.6% for shelter clients, and 10.4% for all clients. The missing rates we report here were obtained after we cross-imputed missing responses for monthly and yearly income variables.

For income as percentage of the federal poverty level, missing, don't know, and refusal responses combined are 10.9% for pantry clients, 9.2% for kitchen clients, 9.0% for shelter clients, and 10.5% for all clients.

[a]For the calculation of the average and the median, responses given as a range were recoded to be the midpoint of the bracket.

[b]See Table 5.8.1.1 for the federal poverty levels.

[c]The percentages in this row may not be equal to those in the corresponding row of the upper panel of this table, because the two panels of data may have different item nonresponse rates. The calculation in the lower panel required information about household size as well as household income.

In the year 2004, 51.5% of all clients had a household income less than $10,000. More information about annual income of client households follows:

- Average household income among all clients in year 2004 was $11,210.

- 75.8% of the clients' households had an income of 130% or below the federal poverty level.

- Average household income as percentage of the federal poverty level was 82% (median: 70%).

In light of interest in overlaps between the A2H clientele and the public assistance system, it is also useful to translate the previous data on the use of TANF and General Assistance into estimates of the absolute numbers of people who receive A2H help and are in these programs. This is done in Table 5.8.4.1N.

TABLE 5.8.4.1N

ESTIMATED NUMBER OF CLIENT HOUSEHOLDS RECEIVING TANF OR GA
DURING PREVIOUS MONTH

Did You (or Anyone in Your Household) Get Money in the Last Month from Any of the Following?[a]	Pantry Client Households	Kitchen Client Households	Shelter Client Households	All Client Households
Temporary Assistance for Needy Families (TANF)	472,400	38,200	22,300	519,300
General Assistance (GA)	566,000	92,100	75,400	755,700
ESTIMATED TOTAL NUMBER CLIENT HOUSEHOLDS	**8,600,000**	**1,000,000**	**670,000**	**10,270,000**

NOTES: See Appendix B for the estimated number of people served in subgroups of A2H clients.

Columns in this table do not exactly add up to the column total. This discrepancy occurs because tables showing percentage distributions are weighted with the monthly weight, while the number of clients presented in this table is estimated at the annual level. Because the relationship between the monthly and annual weights varies across individuals depending on the frequency of visits to program sites, applying annual estimates to a monthly snapshot of percentage distributions results in small discrepancies in column totals.

[a]Multiple responses were accepted.

Nearly 1.3 million A2H client households receive TANF or General Assistance:

- Approximately 0.5 million pantry client households receiving TANF and almost 0.6 million receiving General Assistance.

- The relevant numbers for kitchen and shelter clients are lower, with approximately 40,000 and 90,000 kitchen client households receiving TANF and General Assistance, respectively; the comparable numbers for shelter clients are 22,000 and 76,000.

CH 5. CLIENTS: DEMOGRAPHIC PROFILE

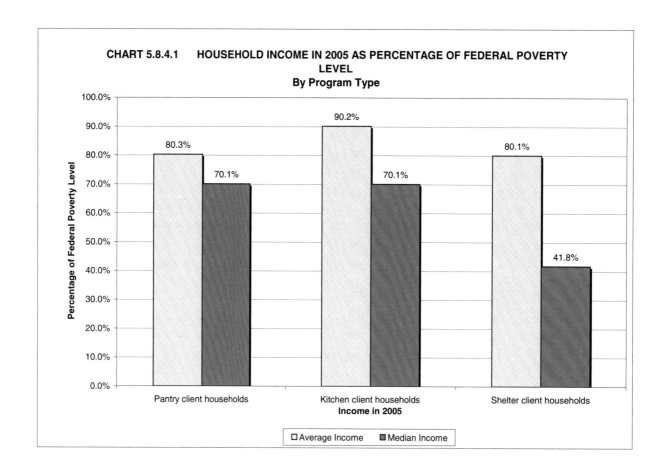

CHART 5.8.4.1   HOUSEHOLD INCOME IN 2005 AS PERCENTAGE OF FEDERAL POVERTY LEVEL
By Program Type

CH 5. CLIENTS: DEMOGRAPHIC PROFILE

5.9   HOUSING

5.9.1   Housing Status

Table 5.9.1.1 shows the housing status of the client households. It shows whether they have a place to live, what kind of housing they have, whether they own or rent, and what their other housing-related experiences have been. Chart 5.9.1.1 shows percentage of clients, by program type, with and without a place to live.

TABLE 5.9.1.1

HOUSING STATUS

	Pantry Client Households	Kitchen Client Households	Shelter Client Households	All Client Households
The kind of place you live now?				
Clients with a place to live				
House	42.3%	27.7%	7.1%	37.4%
Mobile home/trailer	11.4%	3.3%	1.4%	9.3%
Apartment	37.9%	31.7%	4.9%	34.6%
Room	4.0%	8.5%	4.8%	4.8%
Live with family, friends	1.4%	2.8%	1.4%	1.6%
SUBTOTAL	97.0%	73.9%	19.6%	87.9%
Clients without a place to live				
Homeless, living in shelter or mission	1.5%	16.4%	75.0%	9.0%
Homeless, living on the street	1.0%	8.0%	4.5%	2.4%
Car, van, or recreational vehicle	0.4%	1.6%	0.6%	0.6%
Abandoned building	0.1%	0.1%	0.3%	0.1%
SUBTOTAL	3.0%	26.1%	80.4%	12.1%
TOTAL	100.0%	100.0%	100.0%	100.0%
SAMPLE SIZE (N)	**37,986**	**10,667**	**4,225**	**52,878**
Among clients who have a place to live				
Own the place you live	26.3%	15.5%	16.7%	24.6%
Rent your place	65.8%	70.3%	56.6%	66.3%
Live free with someone else	5.7%	10.9%	16.7%	6.6%
Other[a]	2.2%	3.4%	10.0%	2.5%
TOTAL	100.0%	100.0%	100.0%	100.0%

CH 5. CLIENTS: DEMOGRAPHIC PROFILE

TABLE 5.9.1.1 *(continued)*

	Pantry Client Households	Kitchen Client Households	Shelter Client Households	All Client Households
Clients late paying the last month's rent or mortgage	20.2%	17.2%	21.3%	19.8%
Clients whose households receive Section 8 or Public Housing Assistance	19.2%	14.0%	5.5%	17.4%
SAMPLE SIZE (N) – Clients with a place to live	**36,877**	**7,715**	**557**	**45,149**

SOURCE: This table was constructed based on usable responses to questions 16, 17, 18, and 81 of the client survey.

NOTES: The percentages presented in this table are based only on usable responses, excluding missing, don't know, and refusal responses. All usable responses were weighted as described in Chapter 3 and in the Technical Appendix volume to represent all emergency food clients of the A2H National Network. The sample sizes (N) also include missing data.

For the kind of place where living, missing, don't know, and refusal responses combined are 0.8% for pantry clients, 1.2% for kitchen clients, 2.2% for shelter clients, and 1.0% for all clients.

For those with a place to live, missing, don't know, and refusal responses combined are 2.3% for pantry clients, 2.1% for kitchen clients, 3.1% for shelter clients, and 2.3% for all clients.

For those late paying rent or mortgage, missing, don't know, and refusal responses combined are 3.1% for pantry clients, 1.8% for kitchen clients, 3.0% for shelter clients, and 2.8% for all clients.

For those receiving Section 8, missing, don't know, and refusal responses combined are 6.7% for pantry clients, 6.4% for kitchen clients, 4.6% for shelter clients, and 6.5% for all clients.

[a]This includes "working for rent" and halfway houses.

Among all client households, 12.1% were without a place to live. More details on housing status of the clients follow:

- 80.4% of shelter client households were homeless.

- 26.1% of kitchen client households were homeless.

- 3.0% of pantry client households were homeless.

- 26.3% of pantry client households with a place to live own the place where they live.

- 19.8% of the client households with a place to live were late paying the previous month's rent or mortgage.

- 17.4% of the client households with a place to live said they received Section 8 or Public Housing Assistance at the time of the interview.

CH 5. CLIENTS: DEMOGRAPHIC PROFILE

Table 5.9.1.1N translates selected findings about housing into total numbers of A2H clients.

TABLE 5.9.1.1N

ESTIMATED NUMBER OF CLIENTS WITH OR WITHOUT A PLACE TO LIVE

	Adult Clients Who Pick Up Food at a Pantry	Adult Clients at a Kitchen	Adult Clients at a Shelter	All Adult Clients
Clients with a place to live	8,341,400	739,300	131,100	9,022,300
Clients without a place to live	258,600	260,700	538,900	1,247,700
ESTIMATED TOTAL NUMBER OF ADULT CLIENTS AT PROGRAM SITES	**8,600,000**	**1,000,000**	**670,000**	**10,270,000**

NOTES: See Appendix B for the estimated number of people served in subgroups of A2H clients.

Columns in this table do not exactly add up to the column total. This discrepancy occurs because tables showing percentage distributions are weighted with the monthly weight, while the number of clients presented in this table is estimated at the annual level. Because the relationship between the monthly and annual weights varies across individuals depending on the frequency of visits to program sites, applying annual estimates to a monthly snapshot of percentage distributions results in small discrepancies in column totals.

As shown, 1.3 million A2H clients do not have a permanent place to live.

- This includes approximately 0.3 million pantry clients and another 0.3 million kitchen clients.

- As might be expected, homelessness is particularly concentrated among the shelter clients, over half a million of whom lack permanent housing.

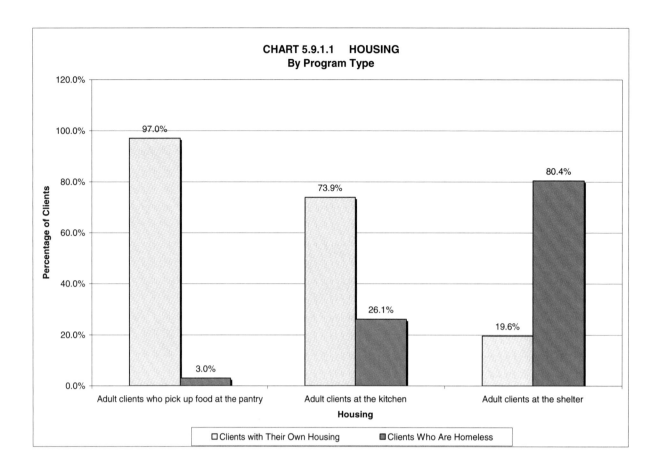

CH 5. CLIENTS: DEMOGRAPHIC PROFILE

5.9.2   Household Resources

Clients indicated whether their households have access to a kitchen, a working telephone, or a working car. Responses are presented in Table 5.9.2.1 and Chart 5.9.2.1.

TABLE 5.9.2.1

HOUSEHOLD RESOURCES

Household Resources	Pantry Client Households	Kitchen Client Households	Shelter Client Households	All Client Households
Clients with access to a place where they can prepare a meal				
Yes	96.6%	76.5%	36.6%	89.1%
No	3.4%	23.5%	63.4%	10.9%
TOTAL	100.0%	100.0%	100.0%	100.0%
Clients have access to a working telephone				
Yes	84.7%	74.1%	69.9%	81.9%
No	15.3%	25.9%	30.1%	18.1%
TOTAL	100.0%	100.0%	100.0%	100.0%
Clients have access to a working car				
Yes	60.3%	37.4%	24.4%	54.0%
No	39.7%	62.6%	75.6%	46.0%
TOTAL	100.0%	100.0%	100.0%	100.0%
SAMPLE SIZE (N)	**37,986**	**10,667**	**4,225**	**52,878**

SOURCE: This table was constructed based on usable responses to Question 19 of the client survey.

NOTES: The percentages presented in this table are based only on usable responses, excluding missing, don't know, and refusal responses. All usable responses were weighted as described in Chapter 3 and in the Technical Appendix volume to represent all emergency food clients of the A2H National Network. The sample sizes (N) also include missing data.

For access to a place, missing, don't know, and refusal responses combined are 1.0% for pantry clients, 1.1% for kitchen clients, 1.9% for shelter clients, and 1.1% for all clients.

For working telephone, missing, don't know, and refusal responses combined are 1.1% for pantry clients, 1.3% for kitchen clients, 2.2% for shelter clients, and 1.2% for all clients.

For clients with working cars, missing, don't know, and refusal responses combined are 1.3% for pantry clients, 1.5% for kitchen clients, 2.0% for shelter clients, and 1.4% for all clients.

Findings about selected household resources presented in Table 5.9.2.1 include:

- Overall, 89.1% of the clients have access to a place where they can prepare a meal.
  - 96.6% of the pantry clients have access to such a place.
  - 76.5% of the kitchen clients have access to such a place.
  - 36.6% of the shelter clients have access to such a place.
- Overall, 81.9% of the clients have access to a working telephone.
  - 84.7% of the pantry clients have access to a working telephone.
  - 74.1% of the kitchen clients have access to a working telephone.
  - 69.9% of the shelter clients have access to a working telephone.
- Overall, 54.0% of the clients have access to a working car.
  - 60.3% of the pantry clients have access to a working car.
  - 37.4% of the kitchen clients have access to a working car.
  - 24.4% of the shelter clients have access to a working car.

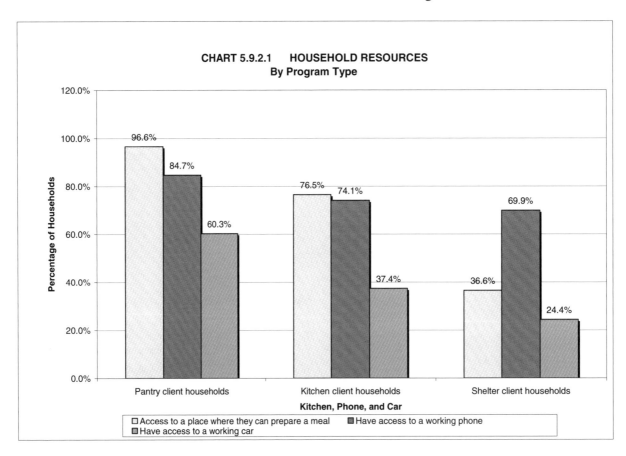

CH 5. CLIENTS: DEMOGRAPHIC PROFILE

6. CLIENTS: FOOD INSECURITY AND HUNGER

Food insecurity is a complex, multifaceted phenomenon that varies along a continuum of successive stages as it becomes more severe. A scaling tool developed by the USDA provides an important approach being used increasingly to assess food security and hunger among households. Six questions in a six-item short module, the minimal information required to construct the scale, were included in the client survey.[35] Food security and food insecurity are conceptually defined as the following[36]:

- Food security: "Access by all people at all times to enough food for an active, healthy life. Food security includes at a minimum: (1) the ready availability of nutritionally adequate and safe foods, and (2) an assured ability to acquire acceptable foods in socially acceptable ways (e.g., without resorting to emergency food supplies, scavenging, stealing, or other coping strategies)."

- Food insecurity: "Limited or uncertain availability of nutritionally adequate and safe foods or limited or uncertain ability to acquire acceptable foods in socially acceptable ways."

The approach to examining food security which we will use in this chapter involves an *approximation* of this conceptual framework. Indeed, in the current study population, *all* of the respondents are reliant to at least some degree on "emergency food supplies" as specified in the first bullet above, simply by the way the sample was assembled (i.e., at emergency food providers). However, despite the conceptual underpinnings summarized above, the *actual questions* which are customarily used to measure food security (Bickel et al. 2000) do not

---

[35] Bickel, Gary, Mark Nord, Cristofer Price, William Hamilton, and John Cook. "Guide to Measuring Household Food Security, Revised 2000." U.S. Department of Agriculture, Food and Nutrition Service, March 2000.

[36] "Core Indicators of Nutritional State for Difficult-to-Sample Populations." *Journal of Nutrition*, vol. 120, no.11S, November 1990.

directly ask about the use of emergency food. In this study we will essentially examine how the sample members who were interviewed responded to a set of questions which are designed to *approximate operationally* the definition of food insecurity. Use of this measure will allow us to examine a measure of need for our study population which is directly comparable to that used in mnay other studies.

This chapter begins by assessing A2H clients' levels of food security, first for all households and then separately for households with children and for households with elderly members. Subsequent sections then provide data on household responses to the specific questions used in constructing the food security scores.

CH 6. CLIENTS: FOOD INSECURITY AND HUNGER

6.1   HOUSEHOLD FOOD INSECURITY

Clients responded to a six-item short module for classifying households by food security status level. Food security scale scores were assigned to households according to the "Guide to Measuring Household Food Security, Revised 2000."[37] Responses are presented in Table 6.1.1 and in Charts 6.1.1, 6.1.1A, and 6.1.1B.

TABLE 6.1.1

HOUSEHOLD FOOD INSECURITY

Food Security Among Clients' Households	Pantry Client Households	Kitchen Client Households	Shelter Client Households	All Client Households
Food security among all households				
Food secure	29.8%	30.7%	26.1%	29.7%
Food insecure				
Food insecure without hunger	39.1%	29.9%	30.2%	36.9%
Food insecure with hunger	31.1%	39.4%	43.7%	33.3%
SUBTOTAL	70.2%	69.3%	73.9%	70.3%
TOTAL	100.0%	100.0%	100.0%	100.0%
SAMPLE SIZE (N)	**37,986**	**10,667**	**4,225**	**52,878**
Food security among households with children younger than age 18				
Food secure	25.9%	35.0%	37.4%	26.9%
Food insecure				
Food insecure without hunger	42.4%	37.1%	31.5%	41.8%
Food insecure with hunger	31.7%	28.0%	31.1%	31.3%
SUBTOTAL	74.1%	65.0%	62.6%	73.1%
TOTAL	100.0%	100.0%	100.0%	100.0%
SAMPLE SIZE (N) – Households with children younger than age 18	**15,756**	**1,518**	**745**	**18,019**
Food security among households with seniors age 65 or older				
Food secure	47.3%	53.5%	59.2%	48.0%
Food insecure				
Food insecure without hunger	36.6%	29.4%	29.0%	35.8%
Food insecure with hunger	16.1%	17.1%	11.8%	16.2%
SUBTOTAL	52.7%	46.5%	40.8%	52.0%
TOTAL	100.0%	100.0%	100.0%	100.0%

---

[37] Bickel et al. March 2000.

TABLE 6.1.1 (*continued*)

Food Security Among Clients' Households	Pantry Client Households	Kitchen Client Households	Shelter Client Households	All Client Households
SAMPLE SIZE (N) – **Households with seniors age 65 years or older**	**9,541**	**2,087**	**84**	**11,712**

SOURCE: This table was constructed based on usable responses to questions 42, 43, 44, 44a, 45, and 46 of the client survey.

NOTES: The percentages presented in this table are based only on usable responses, excluding missing, don't know, and refusal responses. All usable responses were weighted as described in Chapter 3 and in the Technical Appendix volume to represent all emergency food clients of the A2H National Network. The sample sizes (N) also include missing data.

Constructed according to "Guide to Measuring Household Food Security, Revised 2000."

For all households, missing, don't know, and refusal responses combined are 2.1% for pantry clients, 2.3% for kitchen clients, 2.8% for shelter clients, and 2.2% for all clients.

For households with children younger than age 18, missing, don't know, and refusal responses combined are 1.6% for pantry clients, 0.9% for kitchen clients, 0.2% for shelter clients, and 1.5% for all clients.

For households with seniors, missing, don't know, and refusal responses combined are 2.1% for pantry clients, 7.6% for kitchen clients, 11.2% for shelter clients, and 2.8% for all clients.

According to the six-item short module, 36.9% of all client households of the emergency food programs were food insecure without hunger. Another 33.3% were food insecure with hunger. Combined, a total of 70.3% were food insecure.

- Among the client households with children younger than age 18, 41.8% were food insecure without hunger and 31.3% were food insecure with hunger.

- Among the client households with seniors age 65 years or older, 35.8% were food insecure without hunger and 16.2% were food insecure with hunger.

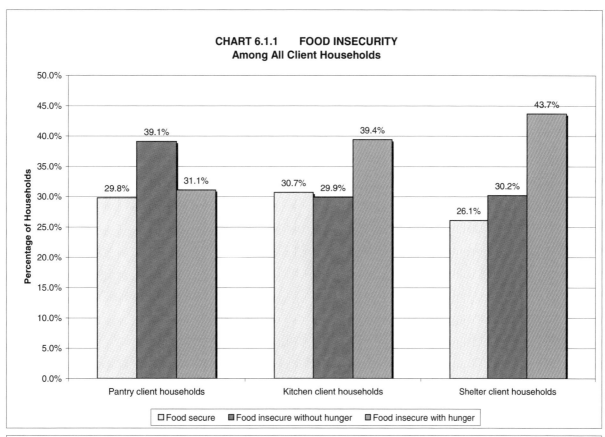

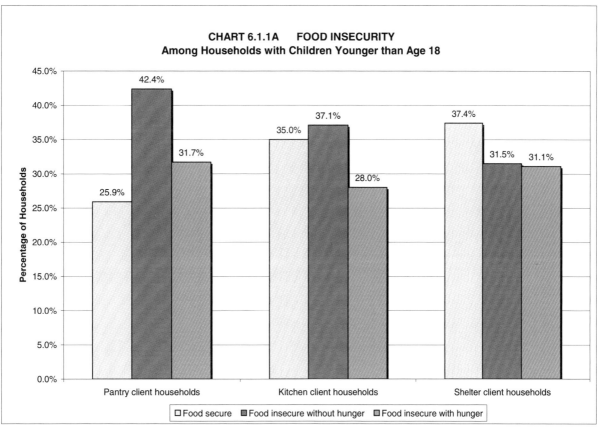

CH 6. CLIENTS: FOOD INSECURITY AND HUNGER

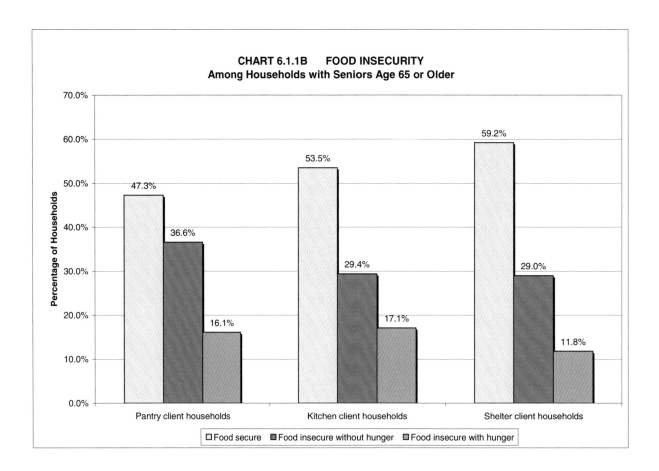

CH 6. CLIENTS: FOOD INSECURITY AND HUNGER

As shown in Table 6.1.1N, the percentages reported above imply that more than 7.2 million A2H client households are food insecure and that more than 3.4 million of them are experiencing hunger.

TABLE 6.1.1N

ESTIMATED NUMBER OF HOUSEHOLDS, BY FOOD SECURITY STATUS

Food Security Among Clients' Households	Pantry Client Households	Kitchen Client Households	Shelter Client Households	All Client Households
Among all households				
Food secure	2,565,500	307,500	174,700	3,053,000
Food insecure				
Food insecure without hunger	3,360,200	299,000	202,500	3,792,300
Food insecure with hunger	2,674,300	393,600	292,800	3,424,800
SUBTOTAL	6,034,500	692,500	495,300	7,217,000
ESTIMATED TOTAL NUMBER OF CLIENT HOUSEHOLDS	**8,600,000[a]**	**1,000,000**	**670,000**	**10,270,000**
Among households with children younger than age 18				
Food secure	906,800	58,600	26,800	1,005,400
Food insecure				
Food insecure without hunger	1,485,800	62,100	22,600	1,562,300
Food insecure with hunger	1,108,100	46,800	22,300	1,172,200
SUBTOTAL	2,593,900	108,900	44,900	2,734,500
ESTIMATED NUMBER OF CLIENT HOUSEHOLDS WITH CHILDREN YOUNGER THAN AGE 18	**3,500,700**	**167,500**	**71,800**	**3,740,000**
Among households with seniors age 65 or older				
Food secure	1,008,400	75,600	11,300	1,101,700
Food insecure				
Food insecure without hunger	781,400	41,500	5,600	821,200
Food insecure with hunger	344,000	24,200	2,300	371,400
SUBTOTAL	1,125,300	65,700	7,800	1,192,600
ESTIMATED TOTAL NUMBER OF HOUSEHOLDS WITH SENIORS AGE 65 OR OLDER	**2,133,800**	**141,300**	**19,200**	**2,294,300**

TABLE 6.1.1N *(continued)*

NOTES: See Appendix B for the estimated number of people served in subgroups of A2H clients.

Columns in this table do not exactly add up to the column total. This discrepancy occurs because tables showing percentage distributions are weighted with the monthly weight, while the number of clients presented in this table is estimated at the annual level. Because the relationship between the monthly and annual weights varies across individuals depending on the frequency of visits to program sites, applying annual estimates to a monthly snapshot of percentage distributions results in small discrepancies in column totals.

[a]The total number of pantry households used in the table is equal to the range specified in Table 4.4.1, line 8, multiplied by a factor of 1.23 to correct for the A2H food banks that did not participate in the study.

Key findings include:

- Of households with children under 18, approximately 2.7 million are food insecure, of which approximately 1.2 million are experiencing hunger.

- The comparable numbers of households with a senior member age 65 or older are 1.2 million and 0.4 million.

TABLE 6.1.2

FOOD STAMP PROGRAM PARTICIPATION AND FOOD SECURITY

Food Security Among Clients' Households	Pantry Client Households	Kitchen Client Households	Shelter Client Households	All Client Households
Among Food Stamp Program participants				
Food secure	25.5%	25.7%	20.5%	25.2%
Food insecure				
Food insecure without hunger	40.0%	33.3%	31.3%	38.4%
Food insecure with hunger	34.5%	41.0%	48.2%	36.4%
SUBTOTAL	74.5%	74.3%	79.5%	74.8%
TOTAL	100.0%	100.0%	100.0%	100.0%
SAMPLE SIZE (N) – Food Stamp Program participants	**14,028**	**3,557**	**1,598**	**19,183**
Among Food Stamp Program nonparticipants				
Food secure	32.3%	33.6%	28.7%	32.3%
Food insecure				
Food insecure without hunger	38.5%	28.0%	29.7%	36.1%
Food insecure with hunger	29.2%	38.5%	41.6%	31.6%
SUBTOTAL	67.7%	66.4%	71.3%	67.7%
TOTAL	100.0%	100.0%	100.0%	100.0%
SAMPLE SIZE (N) – Food Stamp Program nonparticipants	**23,958**	**7,110**	**2,627**	**33,695**

SOURCE: This table was constructed based on usable responses to questions 42, 43, 44, 44a, 45, and 46 of the client survey.

NOTES: The percentages presented in this table are based only on usable responses, excluding missing, don't know, and refusal responses. All usable responses were weighted as described in Chapter 3 and in the Technical Appendix volume to represent all emergency food clients of the A2H National Network. The sample sizes (N) also include missing data.

Constructed according to "Guide to Measuring Household Food Security, Revised 2000."

For participating households, missing, don't know, and refusal responses combined are 0.8% for pantry clients, 0.2% for kitchen clients, 0.1% for shelter clients, and 0.7% for all clients.

For nonparticipating households with seniors, missing, don't know, and refusal responses combined are 2.8% for pantry clients, 3.5% for kitchen clients, 4.0% for shelter clients, and 3.0% for all clients.

As will be discussed in detail in Chapter 7 below, about 35.4% of client households also receive benefits from the Food Stamp Program. Table 6.1.2 compares food security status among Food Stamp Program participants to that of nonparticipants.

- 38.4% of the client household receiving food stamps were food insecure without hunger. Another 36.4% were food insecure with hunger.

- In comparison, among the client households not receiving food stamps, 36.1% were food insecure without hunger, and 31.6% were food insecure with hunger.

CH 6. CLIENTS: FOOD INSECURITY AND HUNGER

As shown in Table 6.1.2N, when these percentages are translated to numbers of households, they imply that the A2H system serves nearly 3 million client households who are receiving food stamps but are food insecure (Table 6.1.2N).

TABLE 6.1.2N

ESTIMATED NUMBER OF HOUSEHOLDS, BY FOOD STAMP PROGRAM PARTICIPATION
AND FOOD SECURITY

Food Security Among Clients' Households	Pantry Client Households	Kitchen Client Households	Shelter Client Households	All Client Households
Among Food Stamp Program participants				
Food secure	810,200	85,700	51,800	949,600
Food insecure				
Food insecure without hunger	1,271,100	111,200	79,300	1,444,000
Food insecure with hunger	1,094,600	136,600	122,300	1,369,100
SUBTOTAL	2,365,700	247,700	201,600	2,813,200
ESTIMATED TOTAL NUMBER OF CLIENT HOUSEHOLDS PARTICIPATING IN FOOD STAMP PROGRAM	**3,175,900**	**333,500**	**253,400**	**3,762,800**
Among Food Stamp Program nonparticipants				
Food secure	1,752,100	223,600	119,600	2,098,600
Food insecure				
Food insecure without hunger	2,089,800	186,500	123,800	2,349,700
Food insecure with hunger	1,582,200	256,400	173,200	2,058,800
SUBTOTAL	3,672,000	442,900	297,000	4,408,600
ESTIMATED TOTAL NUMBER OF CLIENT HOUSEHOLDS NOT PARTICIPATING IN FOOD STAMP PROGRAM	**5,424,100**	**666,500**	**416,600**	**6,507,200**

NOTE: See Appendix B for the estimated number of people served in subgroups of A2H clients.

Columns in this table do not exactly add up to the column total. This discrepancy occurs because tables showing percentage distributions are weighted with the monthly weight, while the number of clients presented in this table is estimated at the annual level. Because the relationship between the monthly and annual weights varies across individuals depending on the frequency of visits to program sites, applying annual estimates to a monthly snapshot of percentage distributions results in small discrepancies in column totals.

CH 6. CLIENTS: FOOD INSECURITY AND HUNGER

Other key findings in the table include:

- Among food stamp participants in the A2H Network, an estimated 1.4 million households are experiencing hunger

- Among A2H households not participating in the Food Stamp Program, over 4.4 million are food insecure, of which over 2 million are experiencing hunger.

6.2 INDICATORS OF FOOD INSECURITY IN HOUSEHOLDS

Table 6.2.1 presents responses to two of the questions involved in the six-item short module.

TABLE 6.2.1

INDICATORS OF FOOD INSECURITY IN HOUSEHOLDS

	Pantry Client Households	Kitchen Client Households	Shelter Client Households	All Client Households
"The food we bought just didn't last, and we didn't have money to get more." In the last 12 months, was that…?				
Often true	32.1%	33.3%	27.3%	32.0%
Sometimes true	43.8%	38.7%	43.3%	42.9%
Never true	24.1%	28.0%	29.3%	25.1%
TOTAL	100.0%	100.0%	100.0%	100.0%
"We couldn't afford to eat balanced meals." In the last 12 months, was that…?				
Often true	23.7%	27.5%	30.8%	24.8%
Sometimes true	42.6%	34.9%	38.2%	41.0%
Never true	33.6%	37.7%	31.0%	34.1%
TOTAL	100.0%	100.0%	100.0%	100.0%
SAMPLE SIZE (N)	**37,986**	**10,667**	**4,225**	**52,878**

SOURCE: This table was constructed based on usable responses to questions 42 and 43 of the client survey.

NOTES: The percentages presented in this table are based only on usable responses, excluding missing, don't know, and refusal responses. All usable responses were weighted as described in Chapter 3 and in the Technical Appendix volume to represent all emergency food clients of the A2H National Network. The sample sizes (N) also include missing data.

For food didn't last, missing, don't know, and refusal responses combined are 3.6% for pantry clients, 3.9% for kitchen clients, 6.2% for shelter clients, and 3.8% for all clients.

For not eating balanced meals, missing, don't know, and refusal responses combined are 3.6% for pantry clients, 3.7% for kitchen clients, 5.5% for shelter clients, and 3.8% for all clients.

Overall, 74.9% of the client households reported that, during the previous 12 months, they had been in a situation where the food they bought "just didn't last and they didn't have money to get more." In addition, 65.8% of the client households were, often or sometimes during the previous 12 months, in a situation where they "couldn't afford to eat balanced meals."

Table 6.2.1N shows that more than 3.3 million A2H households feel that in the last 12 months, the food they bought often "just didn't last" and they lacked money to buy more.

TABLE 6.2.1N

ESTIMATED NUMBER OF HOUSEHOLDS, BY INDICATORS OF FOOD INSECURITY

	Pantry Client Households	Kitchen Client Households	Shelter Client Households	Adult Clients at All Program Sites
"The food we bought just didn't last, and we didn't have money to get more." In the last 12 months, was that …?				
Often true	2,757,600	333,300	183,200	3,282,400
Sometimes true	3,771,000	386,700	290,300	4,410,400
Never true	2,071,400	279,900	196,500	2,577,200
"We couldn't afford to eat balanced meals." In the last 12 months, was that …?				
Often true	2,040,800	274,600	206,500	2,550,800
Sometimes true	3,666,500	348,900	255,900	4,213,800
Never true	2,892,800	376,500	207,500	3,505,300
ESTIMATED TOTAL NUMBER OF CLIENT HOUSEHOLDS	**8,600,000**	**1,000,000**	**670,000**	**10,270,000**

NOTE: See Appendix B for the estimated number of people served in subgroups of A2H clients.

Columns in this table do not exactly add up to the column total. This discrepancy occurs because tables showing percentage distributions are weighted with the monthly weight, while the number of clients presented in this table is estimated at the annual level. Because the relationship between the monthly and annual weights varies across individuals depending on the frequency of visits to program sites, applying annual estimates to a monthly snapshot of percentage distributions results in small discrepancies in column totals.

Other findings are:

- More than 4 million households indicated that it was *sometimes true* their food did not last.

- 2.6 million households said they often could not afford to eat balanced meals, and 4.2 million said this was sometimes true.

6.3   INDICATORS OF FOOD INSECURITY AND HUNGER AMONG ADULTS

Table 6.3.1 presents responses to the four questions about adults in the six-item short module.

TABLE 6.3.1

INDICATORS OF FOOD INSECURITY AND HUNGER AMONG ADULTS

	Pantry Client Households	Kitchen Client Households	Shelter Client Households	All Client Households
How often adult clients or other adults in the household cut the size of meals or skipped meals because there wasn't enough money for food for the previous 12 months[a]				
Almost every month	23.6%	28.2%	28.1%	24.7%
Some months but not every month	18.7%	17.3%	18.3%	18.5%
Only one or two months	6.6%	7.1%	9.4%	6.9%
Never	51.0%	47.4%	44.1%	49.9%
Clients who ate less than they felt they should because there wasn't enough money to buy food for the previous 12 months				
Yes	51.1%	53.4%	57.3%	51.9%
No	48.9%	46.6%	42.7%	48.1%
TOTAL	100.0%	100.0%	100.0%	100.0%
Clients who were hungry but didn't eat because they couldn't afford enough food for the previous 12 months				
Yes	35.8%	46.0%	50.6%	38.5%
No	64.2%	54.0%	49.4%	61.5%
TOTAL	100.0%	100.0%	100.0%	100.0%
Clients or other adults in the household ever did not eat for a whole day because there wasn't enough money for food				
Yes	23.0%	35.0%	41.6%	26.3%
No	77.0%	65.0%	58.4%	73.7%
TOTAL	100.0%	100.0%	100.0%	100.0%
SAMPLE SIZE (N)	**37,986**	**10,667**	**4,225**	**52,878**

SOURCE: This table was constructed based on usable responses to questions 44a, 45, 46, and 47 of the client survey.

NOTES: The percentages presented in this table are based only on usable responses, excluding missing, don't know, and refusal responses. All usable responses were weighted as described in Chapter 3 and in the

TABLE 6.3.1 *(continued)*

Technical Appendix volume to represent all emergency food clients of the A2H National Network. The sample sizes (N) also include missing data.

For cutting meal size, missing, don't know, and refusal responses combined are 3.2% for pantry clients, 3.8% for kitchen clients, 3.8% for shelter clients, and 3.3% for all clients.

For eating less, missing, don't know, and refusal responses combined are 3.3% for pantry clients, 3.3% for kitchen clients, 4.0% for shelter clients, and 3.3% for all clients.

For being hungry because could not afford food, missing, don't know, and refusal responses combined are 3.0% for pantry clients, 3.1% for kitchen clients, 3.8% for shelter clients, and 3.1% for all clients.

For not eating for a whole day, missing, don't know, and refusal responses combined are 3.3% for pantry clients, 2.9% for kitchen clients, 5.3% for shelter clients, and 3.4% for all clients.

[a]Responses may not add up to 100% because this panel was constructed from two questions: "Never" came from Question 44, and the other responses from Question 44a.

Adults in 24.7% of the client households had to cut the size of meals or skip meals because there wasn't enough money for food *almost every month* of the previous 12 months. Responses to the remaining three questions are:

- 51.9% of the clients ate less than they felt they should because there was not enough money to buy food during the previous 12 months.

- Adults in 38.5% of the client households were hungry but did not eat because they could not afford enough food during the previous 12 months.

- Adults in 26.3% of the client households did not eat for a whole day at least once during the previous 12 months because there was not enough money for food.

As shown in Table 6.3.1N, more than 4.4 million A2H households reported that adults in the households had had to cut the size of their meals or had had to skip meals altogether at least during some months of the previous 12 months because there wasn't enough money for food.

TABLE 6.3.1N

ESTIMATED NUMBER OF HOUSEHOLDS, BY INDICATORS OF FOOD INSECURITY

	Pantry Client Households	Kitchen Client Households	Shelter Client Households	All Client Households
How often adult clients or other adults in the household cut the size of meals or skipped meals because there wasn't enough money for food for the previous 12 months				
Almost every month	2,029,500	282,200	188,000	2,534,700
Some months but not every month	1,611,900	173,000	122,900	1,897,100
Only one or two months	571,900	71,200	63,300	710,600
Never	4,384,500	473,600	295,800	5,125,300
Clients who ate less than they felt they should because there wasn't enough money to buy food for the previous 12 months				
Yes	4,396,700	534,300	384,100	5,333,900
No	4,203,300	465,700	285,900	4,936,100
Clients who were hungry but didn't eat because they couldn't afford enough food for the previous 12 months				
Yes	3,076,900	459,900	338,800	3,954,700
No	5,523,100	540,100	331,200	6,315,300
Clients or other adults in the household did not eat for a whole day because there wasn't enough money for food				
Yes	1,981,700	349,800	278,600	2,702,300
No	6,618,300	650,200	391,400	7,567,700
ESTIMATED TOTAL NUMBER OF CLIENT HOUSEHOLDS	**8,600,000**	**1,000,000**	**670,000**	**10,270,000**

NOTE: See Appendix B for the estimated number of people served in subgroups of A2H clients.

Columns in this table do not exactly add up to the column total. This discrepancy occurs because tables showing percentage distributions are weighted with the monthly weight, while the number of clients presented in this table is estimated at the annual level. Because the relationship between the monthly and annual weights varies across individuals depending on the frequency of visits to program sites, applying annual estimates to a monthly snapshot of percentage distributions results in small discrepancies in column totals.

CH 6. CLIENTS: FOOD INSECURITY AND HUNGER

Other findings include:

- Adults in 5.3 million A2H households ate less than they felt they should due to lack of resources to buy food.

- Nearly 4 million A2H households contained adults were hungry but did not eat because they could not afford enough food.

- 2.7 million A2H households included adults who did not eat for a while day because there was not enough money for food.

6.4 INDICATORS OF FOOD INSECURITY AND HUNGER AMONG CHILDREN

In addition to the six questions shown in tables 6.2.1 and 6.3.1, clients were asked three additional questions about their children's skipping meals, being hungry, and not eating enough. Results are presented in Table 6.4.1 and Charts 6.4.1A, 6.4.1B, and 6.4.1C.

TABLE 6.4.1

INDICATORS OF FOOD INSECURITY AND HUNGER AMONG CHILDREN

	Pantry Client Households	Kitchen Client Households	Shelter Client Households	All Client Households
How often during the previous 12 months clients' child/children was/were not eating enough because they just couldn't afford enough food				
Often	5.4%	5.7%	3.5%	5.4%
Sometimes	22.1%	16.3%	23.9%	21.6%
Never	72.6%	78.0%	72.7%	73.0%
TOTAL	100.0%	100.0%	100.0%	100.0%
Clients whose child/children ever skipped meals because there wasn't enough money for food during the previous 12 months				
Yes	13.7%	12.1%	13.9%	13.6%
No	86.3%	87.9%	86.1%	86.4%
TOTAL	100.0%	100.0%	100.0%	100.0%
Clients whose child/children was/were hungry at least once during the previous 12 months, but couldn't afford more food				
Yes	16.5%	15.7%	17.3%	16.5%
No	83.5%	84.3%	82.7%	83.5%
TOTAL	100.0%	100.0%	100.0%	100.0%
SAMPLE SIZE (N) – Households with children younger than age 18	**15,756**	**1,518**	**745**	**18,019**

SOURCE: This table was constructed based on usable responses to questions 3, 6b, 49, 50, and 51 of the client survey.

NOTES: The percentages presented in this table are based only on usable responses, excluding missing, don't know, and refusal responses. All usable responses were weighted as described in Chapter 3 and in the

TABLE 6.4.1 *(continued)*

Technical Appendix volume to represent all emergency food clients of the A2H National Network. The sample sizes (N) also include missing data.

For children not eating enough, missing, don't know, and refusal responses combined are 6.1% for pantry clients, 4.8% for kitchen clients, 10.9% for shelter clients, and 6.1% for all clients.

For children skipping meals, missing, don't know, and refusal responses combined are 6.0% for pantry clients, 4.1% for kitchen clients, 11.3% for shelter clients, and 5.9% for all clients.

For children hungry, missing, don't know, and refusal responses combined are 6.3% for pantry clients, 3.9% for kitchen clients, 11.9% for shelter clients, and 6.2% for all clients.

Among all clients with children, 5.4% stated that, during the previous 12 months, their children were *often* not eating enough because they just couldn't afford enough food. Another 21.6% of the clients experienced such a situation *sometimes* during the previous 12 months.

- 13.6% of the clients with children said that their children skipped meals because there was not enough money for food during the previous 12 months.

- 16.5% of the clients with children said that their children were hungry at least once during the previous 12 months, but they could not afford more food.

Table 6.4.1N provide estimates of the number of A2H households with children which reported various indicators of food insecurity related to the children in the household.

TABLE 6.4.1N

ESTIMATED NUMBER OF CLIENT HOUSEHOLDS WITH CHILDREN,
BY INDICATORS OF FOOD INSECURITY

	Pantry Client Households	Kitchen Client Households	Shelter Client Households	Client Households
How often during the previous 12 months clients' child/children was/were not eating enough because they just couldn't afford enough food				
Often	187,700	9,500	2,500	200,100
Sometimes	772,000	27,400	17,100	808,600
Never	2,541,100	130,600	52,100	2,731,200
Clients whose child/children ever skipped meals because there wasn't enough money for food during the previous 12 months				
Yes	480,300	20,400	10,000	508,400
No	3,020,400	147,200	61,800	3,231,500
Clients whose child/children was/were hungry at least once during the previous 12 months, but couldn't afford more food				
Yes	578,400	26,300	12,400	616,100
No	2,922,300	141,200	59,300	3,123,900
ESTIMATED TOTAL NUMBER OF CLIENT HOUSEHOLDS WITH AT LEAST ONE CHILD YOUNGER THAN AGE 18 YEARS	**3,500,700**	**167,500**	**71,800**	**3,740,000**

NOTE: See Appendix B for the estimated number of people served in subgroups of A2H clients.

Columns in this table do not exactly add up to the column total. This discrepancy occurs because tables showing percentage distributions are weighted with the monthly weight, while the number of clients presented in this table is estimated at the annual level. Because the relationship between the monthly and annual weights varies across individuals depending on the frequency of visits to program sites, applying annual estimates to a monthly snapshot of percentage distributions results in small discrepancies in column totals.

CH 6. CLIENTS: FOOD INSECURITY AND HUNGER

In about 1 million A2H households with children were reported not to be eating enough because the households could not afford enough food. Other findings are:

- In over 0.5 million A2H households, children had to skip meals because of lack of resources to buy food.

- In more than 0.6 million of the households, children were reported to have been hungry, at least once, because of lack of household resources to buy food.

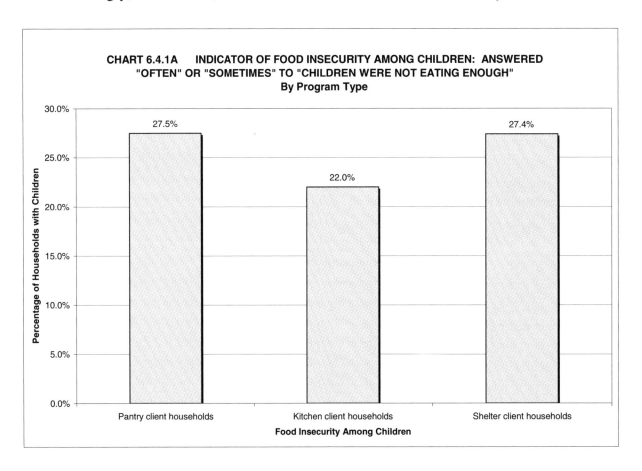

CHART 6.4.1A   INDICATOR OF FOOD INSECURITY AMONG CHILDREN: ANSWERED "OFTEN" OR "SOMETIMES" TO "CHILDREN WERE NOT EATING ENOUGH" By Program Type

CH 6. CLIENTS: FOOD INSECURITY AND HUNGER

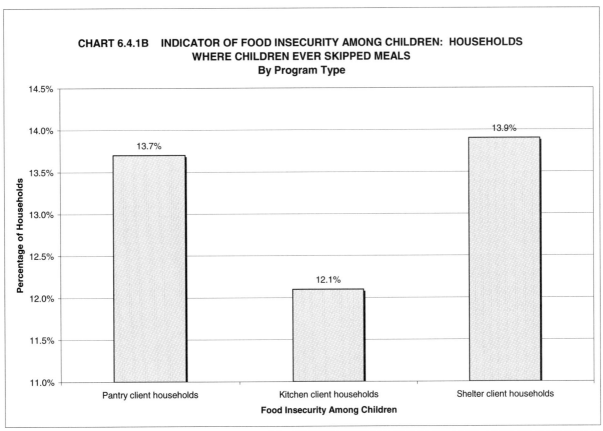

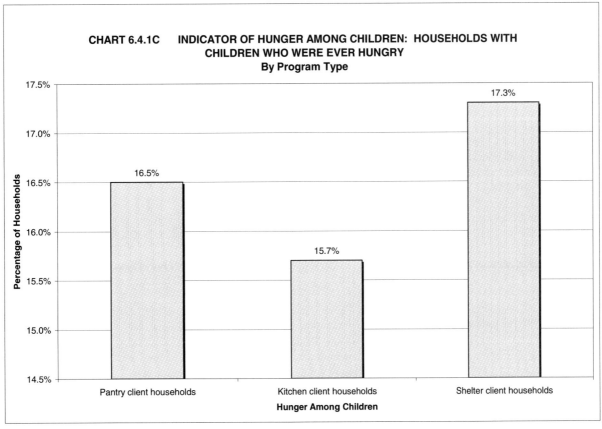

CH 6. CLIENTS: FOOD INSECURITY AND HUNGER

6.5 CHOICE BETWEEN FOOD AND NECESSITIES

Clients were asked whether their families had to choose between food and necessities during the 12-month period prior to the interview. Table 6.5.1 summarizes the results.

TABLE 6.5.1

CHOICE BETWEEN FOOD AND NECESSITIES

	Pantry Client Households	Kitchen Client Households	Shelter Client Households	All Client Households
In the previous 12 months, clients or their family who ever had to choose at least once between				
Paying for food and paying for utilities or heating fuel	44.6%	33.3%	27.7%	41.5%
Paying for food and paying for rent or mortgage	36.4%	31.8%	28.3%	35.0%
Paying for food and paying for medicine or medical care	33.5%	25.5%	25.0%	31.6%
Households with all three situations	19.6%	14.2%	12.5%	18.2%
Households with two, but not three, of the situations	18.9%	15.8%	13.5%	18.0%
Households with just one of the situations	17.3%	15.9%	16.3%	17.0%
SAMPLE SIZE (N)	**37,986**	**10,667**	**4,225**	**52,878**

SOURCE: This table was constructed based on usable responses to Question 52 of the client survey.

NOTES: All usable responses were weighted as described in Chapter 3 and in the Technical Appendix volume to represent all emergency food clients of the A2H National Network. The sample sizes (N) also include missing data.

For choosing between food and utilities, missing, don't know, and refusal responses combined are 2.8% for pantry clients, 3.0% for kitchen clients, 3.5% for shelter clients, and 2.9% for all clients.

For choosing between food and rent (mortgage), missing, don't know, and refusal responses combined are 2.9% for pantry clients, 3.1% for kitchen clients, 3.7% for shelter clients, and 3.0% for all clients.

For choosing between food and medical care, missing, don't know, and refusal responses combined are 2.7% for pantry clients, 3.1% for kitchen clients, 3.4% for shelter clients, and 2.8% for all clients.

For number of situations, missing, don't know, and refusal responses combined are 2.3% for pantry clients, 2.6% for kitchen clients, 3.2% for shelter clients, and 2.4% for all clients.

As shown in Table 6.5.1, among pantry client households, 44.6% had to choose between paying for food and paying for utilities or heating; 36.4% had to choose between food and rent or mortgage; and 33.5% had to choose between food and medicine or medical care. Results for kitchen and shelter client households are:

- Among kitchen client households, 33.3% had to choose between paying for food and paying for utilities or heating; 31.8% between food and rent or mortgage; and 25.5% between food and medicine or medical care.

- Among shelter client households, 27.7% had to choose between paying for food and paying for utilities or heating; 28.3% between food and rent or mortgage; and 25.0% between food and medicine or medical care.

CH 6. CLIENTS: FOOD INSECURITY AND HUNGER

7. CLIENTS: USE OF FOOD ASSISTANCE PROGRAMS

Given the high levels of need evidenced by many clients in the A2H Network, it is important to assess whether the clients of the A2H National Network are getting all the governmental nutrition assistance they are entitled to. This issue is examined here. The analysis begins by examining client participation in the Food Stamp Program, since it is the largest and most widely available government nutrition assistance program. Both levels of participation and reasons for non-participation are examined. A subsequent section examines participation in other government nutrition programs.

7.1   USE OF THE FOOD STAMP PROGRAM

Clients were asked a series of questions relating to the Food Stamp Program. Table 7.1.1 and Chart 7.1.1 summarize the findings.

TABLE 7.1.1

USE OF FOOD STAMP PROGRAM

Participation in Food Stamp Program	Pantry Client Households	Kitchen Client Households	Shelter Client Households	All Client Households
Client or anyone in the household had applied for food stamps	67.1%	70.2%	71.4%	67.9%
Client or anyone in the household currently receiving food stamps	35.9%	35.0%	31.1%	35.4%
Client or anyone in the household currently not receiving but received food stamps during the previous 12 months	7.3%	11.2%	13.1%	8.3%
Client or anyone in the household had applied for but had not received food stamps during the previous 12 months	22.5%	22.6%	25.1%	22.7%
SAMPLE SIZE (N)	**37,986**	**10,667**	**4,225**	**52,878**

TABLE 7.1.1 *(continued)*

Participation in Food Stamp Program	Pantry Client Households	Kitchen Client Households	Shelter Client Households	All Client Households
Number of weeks clients or their households have currently been receiving food stamps (for those who are receiving)				
Less than 2 weeks	1.3%	3.0%	5.1%	1.8%
2-4 weeks	5.1%	6.6%	12.4%	5.8%
5-12 weeks	4.9%	7.2%	9.5%	5.6%
13-51 weeks	19.9%	25.8%	36.9%	22.0%
1-2 years (52-103 weeks)	15.5%	17.5%	14.5%	15.8%
2-4 years (104-207 weeks)	21.2%	17.9%	11.1%	20.0%
4 years or more	32.1%	21.9%	10.5%	29.0%
TOTAL	100.0%	100.0%	100.0%	100.0%
Average number of weeks clients or their households have currently been receiving food stamps	203.2	157.4	69.1	187.2
Median number of weeks clients or their households have currently been receiving food stamps	104	52	26	78
Number of weeks during which food stamps usually last				
1 week or less	25.8%	20.1%	17.4%	24.4%
2 weeks	30.3%	28.9%	26.2%	29.8%
3 weeks	26.9%	30.0%	29.8%	27.5%
4 weeks	15.8%	19.0%	23.5%	16.8%
More than 4 weeks	1.2%	2.0%	3.2%	1.4%
TOTAL	100.0%	100.0%	100.0%	100.0%
Average number of weeks during the month over which food stamps usually last	2.4	2.6	2.8	2.5
Median number of weeks during the month over which food stamps usually last	2	3	3	2
SAMPLE SIZE (N) – Clients who are currently receiving food stamps	**14,028**	**3,557**	**1,598**	**19,183**

SOURCE: This table was constructed based on usable responses to questions 32, 33, 34, 36, and 37 of the client survey.

NOTES: The percentages presented in this table are based only on usable responses, excluding missing, don't know, and refusal responses. All usable responses were weighted as described in Chapter 3 and in the Technical Appendix volume to represent all emergency food clients of the A2H National Network. The sample sizes (N) also include missing data.

The second, third, and fourth rows of the first panel do not add up exactly to the first row due to varying item nonresponses to the question involved.

CH 7. CLIENTS: USE OF FOOD ASSISTANCE PROGRAMS

TABLE 7.1.1 *(continued)*

For length of receipt of food stamps, missing, don't know, and refusal responses combined are 8.0% for pantry clients, 6.6% for kitchen clients, 4.6% for shelter clients, and 7.6% for all clients.

For period of time food stamps lasted, missing, don't know, and refusal responses combined are 3.1% for pantry clients, 4.8% for kitchen clients, 6.6% for shelter clients, and 3.6% for all clients.

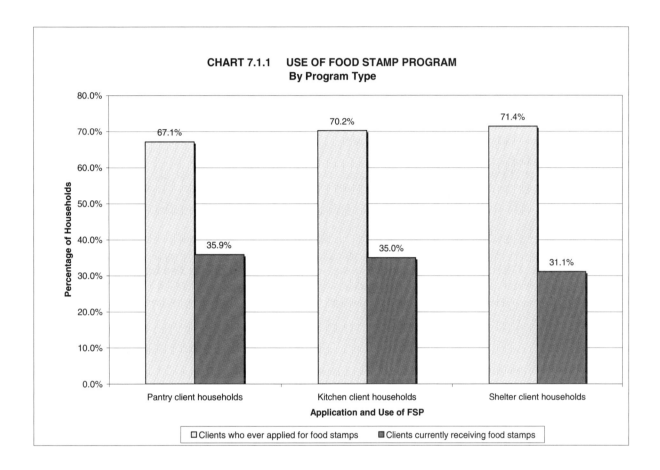

Overall, 67.9% of the clients have applied for and 35.4% are currently receiving food stamps. More information includes:

- 49.1% of the clients who are receiving food stamps have been receiving them for more than two years.

- For 81.8% of the clients who are receiving food stamps, the stamps last for three weeks or less.

- On average, food stamps last for 2.5 weeks.

CH 7. CLIENTS: USE OF FOOD ASSISTANCE PROGRAMS

As shown in Table 7.1.1N, the data reviewed above imply that substantial numbers of A2H clients participate in the food stamp program.

TABLE 7.1.1N

USE OF FOOD STAMP PROGRAM

	Pantry Client Households	Kitchen Client Households	Shelter Client Households	All Client Households
Client or anyone in the household had applied for food stamps	5,769,400	702,200	478,700	6,974,700
Client or anyone in the household currently receiving food stamps	3,175,900	333,500	253,400	3,762,800
ESTIMATED TOTAL NUMBER OF CLIENT HOUSEHOLDS	**8,600,000**	**1,000,000**	**670,000**	**10,270,000**

NOTE: See Appendix B for the estimated number of people served in subgroups of A2H clients.

Columns in this table do not exactly add up to the column total. This discrepancy occurs because tables showing percentage distributions are weighted with the monthly weight, while the number of clients presented in this table is estimated at the annual level. Because the relationship between the monthly and annual weights varies across individuals depending on the frequency of visits to program sites, applying annual estimates to a monthly snapshot of percentage distributions results in small discrepancies in column totals.

Key findings are:

- Approximately 3.8 million A2H households participate in the Food Stamp Program.

- This number includes: approximately 3.2 million pantry households, 0.3 million kitchen household and 0.3 million shelter households. (Numbers do not add due to rounding.)

7.2 REASONS WHY CLIENTS NEVER APPLIED FOR FOOD STAMPS

Clients who had not applied for food stamps were asked why they or their households

never applied for food stamps. Table 7.2.1 and Chart 7.2.1 show the results.

TABLE 7.2.1

REASONS WHY CLIENTS NEVER APPLIED FOR FOOD STAMPS

Reasons Why Clients or Their Households Never Applied for Food Stamps[a]	Pantry Client Households	Kitchen Client Households	Shelter Client Households	All Client Households
Factors associated with eligibility[b]				
Don't think eligible because of income or assets				
All clients	36.6%	29.9%	18.5%	34.5%
Clients with income 130% of the federal poverty level or lower	23.0%	15.0%	9.4%	20.9%
Clients with income higher than 130% of the federal poverty level	10.1%	11.1%	8.8%	10.2%
Unknown	3.5%	3.8%	0.3%	3.3%
Don't think eligible because of citizenship status	5.4%	3.3%	3.7%	5.0%
Eligible for only a low benefit amount	4.9%	3.5%	1.6%	4.5%
SUBTOTAL[c]	45.1%	35.2%	23.4%	42.3%
Factors associated with program access and operation				
Don't know where to go or who to contact to apply	5.9%	5.4%	10.3%	6.1%
Hard to get to the food stamp office	4.8%	2.9%	2.9%	4.4%
Application process is too long and complicated	5.3%	3.5%	4.0%	4.9%
Questions are too personal	1.6%	1.1%	2.1%	1.5%
Food stamp office staff are disrespectful	2.0%	1.0%	0.4%	1.7%
Food stamp office is unpleasant or in unsafe area	0.9%	0.3%	0.0%	0.8%
SUBTOTAL	17.3%	12.7%	16.4%	16.5%
Factors associated with need				
No need for benefit	13.5%	18.2%	17.5%	14.5%
Others need benefits more	5.9%	4.2%	3.2%	5.4%
Need is only temporary	2.7%	2.6%	3.8%	2.8%
SUBTOTAL	20.2%	23.5%	23.1%	20.9%

CH 7. CLIENTS: USE OF FOOD ASSISTANCE PROGRAMS

TABLE 7.2.1 (continued)

Reasons Why Clients or Their Households Never Applied for Food Stamps[a]	Pantry Client Households	Kitchen Client Households	Shelter Client Households	All Client Households
Social stigma				
Feel embarrassed applying for benefits	3.3%	1.0%	1.6%	2.8%
Family or friends do not approve of my receiving benefits	0.6%	0.2%	0.0%	0.5%
Dislike relying on the government for assistance	2.7%	2.8%	4.2%	2.8%
Feel embarrassed using benefits	2.6%	1.2%	9.7%	2.8%
SUBTOTAL	7.6%	4.6%	12.0%	7.4%
Other				
Planning to apply, but not yet applied	4.1%	2.5%	5.0%	3.9%
Other[d]	14.9%	27.1%	25.3%	17.4%
SAMPLE SIZE (N) – Clients or their households who never applied for food stamps	**11,405**	**3,286**	**1,038**	**15,729**

SOURCE: This table was constructed based on usable responses to Question 38 of the client survey.

NOTES: All usable responses were weighted as described in Chapter 3 and in the Technical Appendix volume to represent all emergency food clients of the A2H National Network. The sample sizes (N) also include missing data.

Missing, don't know, and refusal responses combined are 6.9% for pantry clients, 7.2% for kitchen clients, 9.8% for shelter clients, and 7.1% for all clients.

[a]Multiple responses were accepted.

[b]See Appendix C for food stamp eligibility criteria.

[c]The subtotal in this table indicates the percentage of people who provided one or more component items as their responses; thus, it may differ from the sum of component items.

[d]This includes working, having no mailing address, and being in a temporary living situation.

Reasons for not having applied for food stamps include:

- Overall, 42.3% of the clients who had not applied for food stamps did not do so because they believe they are not eligible or eligible for only a low benefit amount; 16.5% because of program access and operation; 20.9% either because there is no need or because they think others would need the benefits more; and 7.4% because they associate a social stigma with food stamps.

- 34.5% of the clients indicated income above the eligible level as a reason for having not applied for food stamps.

- That 34.5% was broken down into two categories: those who had an income that is at or below 130% of the federal poverty level (20.9%), and those who had an income that is higher than 130% of the federal poverty level (10.2%).[38,39]

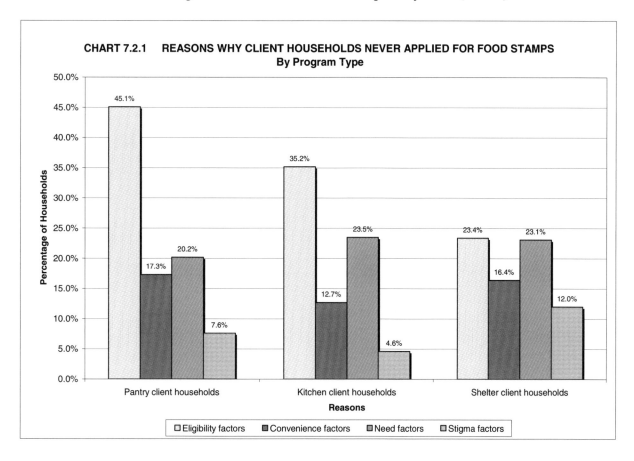

CHART 7.2.1   REASONS WHY CLIENT HOUSEHOLDS NEVER APPLIED FOR FOOD STAMPS
By Program Type

---

[38] Generalizing this result requires caution, as the income data collected through our client survey were not validated.

[39] Broadly speaking, a household usually meets the income eligibility requirements for the Food Stamp Program if its gross income is less than 130% of the poverty level. However, it was not possible during the survey to collect all the detailed data necessary to assess eligibility. See Appendix B for the eligibility criteria.

7.3 REASONS WHY CLIENTS OR THEIR HOUSEHOLDS ARE NOT CURRENTLY RECEIVING FOOD STAMPS, FOR THOSE WHO HAVE APPLIED

Clients who have applied but are not currently receiving food stamps were asked why this is so. Results are shown in Table 7.3.1 and Chart 7.3.1.

TABLE 7.3.1

REASONS WHY CLIENTS OR THEIR HOUSEHOLDS ARE NOT CURRENTLY
RECEIVING FOOD STAMPS, FOR THOSE WHO HAVE APPLIED

Reasons Why Clients or Their Households Are Not Currently Receiving Food Stamps, for Those Who Have Applied for Food Stamps[a]	Pantry Client Households	Kitchen Client Households	Shelter Client Households	All Client Households
Factors associated with eligibility				
Ineligible income level	44.2%	35.2%	22.4%	40.7%
Change of household makeup	3.7%	4.3%	5.0%	3.9%
Time limit for receiving the help ran out	5.5%	9.5%	8.3%	6.5%
Citizenship status	1.0%	0.1%	0.1%	0.8%
SUBTOTAL[b]	52.6%	46.0%	34.6%	49.8%
Factors associated with program access and operation				
Too much hassle	16.1%	16.4%	12.0%	15.8%
Hard to get to food stamp office	5.9%	5.4%	7.2%	5.9%
SUBTOTAL	19.2%	19.9%	18.2%	19.2%
Factors associated with need				
No need for benefits	5.4%	9.1%	6.0%	6.1%
Others need benefits more	2.2%	5.1%	3.3%	2.8%
Need is only temporary	3.6%	5.9%	5.9%	4.2%
SUBTOTAL	9.4%	14.8%	14.0%	10.8%
Other				
Other reasons[c]	24.0%	26.9%	31.1%	25.2%
SAMPLE SIZE (N) – Clients who have applied for but are not currently receiving food stamps	**12,553**	**3,824**	**1,589**	**17,966**

SOURCE: This table was constructed based on usable responses to Question 35 of the client survey.

NOTES: All usable responses were weighted as described in Chapter 3 and in the Technical Appendix volume to represent all emergency food clients of the A2H National Network. The sample sizes (N) also include missing data.

TABLE 7.3.1 *(continued)*

Missing, don't know, and refusal responses combined are 4.8% for pantry clients, 4.0% for kitchen clients, 7.6% for shelter clients, and 4.9% for all clients.

[a]Multiple responses were accepted.

[b]The subtotal in this table indicates the percentage of people who provided one or more component items as their responses; thus it may differ from the sum of component items.

[c]This includes "waiting" and "in progress."

Other findings include:

- Overall, 49.8% of the clients believe that they are not receiving food stamps because they are not eligible.

- 19.2% are not receiving food stamps because it is too much hassle.

- 10.8% are not receiving food stamps either because there is no need or because they think others would need the benefits more.

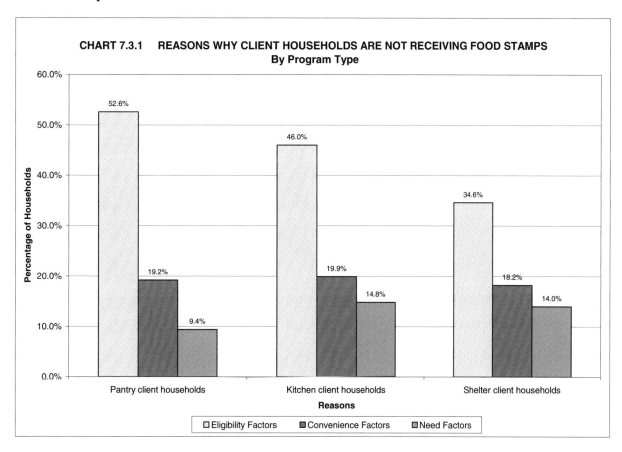

CHART 7.3.1   REASONS WHY CLIENT HOUSEHOLDS ARE NOT RECEIVING FOOD STAMPS
By Program Type

CH 7. CLIENTS: USE OF FOOD ASSISTANCE PROGRAMS

TABLE 7.3.2

REPORTED INCOME LEVELS OF CLIENTS WHO INDICATED INELIGIBLE INCOME
AS A REASON FOR NOT RECEIVING FOOD STAMPS

Reported Income Levels of Clients Who Indicated Ineligible Income as a Reason for Not Receiving Food Stamps	Pantry Client Households	Kitchen Client Households	Shelter Client Households	All Client Households
Ineligible income level	44.2%	35.2%	22.4%	40.7%
Income 130% of the federal poverty level or lower	31.9%	24.7%	15.9%	29.2%
Income higher than 130% of the federal poverty level	9.7%	9.2%	5.6%	9.3%
Income unknown	2.6%	1.3%	0.9%	2.2%
SAMPLE SIZE (N) – Clients who have applied for but are not currently receiving food stamps	**12,553**	**3,824**	**1,589**	**17,966**

As Table 7.3.2 shows, 40.7% of the clients indicated a higher-than-required income level as a reason they were not currently receiving food stamps. Those clients are further broken down into two categories based on the information about their previous month's household income: those whose income is 130% of the federal poverty level or lower (29.2%); and those whose income is higher than 130% of the federal poverty level (9.3%).

7.4   USE OF OTHER PROGRAMS

Clients also reported on other federal nutrition or child care programs they use. Table

7.4.1 shows the results.

TABLE 7.4.1

USE OF OTHER PROGRAMS

Other Program(s) Clients or Their Families Currently Participate in[a]	Pantry Client Households	Kitchen Client Households	Shelter Client Households	All Client Households
Government Mass Distribution Program or TEFAP (cheese, butter, etc., not from pantries)	27.0%	13.2%	9.5%	23.4%
SAMPLE SIZE (N)	**37,986**	**10,667**	**4,225**	**52,878**
Senior nutrition sites, such as senior centers that serve lunch	16.3%	32.5%	34.5%	18.3%
Home-delivered meals or meals-on-wheels (usually for seniors or people with disabilities)	5.1%	9.8%	7.9%	5.7%
Senior brown-bag programs that give out groceries and produce	12.2%	8.5%	4.6%	11.7%
SAMPLE SIZE (N) – Households with at least one senior member age 65 or older	**9,541**	**2,087**	**84**	**11,712**
Special Supplemental Nutrition Program for Women, Infants, and Children (WIC)[b]	50.4%	59.8%	46.6%	51.0%
SAMPLE SIZE (N) – Households with at least one child ages 0-3 years	**4,547**	**407**	**334**	**5,288**
Child day care	21.1%	16.1%	36.7%	21.1%
Government assistance for child day care among those using child day care[c]	45.0%	61.3%	45.1%	46.0%
SAMPLE SIZE (N) – Households with at least one child ages 0-5 years	**7,112**	**644**	**481**	**8,237**
School lunch program	62.4%	59.7%	53.1%	62.0%
School breakfast program	51.7%	48.8%	43.2%	51.3%
After-school snack program	11.5%	20.7%	17.1%	12.4%
Child care food program, such as meals at subsidized child care centers	5.2%	7.6%	9.4%	5.5%
Summer food program providing free lunches for children	12.9%	20.3%	10.7%	13.4%
SAMPLE SIZE (N) – Households with at least one child younger than age 18	**15,756**	**1,518**	**745**	**18,019**

TABLE 7.4.1 *(continued)*

SOURCE: This table was constructed based on usable responses to questions 7a, 8, and 41 of the client survey.

NOTES: All usable responses were weighted as described in Chapter 3 and in the Technical Appendix volume to represent all emergency food clients of the A2H National Network. The sample sizes (N) also include missing data.

[a]Multiple responses were accepted.

[b]Note that in *Hunger in America 2001* households with children ages 0 to 5 years were used as the base of the WIC participation percentage. At the suggestion of an earlier reviewer, the current study uses a base of children ages 0 to 3 years, in order to better approximate the main population of children who actually use WIC. Because a smaller denominator leads to a larger percentage, this percentage may appear substantially larger than in 2001 for some food banks, which may not reflect the actual change in the rate of WIC participation. Therefore, readers must use caution when comparing this percentage between the two studies.

[c]The sample size is 784 for the pantries, 90 for the kitchens, 136 for the shelters, and 1,010 for all.

Among all client households, 23.4% participate in government mass distribution programs or TEFAP. Participation in other programs is as follows:

- Among the households with at least one senior member age 65 or older, 18.3% use senior nutrition sites; 5.7% use home-delivered meals or meals-on-wheels; and 11.7% participate in senior brown-bag programs.

- Among the households with at least one child younger than age 18, 62.0% and 51.3% benefit from the school lunch and the school breakfast program, respectively; 12.4% use an after-school snack program; 5.5% use a child care food program; and 13.4% participate in the summer food program.

CH 7. CLIENTS: USE OF FOOD ASSISTANCE PROGRAMS

7.5   GENERAL ASSISTANCE, WELFARE, AND TANF IN THE PREVIOUS TWO YEARS

Clients were asked whether they received general assistance, welfare, or TANF in the previous two years and, if so, whether the assistance had been discontinued. They also provided reasons for the discontinuation. Table 7.5.1 presents the results.

TABLE 7.5.1

GENERAL ASSISTANCE, WELFARE, AND TANF IN THE PREVIOUS TWO YEARS

	Pantry Client Households	Kitchen Client Households	Shelter Client Households	All Client Households
Clients who received general assistance, welfare, or TANF during the past two years				
Yes	13.9%	15.1%	14.4%	14.2%
No	86.1%	84.9%	85.6%	85.8%
TOTAL	100.0%	100.0%	100.0%	100.0%
SAMPLE SIZE (N)	**37,986**	**10,667**	**4,225**	**52,878**
Clients for whom the assistance stopped during the past two years	39.4%	49.3%	50.4%	42.0%
SAMPLE SIZE (N) – Clients who received specified assistance	**4,841**	**1,342**	**807**	**6,990**
Reasons for the discontinuation of the assistance[a]				
Ineligible income level	38.3%	27.6%	26.3%	34.9%
Change in household makeup	7.6%	4.5%	16.6%	7.7%
Time limit for receiving the help ran out	14.6%	15.9%	20.1%	15.3%
Sanctioned by welfare or another agency	7.2%	16.8%	2.7%	9.0%
Citizenship status	0.1%	0.3%	0.3%	0.2%
Too much hassle	4.9%	9.3%	8.2%	6.2%
Chose to stop receiving it	5.8%	5.9%	13.4%	6.5%
Other[b]	25.4%	31.1%	31.6%	27.2%
SAMPLE SIZE (N) – Clients who received specified assistance, which then stopped during the previous two years	**1,757**	**595**	**352**	**2,704**

SOURCE: This table was constructed based on usable responses to questions 26, 27, and 28 of the client survey.

TABLE 7.5.1 *(continued)*

NOTES: The percentages presented in this table are based only on usable responses, excluding missing, don't know, and refusal responses. All usable responses were weighted as described in Chapter 3 and in the Technical Appendix volume to represent all emergency food clients of the A2H National Network. The sample sizes (N) also include missing data.

For receiving assistance, missing, don't know, and refusal responses combined are 3.8% for pantry clients, 3.0% for kitchen clients, 3.3% for shelter clients, and 3.7% for all clients.

For reasons for discontinuation of assistance, missing, don't know, and refusal responses combined are 3.5% for pantry clients, 2.0% for kitchen clients, 0.9% for shelter clients, and 2.9% for all clients.

[a]Multiple responses were accepted.

[b]This category includes having not reapplied, relocation, and found work.

During the previous two years, 14.2% of the clients received general assistance, welfare, or TANF. Details include:

- Among those who had received the specified assistance, 42.0% indicated that the assistance was discontinued.

- As for the reasons for the discontinuation, 34.9% ascribed it to having an ineligible income level, 7.7% to change of household makeup, and 15.3% to time limit for the assistance.

- In addition, 9.0% of the clients indicated that the assistance was discontinued because they were sanctioned by welfare or another agency, and 0.2% mentioned their citizenship status as a factor.

- Also, 6.2% of the clients no longer received the assistance because it was too much hassle for them, and 6.5% chose to stop receiving the assistance.

7.6   GROCERY SHOPPING PATTERNS

Clients were asked where they do most of their grocery shopping. Results are shown in

Table 7.6.1.

TABLE 7.6.1

GROCERY SHOPPING PATTERNS

Where do you do <u>most</u> of your grocery shopping?	Adult Clients Who Pick Up Food at a Pantry	Adult Clients at a Kitchen	Adult Clients at a Shelter	Adult Clients at All Program Sites
Supermarkets or grocery stores	73.4%	69.1%	61.3%	71.8%
Discount stores (e.g., Wal-Mart, Target, K-Mart)	17.7%	13.6%	12.7%	16.7%
Warehouse clubs (e.g., Price Club, Costco, Pace, Sam's Club, BJ's)	0.9%	1.1%	0.4%	0.9%
Convenience stores (e.g., 7-11, Quickshop, Wawa)	0.9%	3.4%	5.4%	1.6%
Ethnic food stores (e.g., bodegas, Asian food markets, or Caribbean markets)	1.0%	1.0%	0.7%	1.0%
Farmer's market	0.3%	0.4%	0.1%	0.3%
Other (including "dollar" stores)	3.9%	3.2%	5.4%	3.9%
Don't know because someone else in family shops	0.3%	0.7%	2.2%	0.5%
Don't buy groceries, free food only	1.6%	7.5%	12.1%	3.3%
TOTAL	100.0%	100.0%	100.0%	100.0%
SAMPLE SIZE (N)	**37,986**	**10,667**	**4,225**	**52,878**

SOURCE: This table was constructed based on usable responses to Question 40 of the client survey.

NOTES: The percentages presented in this table are based only on usable responses, excluding missing, don't know, and refusal responses. All usable responses were weighted as described in Chapter 3 and in the Technical Appendix volume to represent all emergency food clients of the A2H National Network. The sample sizes (N) also include missing data.

Missing, don't know, and refusal responses combined are 4.4% for pantry clients, 4.5% for kitchen clients, 4.5% for shelter clients, and 4.5% for all clients.

Among all clients, 71.8% shop mostly at supermarkets or grocery stores. Information about other places where some of the clients do most their grocery shopping follows:

- 1.6% of the clients use convenience stores for most of their grocery shopping.

- 16.7% of the clients shop mostly at discount stores such as Wal-Mart, Target, or K-Mart.

- 3.3% of the clients do not buy groceries. They rely only on free food.

CH 7. CLIENTS: USE OF FOOD ASSISTANCE PROGRAMS

8. CLIENTS: HEALTH STATUS

Health status can be an important determinant of overall household circumstances and need. Therefore, the survey asked clients for information on the health of both themselves and other household members. The responses to these questions are presented below. In addition, data are presented on clients' access to health insurance and health care.

8.1   HEALTH STATUS

Clients were asked to indicate their health status, then to indicate whether anyone (or anyone else) in their household was in poor health. Table 8.1.1 and Chart 8.1.1 summarize the results.

TABLE 8.1.1

HEALTH STATUS

	Adult Clients Who Pick Up Food at a Pantry	Adult Clients at a Kitchen	Adult Clients at a Shelter	Adult Clients at All Program Sites
Clients who indicated that their health was…				
Excellent	9.5%	15.9%	14.4%	10.9%
Very good	14.1%	16.8%	18.6%	14.9%
Good	28.0%	27.5%	27.4%	27.9%
Fair	31.0%	27.0%	24.6%	29.9%
Poor	17.4%	12.8%	15.0%	16.4%
TOTAL	100.0%	100.0%	100.0%	100.0%
Clients who indicated that someone else in the household was in poor health				
Yes	19.9%	9.8%	3.7%	17.1%
No	46.6%	28.9%	13.0%	41.3%
Live alone	33.5%	61.3%	83.3%	41.6%
TOTAL	100.0%	100.0%	100.0%	100.0%
Households with at least one member reported to be in poor health	31.7%	20.3%	17.9%	28.8%
SAMPLE SIZE (N)	**37,986**	**10,667**	**4,225**	**52,878**

TABLE 8.1.1 *(continued)*

SOURCE: This table was constructed based on usable responses to questions 20 and 21 of the client survey.

NOTES: The percentages presented in this table are based only on usable responses, excluding missing, don't know, and refusal responses. All usable responses were weighted as described in Chapter 3 and in the Technical Appendix volume to represent all emergency food clients of the A2H National Network. The sample sizes (N) also include missing data.

For client health, missing, don't know, and refusal responses combined are 1.3% for pantry clients, 1.5% for kitchen clients, 1.2% for shelter clients, and 1.3% for all clients.

For poor health of anyone in household, missing, don't know, and refusal responses combined are 2.1% for pantry clients, 1.8% for kitchen clients, 1.9% for shelter clients, and 2.0% for all clients.

Overall, 16.4% of the clients at all program sites are in poor health, and 28.8% of the client households have one or more members in poor health. More details follow:

- Among pantry clients, 9.5% were in excellent health, 14.1% in very good health, 28.0% in good health, and 48.4% in fair or poor health.

- Among kitchen clients, 15.9% were in excellent health, 16.8% in very good health, 27.5% in good health, and 39.8% in fair or poor health.

- Among shelter clients, 14.4% were in excellent health, 18.6% in very good health, 27.4% in good health, and 39.6% in fair or poor health.

- 31.7% of the pantry client households had at least one person in poor health.

- 20.3% of the kitchen client households had at least one person in poor health.

- 17.9% of the shelter client households had at least one person in poor health.

CH 8. CLIENTS: HEALTH STATUS

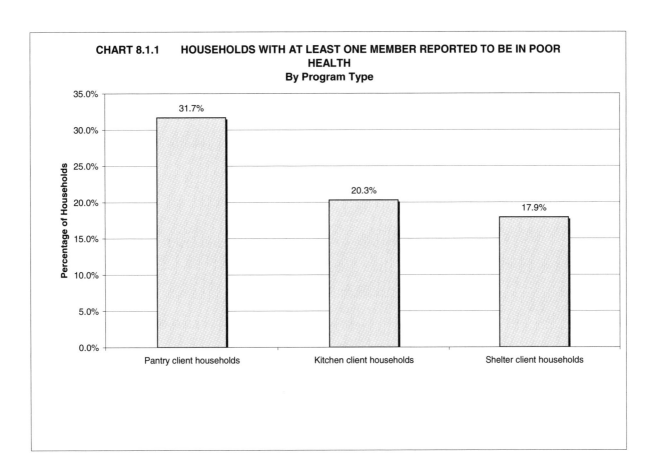

CHART 8.1.1   HOUSEHOLDS WITH AT LEAST ONE MEMBER REPORTED TO BE IN POOR HEALTH
By Program Type

CH 8. CLIENTS: HEALTH STATUS

8.2   HEALTH INSURANCE AND ACCESS TO MEDICAL CARE

Clients were asked whether they or anyone in their households had various kinds of health insurance. Clients also indicated whether they had unpaid medical or hospital bills and whether they had been refused medical care during the previous 12 months. Results are provided in Table 8.2.1 and Chart 8.2.1.

TABLE 8.2.1

HEALTH INSURANCE AND ACCESS TO MEDICAL CARE

	Adult Clients Who Pick Up Food at a Pantry	Adult Clients at a Kitchen	Adult Clients at a Shelter	Adult Clients at All Program Sites
Client or his or her family with following types of health insurance[a]				
Medicare[b]	39.7%	27.5%	13.3%	35.9%
State Medical Assistance Program or Medicaid	48.2%	39.0%	28.6%	45.3%
State Children's Health Insurance Program (SCHIP)	9.3%	3.7%	1.3%	7.8%
Veterans Administration (VA) benefits	5.6%	10.3%	10.8%	6.7%
Private health insurance	14.4%	13.0%	6.2%	13.6%
Other health insurance[c]	7.9%	8.7%	6.9%	8.0%
No insurance	17.4%	28.8%	46.9%	21.4%
Clients who had unpaid medical or hospital bills				
Yes	41.8%	38.2%	45.3%	41.4%
No	58.2%	61.8%	54.7%	58.6%
TOTAL	100.0%	100.0%	100.0%	100.0%
Clients who had been refused medical care because they could not pay or because they had a Medicaid or Medical Assistance card during the previous 12 months				
Yes	9.2%	10.2%	9.1%	9.4%
No	89.8%	88.9%	90.3%	89.7%
Not refused care, but avoid providers who don't accept medical assistance	0.3%	0.5%	0.3%	0.4%
Not refused care, but finding providers that accept medical assistance is a problem	0.6%	0.4%	0.3%	0.6%
TOTAL	100.0%	100.0%	100.0%	100.0%
SAMPLE SIZE (N)	**37,986**	**10,667**	**4,225**	**52,878**

CH 8. CLIENTS: HEALTH STATUS

TABLE 8.2.1 *(continued)*

SOURCE: This table was constructed based on usable responses to questions 22a-f, 23, and 24 of the client survey.

NOTES: The percentages presented in this table are based only on usable responses, excluding missing, don't know, and refusal responses. All usable responses were weighted as described in Chapter 3 and in the Technical Appendix volume to represent all emergency food clients of the A2H National Network. The sample sizes (N) also include missing data.

For types of health insurance, missing, don't know, and refusal responses combined are 1.3% for pantry clients, 1.6% for kitchen clients, 1.7% for shelter clients, and 1.4% for all clients.

For unpaid medical bills, missing, don't know, and refusal responses combined are 2.7% for pantry clients, 2.8% for kitchen clients, 4.2% for shelter clients, and 2.8% for all clients.

For refused medical care, missing, don't know, and refusal responses combined are 1.8% for pantry clients, 1.8% for kitchen clients, 2.5% for shelter clients, and 1.9% for all clients.

[a]Multiple responses were accepted.

[b]At the national level, the percentage of people who reported having Medicare coverage is substantially larger than what appears to be appropriate considering the percentage of households with seniors. One possible explanation for the discrepancy is widespread confusion between Medicare and Medicaid programs.

[c]This category includes government retirement benefits and military health system (TRICARE).

Findings presented in Table 8.2.1 include:

- 17.4% of the pantry, 28.8% of the kitchen, and 46.9% of the shelter clients or their households are without health insurance. This accounts for 21.4% of all clients.

- 41.4% of the clients have unpaid medical or hospital bills.

- 9.4% of the clients report that they have been refused medical care because they could not pay or because they had a Medicaid or Medical Assistance card during the previous 12 months.

As shown in Table 8.2.1N, the findings discussed above indicate that nearly 1 million adult clients of the A2H system had been refused medical care in the previous year, due to not being able to pay or care or because they lacked insurance.

TABLE 8.2.1N

ESTIMATED NUMBER OF CLIENTS AT PROGRAM SITES WHO HAD BEEN REFUSED MEDICAL CARE

	Adult Clients Who Pick Up Food at a Pantry	Adult Clients at a Kitchen	Adult Clients at a Shelter	Adult Clients at All Program Sties
Clients who had been refused medical care because they could not pay or because they had a Medicaid or medical assistance card during the previous 12 months				
Yes	793,800	101,700	61,200	963,600
No	7,722,900	889,100	605,100	9,210,800
Not refused care, but avoid providers who don't accept medical assistance	29,100	5,200	2,000	37,600
Not refused care, but finding providers that accept medical assistance is a problem	54,200	3,900	1,800	58,100
ESTIMATED TOTAL NUMBER OF CLIENTS AT PROGRAM SITES	**8,600,000**	**1,000,000**	**670,000**	**10,270,000**

NOTE: Columns in this table do not exactly add up to the column total. This discrepancy occurs because tables showing percentage distributions are weighted with the monthly weight, while the number of clients presented in this table is estimated at the annual level. Because the relationship between the monthly and annual weights varies across individuals depending on the frequency of visits to program sites, applying annual estimates to a monthly snapshot of percentage distributions results in small discrepancies in column totals.

Related findings are:

- Clients refused care included 0.8 million pantry clients and 0.1 million kitchen clients.

- Another 0.1 million A2H clients reported trying to avoid medical providers who didn't accept medical assistance or find those who do accept.

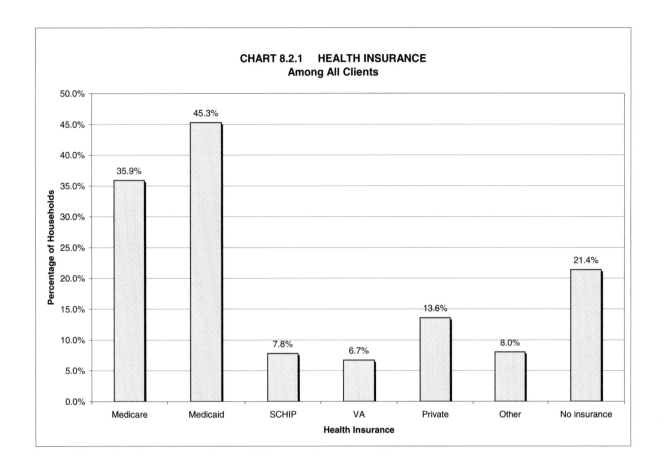

CH 8. CLIENTS: HEALTH STATUS

9.   CLIENTS: SERVICES RECEIVED AT FOOD PROGRAMS

To better understand how clients use the services of the A2H National Network, the survey asked questions about the numbers of kitchens and pantries that households used. Questions were also asked concerning the degree of satisfaction that respondents felt with the food services they were receiving from the providers and about what clients would do if they did not have access to the provider from which they were receiving food on the day of the interview. The answers to these questions are examined below.

9.1   NUMBER OF PANTRIES OR KITCHENS USED

Clients were asked how many different pantries or kitchens they had used during the previous month. The results are shown in Table 9.1.1.

TABLE 9.1.1

NUMBER OF DIFFERENT PANTRIES OR KITCHENS USED

	Pantry Client Households	Kitchen Client Households	Shelter Client Households	All Client Households
Number of different food **pantries** clients or their families used during the previous month				
None	n.a.	54.8%	72.2%	14.0%
One or more pantries				
1 pantry	82.0%	28.6%	16.3%	68.6%
2 pantries	13.5%	9.9%	6.6%	12.4%
3 pantries	3.0%	4.8%	2.2%	3.2%
4 pantries	0.9%	1.2%	1.1%	0.9%
5 or more pantries	0.7%	0.7%	1.6%	0.8%
SUBTOTAL	100.0%	45.2%	27.8%	86.0%
TOTAL	100.0%	100.0%	100.0%	100.0%

TABLE 9.1.1 *(continued)*

	Pantry Client Households	Kitchen Client Households	Shelter Client Households	All Client Households
Number of different soup **kitchens** clients or their families used during the previous month				
None	85.4%	n.a.	50.4%	68.6%
One or more kitchens				
1 kitchen	10.2%	76.6%	27.1%	22.5%
2 kitchens	2.6%	14.3%	11.9%	5.2%
3 kitchens	1.0%	5.7%	4.9%	2.1%
4 kitchens	0.3%	1.8%	2.8%	0.7%
5 or more kitchens	0.5%	1.7%	2.9%	0.9%
SUBTOTAL	14.6%	100.0%	49.6%	31.4%
TOTAL	100.0%	100.0%	100.0%	100.0%
SAMPLE SIZE (N)	**37,986**	**10,667**	**4,225**	**52,878**

SOURCE: This table was constructed based on usable responses to questions 56 and 57 of the client survey.

NOTES: The percentages presented in this table are based only on usable responses, excluding missing, don't know, and refusal responses. All usable responses were weighted as described in Chapter 3 and in the Technical Appendix volume to represent all emergency food clients of the A2H National Network. The sample sizes (N) also include missing data.

For pantries used, missing, don't know, and refusal responses combined are 2.9% for pantry clients, 3.8% for kitchen clients, 5.2% for shelter clients, and 3.2% for all clients.

For kitchens used, missing, don't know, and refusal responses combined are 3.3% for pantry clients, 3.3% for kitchen clients, 3.5% for shelter clients, and 3.3% for all clients.

n.a. = not applicable.

Among the pantry clients, 82.0% used just one food pantry during the previous month.

More information on the clients' use of the emergency food programs follows:

- 76.6% of the kitchen clients used only one soup kitchen, and 45.2% also used one or more pantries.

- 27.8% of the shelter clients used one or more pantries, and 49.6% of the shelter clients also used one or more kitchens.

- 14.6% of the pantry clients also used one or more kitchens.

9.2   SATISFACTION WITH SERVICES AT FOOD PROGRAMS

Clients were asked how satisfied they were with the amount, variety, and overall quality of food provided at the emergency food programs. Clients were also asked how often they were treated with respect by the staff of those programs. Table 9.2.1 and Chart 9.2.1 summarize the findings.

TABLE 9.2.1

SATISFACTION WITH SERVICES AT FOOD PROGRAMS

Level of Satisfaction with Various Aspects of the Service Provided to Clients or Others in the Household:	Adult Clients Who Pick Up Food at a Pantry	Adult Clients at a Kitchen	Adult Clients at a Shelter	Adult Clients at All Program Sites
Amount of food provided				
Very satisfied	59.6%	63.2%	52.7%	59.7%
Somewhat satisfied	33.0%	29.5%	31.0%	32.3%
Somewhat dissatisfied	6.1%	4.6%	9.0%	6.0%
Very dissatisfied	1.3%	2.7%	7.3%	2.0%
TOTAL	100.0%	100.0%	100.0%	100.0%
Variety of food provided				
Very satisfied	56.7%	59.1%	43.6%	56.2%
Somewhat satisfied	34.0%	30.3%	35.1%	33.4%
Somewhat dissatisfied	7.7%	6.6%	11.4%	7.8%
Very dissatisfied	1.7%	4.0%	9.9%	2.7%
TOTAL	100.0%	100.0%	100.0%	100.0%
Overall quality of food provided				
Very satisfied	62.3%	60.4%	45.9%	60.8%
Somewhat satisfied	31.6%	31.2%	37.0%	31.9%
Somewhat dissatisfied	4.9%	4.7%	8.5%	5.2%
Very dissatisfied	1.1%	3.6%	8.6%	2.1%
TOTAL	100.0%	100.0%	100.0%	100.0%
Frequency at which clients are treated with respect by the staff who distribute food				
All of the time	84.6%	80.9%	65.9%	82.7%
Most of the time	7.0%	10.1%	18.3%	8.3%
Some of the time	2.2%	5.2%	8.9%	3.2%
Never	0.3%	0.7%	2.8%	0.6%
Never came before	5.9%	3.0%	4.1%	5.3%
TOTAL	100.0%	100.0%	100.0%	100.0%

TABLE 9.2.1 *(continued)*

Level of Satisfaction with Various Aspects of the Service Provided to Clients or Others in the Household:	Adult Clients Who Pick Up Food at a Pantry	Adult Clients at a Kitchen	Adult Clients at a Shelter	Adult Clients at All Program Sites
SAMPLE SIZE (N)	**37,986**	**10,667**	**4,225**	**52,878**

SOURCE: This table was constructed based on usable responses to questions 53 and 54 of the client survey.

NOTES: The percentages presented in this table are based only on usable responses, excluding missing, don't know, and refusal responses. All usable responses were weighted as described in Chapter 3 and in the Technical Appendix volume to represent all emergency food clients of the A2H National Network. The sample sizes (N) also include missing data.

For amount of food provided, missing, don't know, and refusal responses combined are 9.6% for pantry clients, 5.3% for kitchen clients, 5.4% for shelter clients, and 8.6% for all clients.

For variety of food provided, missing, don't know, and refusal responses combined are 9.8% for pantry clients, 5.4% for kitchen clients, 7.1% for shelter clients, and 8.9% for all clients.

For overall quality of food provided, missing, don't know, and refusal responses combined are 10.0% for pantry clients, 4.7% for kitchen clients, 5.9% for shelter clients, and 1.4% for all clients.

For client treatment by staff, missing, don't know, and refusal responses combined are 3.3% for pantry clients, 2.9% for kitchen clients, 3.0% for shelter clients, and 3.2% for all clients.

Across all three kinds of emergency food programs, the level of satisfaction among clients is high. 92.0% are either very satisfied or somewhat satisfied with the amount of the food they receive at the programs. Client satisfaction with specific aspects of the programs follows:

- 89.6% of the clients are either very satisfied or somewhat satisfied with the variety of the food.

- 92.7% of the clients are either very satisfied or somewhat satisfied with overall quality of the food.

- 82.7% of the clients say that they are treated with respect by the staff all the time.

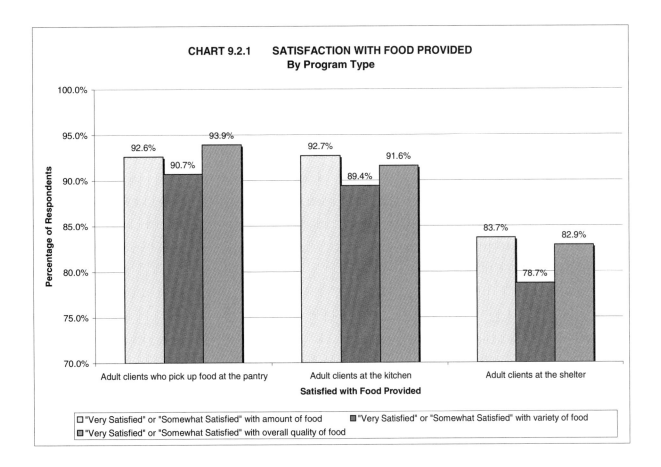

CH 9. CLIENTS: SERVICES RECEIVED AT FOOD PROGRAMS

9.3 WHAT CLIENTS WOULD DO WITHOUT FOOD ASSISTANCE FROM THE AGENCY

Clients were asked what they would do without the agency helping them. Results are shown in Table 9.3.1 and Chart 9.3.1.

TABLE 9.3.1

WHAT CLIENTS WOULD DO WITHOUT FOOD ASSISTANCE FROM THE AGENCY

If this agency weren't here to help you or your household with food, what would you do?[a]	Pantry Client Households	Kitchen Client Households	Shelter Client Households	All Client Households
Go to another agency	55.1%	47.4%	45.7%	53.1%
Get help from relatives, friends	20.8%	16.5%	17.8%	19.9%
Get help from the government	8.3%	7.5%	10.0%	8.3%
Get a job, more hours, an additional job	10.1%	13.1%	15.0%	10.9%
Sell some personal property	5.4%	3.4%	3.3%	4.9%
Lower expenses	6.8%	5.9%	4.2%	6.5%
Eat less, skip meals, reduce size of meals	15.4%	16.9%	12.0%	15.4%
Would get by somehow	25.1%	23.2%	19.5%	24.4%
I have no other place to get help	5.2%	5.4%	7.2%	5.3%
Do something illegal	1.5%	2.9%	4.4%	2.0%
Do not know[b]	11.2%	10.9%	15.3%	11.5%
Other[c]	6.9%	11.3%	11.0%	8.0%
SAMPLE SIZE (N)	**37,986**	**10,667**	**4,225**	**52,878**

SOURCE: This table was constructed based on usable responses to Question 55 of the client survey.

NOTES: All usable responses were weighted as described in Chapter 3 and in the Technical Appendix volume to represent all emergency food clients of the A2H National Network. The sample sizes (N) also include cases with missing data.

Missing and refusal responses combined are 2.9% for pantry clients, 3.1% for kitchen clients, 3.2% for shelter clients, and 2.9% for all clients.

[a]Multiple responses were accepted.

[b]Do not know responses to this question may indicate a feeling of hopelessness, disappointment, or desperation.

[c]This includes eating at home and begging.

In the absence of the agency helping the clients, 53.1% of them said that they would go to another agency. Other responses include:

- 24.4% of the clients said that they would get by somehow.

- 19.9% of the clients said that they would get help from relatives or friends.

- 15.4% of the clients said that they would eat less, skip meals, or reduce the size of meals.

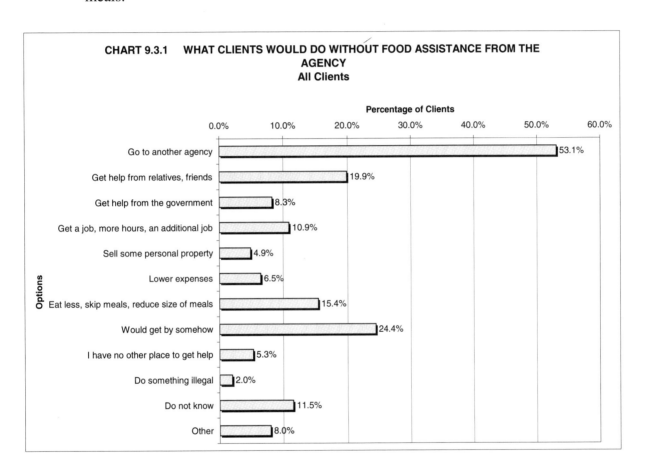

CHART 9.3.1 WHAT CLIENTS WOULD DO WITHOUT FOOD ASSISTANCE FROM THE AGENCY
All Clients

CH 9. CLIENTS: SERVICES RECEIVED AT FOOD PROGRAMS

10. AGENCIES AND FOOD PROGRAMS: PROFILES

Until now, the discussion has focused on information from the *client* survey. This chapter begins the presentation of the results from the survey of *agencies* affiliated with the A2H National Network. The first section below details the numbers of responses received from various types of agencies. Next we present information on what combinations of programs are operated by the responding agencies. Subsequent sections examine characteristics of emergency food programs operated by these agencies, such as years of program operation, services provided other than food distribution, and types of organizations. Agency estimates of the changes in their numbers of clients between 2001 and 2005 are also presented.

10.1 PARTICIPATING AGENCIES AND PROGRAMS REPRESENTED

The agency survey questionnaire was sent to 43,141 agencies affiliated with the A2H National Network. Each agency was asked to provide detailed information about one of each type of emergency food programs it operates (such as one pantry, one kitchen, and one shelter). Agencies operating nonemergency food programs only (referred to as "other programs") were asked to answer several general questions only.

Of the agencies that received the questionnaire, 31,111 agencies completed the survey. Among those that completed the survey, 21,834 operate one or more emergency programs, and the remaining agencies operate other nonemergency food programs. Those 31,111 responding agencies reported on 54,464 programs,[40] of which 47.1% are emergency food programs. Table

---

[40] There are more programs than agencies, because agencies often run two or more programs of different types.

10.1.1 and Chart 10.1.1. show the breakdown of the participating agencies by the type of program they operate.

TABLE 10.1.1

PROGRAMS REPORTED ON BY PARTICIPATING AGENCIES, BY PROGRAM TYPE

Program Type	Number	Unweighted Percentage	Unweighted Percentage Excluding "Other" Type
Pantry	18,436	33.8%	71.9%
Kitchen	4,514	8.3%	17.6%
Shelter	2,704	5.0%	10.5%
Other[a]	28,810	52.9%	n.a.
TOTAL[b]	54,464	100.0%	100.0%

[a]Other programs refer to nonemergency food programs. They are programs that have a primary purpose other than emergency food distribution but also distribute food. Examples include day care programs, senior congregate-feeding programs, and summer camps.

[b]This is the number of programs about which agencies provide detailed or some information. The total number of programs operated by these agencies is larger.

n.a. = not applicable.

Among the total of 54,464 programs reported on by the agencies, 33.8% are pantries, 8.3% are kitchens, and 5.0% are shelters. The remaining 52.9% are other nonemergency food programs, such as child day care, senior-congregate feeding programs, and summer camps.

Excluding other nonemergency food programs makes the percentage breakdown 71.9% pantries, 17.6% kitchens, and 10.5% shelters.

CH 10. AGENCIES AND FOOD PROGRAMS: PROFILES

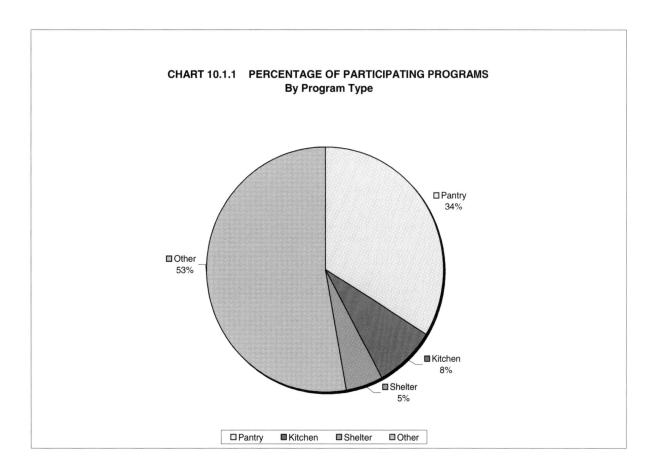

CHART 10.1.1   PERCENTAGE OF PARTICIPATING PROGRAMS
By Program Type

CH 10. AGENCIES AND FOOD PROGRAMS: PROFILES

10.2 NUMBER OF PROGRAMS OPERATED BY AGENCIES

Percentages of the agencies operating various types of programs, as well as the total number of programs operated of each program type, are shown in Table 10.2.1.

TABLE 10.2.1

NUMBER OF PROGRAMS OPERATED BY AGENCIES

Number of Programs of Each Type Operated by Agencies	Percentage of All Agencies That Operate the Specified Number of Each Program Type			
	Agencies with Pantries	Agencies with Kitchens	Agencies with Shelters	Agencies with Others
1	96.0%	93.4%	92.1%	90.7%
2	1.9%	3.0%	3.5%	3.6%
3 or more	2.2%	3.6%	4.4%	5.7%
TOTAL	100.0%	100.0%	100.0%	100.0%
SAMPLE SIZE (N) – Agencies with at least one program for each program type	**18,436**	**4,514**	**2,704**	**28,810**
Total number of participating agencies		31,111		
Total number of programs reported on by participating agencies		54,464		

SOURCE: This table was constructed based on usable responses to Question 1 of the agency survey.

Among the participating agencies, 18,436 operate at least one pantry program, 4,514 at least one kitchen program, and 2,704 at least one shelter program. A total of 31,111 agencies provided information about 54,464 programs.

CH 10. AGENCIES AND FOOD PROGRAMS: PROFILES

10.3   AGENCIES OPERATING VARIOUS TYPE(S) OF PROGRAMS

Table 10.3.1 shows the distribution of agencies by types of programs they operate.

TABLE 10.3.1

AGENCIES OPERATING VARIOUS TYPE(S) OF PROGRAMS

Combinations of Programs the Agency Operates	Agencies
Pantry only	5.1%
Kitchen only	0.4%
Shelter only	0.2%
Other program only	29.6%
Pantry and Kitchen	0.9%
Kitchen and Shelter	0.1%
Shelter and Pantry	0.2%
Pantry and Other	43.8%
Kitchen and Other	5.4%
Shelter and Other	4.6%
Pantry, Kitchen, and Shelter	0.3%
Pantry, Kitchen, and Other	5.8%
Kitchen, Shelter, and Other	0.6%
Shelter, Pantry, and Other	1.5%
Pantry, Kitchen, Shelter, and Other	1.5%
Unknown	0.0%
TOTAL	100.0%
SAMPLE SIZE (N) – Total number of participating agencies	**31,111**

SOURCE: This table was constructed based on responses to Question 1 of the agency survey.

As Table 10.3.1 shows, 5.1% of the participating agencies exclusively operate one or more pantries, while 0.4% and 0.2% operate exclusively kitchen or shelter programs, respectively.

10.4 LENGTH OF PROGRAM OPERATION

Responding agencies identified the year their emergency food programs opened. Table 10.4.1 shows the distribution of the length of program operation and Chart 10.4.1 shows the percentage of programs operating for 11 to 20 years.

TABLE 10.4.1

LENGTH OF PROGRAM OPERATION

How Long the Program Has Been Operating[a]	Percentage of Programs That Have Operated for a Specified Period			Agencies with Pantry, Kitchen, or Shelter
	Pantry Programs	Kitchen Programs	Shelter Programs	
2 years or less	12.4%	12.1%	7.9%	11.4%
3-4 years	11.0%	9.3%	6.8%	10.4%
5-6 years	11.2%	8.4%	7.0%	10.4%
7-10 years	15.1%	13.4%	12.5%	14.5%
11-20 years	26.3%	27.9%	29.7%	26.8%
21-30 years	14.6%	16.4%	20.6%	15.9%
More than 30 years	9.5%	12.5%	15.6%	10.6%
TOTAL	100.0%	100.0%	100.0%	100.0%
SAMPLE SIZE (N)	18,436	4,514	2,704	21,834
Average length of operation among valid responses (in years)	15	17	20	16
Median length of operation among valid responses (in years)	11	13	16	12
SAMPLE SIZE (N)	15,421	3,584	2,121	18,557

SOURCE: This table was constructed based on usable responses to Question 3b of the agency survey.

NOTES: The percentages presented in this table are based only on usable responses, excluding missing, don't know, and refusal responses. All usable responses were weighted as described in Chapter 3 and in the Technical Appendix volume to represent all emergency food programs of the A2H National Network. The sample sizes (N) also include missing data.

Missing, don't know, and refusal responses combined are 16.5% for pantry programs, 20.7% for kitchen programs, 21.4% for shelter programs, and 15.0% for all agencies.

[a]For all programs, responses greater than 70 years of operation were recoded as 70 years. Responses less than 1 year were recoded as 1 year.

The average length of operation among the pantry programs is 15 years. It is 17 years for

the kitchens and 20 years for the shelter programs. Details follow:

- 12.4% of the pantries, 12.1% of the kitchens, and 7.9% of the shelters have been operating for two years or less.

- 26.3% of the pantries, 27.9% of the kitchens, and 29.7% of the shelters have been operating for 11 to 20 years.

- 14.6% of the pantries, 16.4% of the kitchens, and 20.6% of the shelters have been operating for 21 to 30 years.

- 9.5% of the pantries, 12.5% of the kitchens, and 15.6% of the shelters have been operating for more than 30 years.

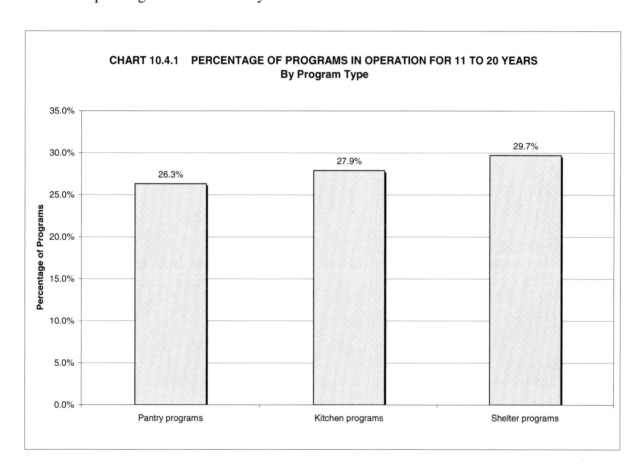

CHART 10.4.1   PERCENTAGE OF PROGRAMS IN OPERATION FOR 11 TO 20 YEARS
By Program Type

CH 10. AGENCIES AND FOOD PROGRAMS: PROFILES

10.5   OTHER SERVICES OR FACILITIES PROVIDED IN ADDITION TO FOOD DISTRIBUTION

Agencies were provided with a list of additional possible services and asked which services their programs provide to their clients. Table 10.5.1 shows what percentage of food programs supply the services listed.

TABLE 10.5.1

OTHER SERVICES OR FACILITIES AGENCIES OR PROGRAMS PROVIDE
IN ADDITION TO FOOD DISTRIBUTION, BY PROGRAM TYPE

	Pantry Programs	Kitchen Programs	Shelter Programs
Food-related support			
Nutrition counseling	22.7%	32.4%	40.7%
Eligibility counseling for WIC	13.1%	7.2%	24.8%
Eligibility counseling for food stamps	19.2%	12.7%	36.5%
Soup kitchen meals	13.4%	n.a.	22.8%
Food pantry bags	n.a.	24.2%	21.2%
Client training			
Employment training	8.6%	21.1%	38.0%
Supported employment (Welfare to Work or job training)	5.1%	8.4%	15.2%
Retraining physically disabled	1.6%	4.6%	5.0%
Retraining mentally ill/challenged	2.5%	8.4%	9.7%
Other assistance			
Eligibility counseling for other government programs	8.7%	13.9%	24.0%
Legal services	3.5%	5.4%	22.1%
Tax preparation help (Earned Income Tax Credit)	5.8%	6.2%	11.9%
Utility bill assistance (Low-Income Heating and Energy Assistance Programs)	20.3%	8.2%	13.0%
Short-term financial assistance	14.2%	6.4%	18.6%
Budget and credit counseling	10.7%	7.2%	37.7%
Consumer protection	2.5%	4.0%	6.7%
Information and referral	39.2%	33.7%	65.8%
Language translation	10.3%	8.6%	19.5%

TABLE 10.5.1 *(continued)*

	Pantry Programs	Kitchen Programs	Shelter Programs
Housing services			
Short-term shelter	7.7%	6.6%	80.1%
Subsidized housing assistance	6.2%	4.3%	18.7%
Housing rehabilitation or repair	3.4%	2.6%	4.8%
Health and other services			
Health services or health clinics	9.3%	19.0%	34.7%
Transportation	16.3%	23.4%	64.4%
Clothing	46.6%	36.6%	76.7%
Furniture	21.4%	11.3%	40.3%
Senior programs	12.0%	15.2%	6.5%
No additional services	25.1%	17.3%	1.9%
SAMPLE SIZE (N)	**18,436**	**4,514**	**2,704**

SOURCE: This table was constructed based on usable responses to Question 4 of the agency survey.

NOTES: All usable responses were weighted as described in Chapter 3 and in the Technical Appendix volume to represent all emergency food programs of the A2H National Network. The sample sizes (N) also include missing data.

Missing, don't know, and refusal responses combined are 10.8% for pantry programs, 20.0% for kitchen programs, and 7.7% for shelter programs.

n.a. = not applicable.

13.1% of pantries and 24.8% of shelters provide counseling for WIC. Other services provided by the programs or the agencies include:

- 19.2% of the pantries, 12.7% of the kitchens, and 36.5% of the shelters provide eligibility counseling for food stamps.

- 24.0% of the shelters provide counseling for other government programs.

- 20.3% of the pantries provide utility bill assistance.

- 39.2% of the pantries, 33.7% of the kitchens, and 65.8% of the shelters provide information and referral services.

- 38.0% of the shelters provide employment training.

- 9.3% of the pantries, 19.0% of the kitchens, and 34.7% of the shelters provide health services or health clinics.

- 64.4% of the shelters provide transportation.

- 46.6% of the pantries, 36.6% of the kitchens, and 76.7% of the shelters provide clothing.

Table 10.5.2 shows the distribution of the number of additional services that emergency food programs offer to their clients.

TABLE 10.5.2

NUMBER OF ADDITIONAL SERVICES, BY PROGRAM TYPE

Number of Additional Services or Facilities Provided by Programs	Pantry Programs	Kitchen Programs	Shelter Programs
None	25.1%	17.3%	1.9%
1	17.0%	23.0%	5.3%
2-5	36.8%	38.9%	28.5%
6-10	16.1%	15.5%	40.2%
More than 10	5.1%	5.3%	24.1%
TOTAL	100.0%	100.0%	100.0%
SAMPLE SIZE (N)	**18,436**	**4,514**	**2,704**
Average number of additional services among those that provide at least one such service	3	3	8
Median number of additional services among those that provide at least one such service	2	2	7
SAMPLE SIZE (N)	**16,480**	**3,614**	**2,489**

SOURCE: This table was constructed based on usable responses to Question 4 of the agency survey.

NOTES: The percentages presented in this table are based only on usable responses, excluding missing, don't know, and refusal responses. All usable responses were weighted as described in Chapter 3 and in the Technical Appendix volume to represent all emergency food programs of the A2H National Network. The sample sizes (N) also include missing data.

Missing, don't know, and refusal responses combined are 10.8% for pantry programs, 20.0% for kitchen programs, and 7.7% for shelter programs.

On average, pantries provide 3 additional services or facilities. Kitchens and shelters provide, on average, 3 and 8 additional services, respectively.

- 25.1% of pantry programs, 17.3% of kitchen programs, and 1.9% of shelter programs do not offer any other services or facilities.

- 17.0% of pantry programs, 23.0% of kitchen programs, and 5.3% of the shelter programs offer one additional service or facility.

- 36.8% of pantry programs, 38.9% of kitchen programs, and 28.5% of shelter programs offer two to five additional services or facilities.

- 16.1% of pantry programs, 15.5% of kitchen programs, and 40.2% of shelter programs offer as many as 6 to 10 additional services or facilities.

- 5.1% of pantry programs, 5.3% of kitchen programs, and 24.1% of shelter programs offer more than 10 additional services or facilities.

CH 10. AGENCIES AND FOOD PROGRAMS: PROFILES

In addition to other services provided by their programs, agencies were asked whether they provide other facilities at the agency level for their clients. Table 10.5.3 summarizes the results.

TABLE 10.5.3

OTHER FACILITIES AGENCIES PROVIDE IN ADDITION TO
FOOD DISTRIBUTION, BY PROGRAM TYPE

	Agencies with Pantry, Kitchen, or Shelter
Health clinic	5.5%
Group home for physically/mentally disadvantaged	3.0%
Other residential facility	10.3%
Child day care program	7.4%
Youth after school program	13.3%
Summer camp serving low-income clients	8.6%
Senior congregate feeding program	6.5%
Other[a]	13.4%
No other facilities/programs	55.6%
SAMPLE SIZE (N)	**21,834**

SOURCE: This table was constructed based on usable responses to Question 27 of the agency survey.

NOTES: All usable responses were weighted as described in Chapter 3 and in the Technical Appendix volume to represent all emergency food programs of the A2H National Network. The sample sizes (N) also include missing data.

Missing, don't know, and refusal responses combined are 18.3%.

[a]This includes learning centers, food delivery services, and day programs for mentally disabled adults.

As many as 5.5% of agencies also operate health clinics. Other facilities run by agencies include:

- 3.0% of agencies run group homes for physically/mentally disadvantaged.

- 10.3% of agencies run other types of residential facilities.

- 7.4% of agencies run child day care programs.

- 13.3% of agencies run youth after-school programs.

- 8.6% of agencies run summer camps serving low-income clients.

- 6.5% of agencies run senior congregate-feeding programs.

- 13.4% of agencies run some other type of facility not mentioned above.

10.6 TYPE OF AGENCY THAT OPERATES THE PROGRAM

Table 10.6.1 shows types of agencies operating each type of program.

TABLE 10.6.1

TYPE OF AGENCY THAT OPERATES THE PROGRAM

Type of Agency That Operates the Program	Pantry Programs	Kitchen Programs	Shelter Programs	Agencies with Pantry, Kitchen, or Shelter	All Agencies
Faith-based or religion-affiliated nonprofit	73.6%	64.7%	43.1%	68.5%	56.1%
Other private nonprofit	18.3%	27.9%	50.1%	23.4%	33.3%
Governmental	2.3%	2.5%	1.8%	2.4%	3.5%
Community Action Program (CAP)	3.2%	1.8%	1.6%	2.9%	2.6%
Other[a]	2.6%	3.0%	3.4%	2.8%	4.5%
TOTAL	100.0%	100.0%	100.0%	100.0%	100.0%
SAMPLE SIZE (N)	18,436	4,514	2,704	21,834	31,111

SOURCE: This table was constructed based on usable responses to Question 28 of the agency survey.

NOTES: The percentages presented in this table are based only on usable responses, excluding missing, don't know, and refusal responses. All usable responses were weighted as described in Chapter 3 and in the Technical Appendix volume to represent all emergency food programs of the A2H National Network. The sample sizes (N) also include missing data.

Missing, don't know, and refusal responses combined are 4.8% for pantry programs, 5.5% for kitchen programs, 4.5% for shelter programs, 4.8% for agencies with pantry, kitchen, or shelter programs, and 4.5% for all agencies.

[a]This includes various community-based organizations.

Table 10.6.1 shows that 73.6% of the pantries, 64.7% of the kitchens, and 43.1% of the shelters are run by faith-based or religion-affiliated nonprofit agencies. In addition:

- 68.5% of agencies operating emergency feeding programs are faith-based.

- 2.3% of the pantries, 2.5% of the kitchens, and 1.8% of the shelters are run by government-affiliated agencies.

- The remaining agencies are operated by other kinds of private nonprofit organizations, such as community-based charities or philanthropic organizations.

10.7   PROGRAMS SERVING SELECTED TYPES OF CLIENTS

Agencies were asked whether their programs serve migrant workers, legal immigrants, or undocumented immigrants.[41] Results are presented in Table 10.7.1 and Chart 10.7.1.

TABLE 10.7.1

PROGRAMS SERVING SELECTED TYPES OF CLIENTS

	Pantry Programs	Kitchen Programs	Shelter Programs
Migrant Workers			
Yes	32.9%	30.2%	30.5%
No	67.1%	69.8%	69.5%
TOTAL	100.0%	100.0%	100.0%
Legal Immigrants			
Yes	54.9%	51.1%	58.4%
No	45.1%	48.9%	41.6%
TOTAL	100.0%	100.0%	100.0%
Undocumented Immigrants			
Yes	36.1%	36.0%	41.3%
No	63.9%	64.0%	58.7%
TOTAL	100.0%	100.0%	100.0%
SAMPLE SIZE (N)	**18,436**	**4,514**	**2,704**

SOURCE: This table was constructed based on usable responses to Question 18 of the agency survey.

NOTES: The percentages presented in this table are based only on usable responses, excluding missing, don't know, and refusal responses. All usable responses were weighted as described in Chapter 3 and in the Technical Appendix volume to represent all emergency food programs of the A2H National Network. The sample sizes (N) also include missing data.

For migrant workers, missing, don't know, and refusal responses combined are 37.9% for pantry programs, 44.5% for kitchen programs, and 35.7% for shelter programs.

For legal immigrants, missing, don't know, and refusal responses combined are 31.7% for pantry programs, 40.6% for kitchen programs, and 27.7% for shelter programs.

For undocumented immigrants, missing, don't know, and refusal responses combined are 44.4% for pantry programs, 50.4% for kitchen programs, and 35.0% for shelter programs.

---

[41] At the national level, a large number of the responding agencies left these three questions unanswered.

Findings in Table 10.7.1 include:

- 32.9% of the pantries, 30.2% of the kitchens, and 30.5% of the shelters serve migrant workers.

- 54.9% of the pantries, 51.1% of the kitchens, and 58.4% of the shelters serve legal immigrants.

- 36.1% of the pantries, 36.0% of the kitchens, and 41.3% of the shelters serve undocumented immigrants.

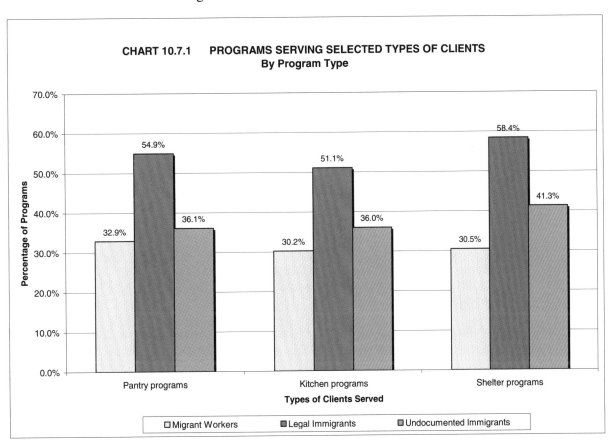

CHART 10.7.1   PROGRAMS SERVING SELECTED TYPES OF CLIENTS
By Program Type

CH 10. AGENCIES AND FOOD PROGRAMS: PROFILES

10.8 AGENCY ESTIMATES OF CHANGE IN NUMBER OF CLIENTS FROM 2001 TO 2005

Agencies were asked whether they serve more or fewer clients than they did in 2001.

Table 10.8.1 and Chart 10.8.1 show the findings.

TABLE 10.8.1

AGENCY ESTIMATES OF CHANGE IN NUMBER OF CLIENTS FROM 2001 TO 2005

Agency Estimate of Change in the Number of Clients Compared with Year 2001	Pantry Programs	Kitchen Programs	Shelter Programs
More clients	64.6%	61.0%	52.4%
Fewer clients	8.2%	8.0%	6.3%
About the same number of clients	20.1%	25.3%	37.2%
Program did not exist in 2001	7.1%	5.8%	4.2%
TOTAL	100.0%	100.0%	100.0%
SAMPLE SIZE (N)	18,436	4,514	2,704

SOURCE: This table was constructed based on usable responses to Question 7 of the agency survey.

NOTES: The percentages presented in this table are based only on usable responses, excluding missing, don't know, and refusal responses. All usable responses were weighted as described in Chapter 3 and in the Technical Appendix volume to represent all emergency food programs of the A2H National Network. The sample sizes (N) also include missing data.

Missing, don't know, and refusal responses combined are 7.0% for pantry programs, 11.3% for kitchen programs, and 11.7% for shelter programs.

Regarding the volume of the clients, 64.6% of the pantries, 61.0% of the kitchens, and 52.4% of the shelters indicate that they serve more clients now than they did in 2001.

- 20.1% of the pantries, 25.3% of the kitchens, and 37.2% of the shelters indicated that they serve about the same number of clients in 2005 as in 2001.

- 8.2% of the pantries, 8.0% of the kitchens, and 6.3% of the shelters indicated that they serve fewer clients in 2005 than they did in 2001.

- 7.1% of the pantries, 5.8% of the kitchens, and 4.2% of the shelters did not exist in 2001.

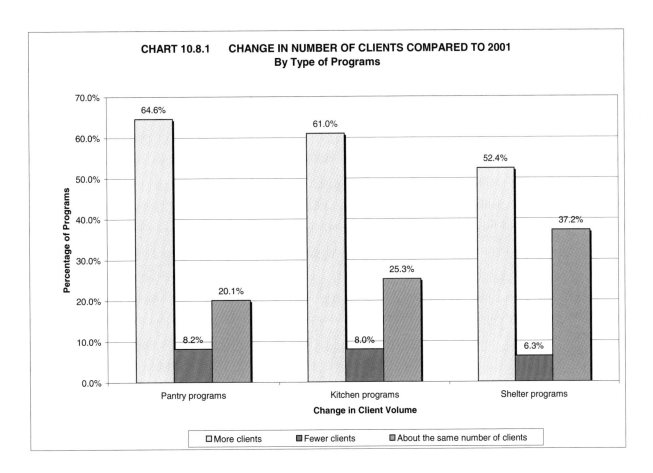

CHART 10.8.1   CHANGE IN NUMBER OF CLIENTS COMPARED TO 2001
By Type of Programs

CH 10. AGENCIES AND FOOD PROGRAMS: PROFILES

10.9   SEASONALITY OF CLIENT MIX

Agencies were asked whether their programs experience significant change in client mix by season and, if so, what kinds of change. Results are shown in Table 10.9.1.

TABLE 10.9.1

SEASONALITY OF CLIENT MIX

Nature of Changes in Client Mix During the Year[a]	Pantry Programs	Kitchen Programs	Shelter Programs
Ratio of men to women changes	17.8%	23.7%	21.5%
Mix of ethnic groups changes	17.6%	22.4%	39.6%
Many more children in summer	29.4%	40.9%	16.4%
Many more migrant workers in summer	5.9%	6.5%	3.2%
Many more migrant workers in winter	4.1%	3.2%	1.8%
Different group of people at the holidays	57.3%	36.4%	27.8%
Other[b]	5.5%	5.5%	5.5%
Do not experience change in client mix	29.4%	32.7%	31.0%
SAMPLE SIZE (N)	**17,456**	**3,976**	**2,446**

SOURCE: This table was constructed based on usable responses to Questions 19 of the agency survey.

NOTES: All usable responses were weighted as described in Chapter 3 and in the Technical Appendix volume to represent all emergency food programs of the A2H National Network. The sample sizes (N) also include missing data.

Missing, don't know, and refusal responses combined are 5.4% for pantry programs, 11.9% for kitchen programs, and 9.4% for shelter programs.

[a]Multiple responses were accepted.

[b]This includes fewer elderly people in winter and more families in winter.

29.4% of the pantries, 32.7% of the kitchens, and 31.0% of the shelters indicated that they do not experience seasonal changes in the mix of clients during the year. As to the nature of seasonal changes in client mix among programs that experience such changes:

- 17.8% of the pantries, 23.7% of the kitchens, and 21.5% of the shelters said they experience changes in the ratio of men to women.

- 29.4% of the pantries, 40.9% of the kitchens, and 16.4% of the shelters said they serve more children in summer.

- 57.3% of the pantries, 36.4% of the kitchens, and 27.8% of the shelters said they serve a different group of people during the holidays.

CH 10. AGENCIES AND FOOD PROGRAMS: PROFILES

11. AGENCIES AND FOOD PROGRAMS: FOOD SERVICES

In understanding the workings of the A2H Network, it is important to understand the broad differences between providers in their scales of operations. The chapter discusses a number of indicators of the size of provider food service operations. As will be seen, providers vary dramatically in size, from pantries that serve just a few clients a day to pantries and kitchens that provide food to hundreds of clients on a given day of operation.

There is great variation among providers in the detail with which they keep long-term records such as service and client counts. Therefore, the analysis below focuses on measures of size based on either a "typical week" or on the "most recent day the provider was open," since these are the size concepts that respondents were in general best able to relate to.

11.1 NUMBER OF BOXES OR BAGS DISTRIBUTED IN A TYPICAL WEEK

Agencies were asked how much food their pantries distribute during a typical week and how much a typical box or bag weighs. Table 11.1.1 shows the results.

TABLE 11.1.1

NUMBER OF BOXES OR BAGS DISTRIBUTED IN A TYPICAL WEEK

	Pantry Programs
Programs distributing the following number of boxes or bags of food in a typical week[a]:	
1-9	13.9%
10-29	23.4%
30-49	13.1%
50-99	19.4%
100-299	21.4%
300-499	4.1%
500 or more	4.6%
TOTAL	100.0%
SAMPLE SIZE (N)	**18,436**

TABLE 11.1.1 *(continued)*

	Pantry Programs
Average number of boxes or bags of food distributed in a typical week among valid responses[b]	140
Median number of boxes or bags of food distributed in a typical week among valid responses[b]	46
Average weight of a typical bag/box among valid responses (in pounds)	22
Median weight of a typical bag/box among valid responses (in pounds)	20
SAMPLE SIZE (N)	**14,070**

SOURCE: This table was constructed based on usable responses to questions 6 and 6a of the agency survey.

NOTES: The percentages presented in this table are based only on usable responses, excluding missing, don't know, and refusal responses. All usable responses were weighted as described in Chapter 3 and in the Technical Appendix volume to represent all pantries (as noted earlier in this footnote only) of the A2H National Network. The sample sizes (N) also include missing data.

Missing, don't know, and refusal responses combined are 24.3% for pantry programs.

[a]For pantries, responses greater than 5,000 bags or boxes distributed were recoded as 5,000 bags or boxes. Responses greater than 40 pounds per bag or box were recoded as 40 pounds.

[b]Zeros as responses were not included as valid responses for calculating the average and the median.

On average, the participating pantries distributed 140 boxes or bags (median: 46) of food during a typical week, with the average weight of a typical box or bag being 22 pounds. More details on the amount of food distributed during a typical week follow:

- 23.4% of the pantries distributed 10 to 29 boxes or bags of food.

- 13.1% of the pantries distributed 30 to 49 boxes or bags of food.

- 19.4% of the pantries distributed 50 to 99 boxes or bags of food.

- 21.4% of the pantries distributed 100 to 299 boxes or bags of food.

- 4.1% of the pantries distributed 300 to 499 boxes or bags of food.

- 4.6% of the pantries distributed 500 or more boxes or bags.

11.2   AMOUNT OF FOOD SERVED ON THE DAY THE PROGRAM WAS LAST OPEN

Agencies were asked how much food their programs distributed when they were last open. Results are presented in Table 11.2.1.

TABLE 11.2.1

AMOUNT OF FOOD SERVED ON THE DAY THE PROGRAM WAS LAST OPEN

	Pantry Programs (in Bags or Boxes)	Kitchen Programs (in Meals)	Shelter Programs (in Meals)
Programs that distributed the following number of boxes/bags or meals of food[a,b]			
1-9	19.7%	5.8%	17.6%
10-29	24.6%	12.4%	19.2%
30-49	14.5%	14.4%	15.2%
50-99	18.4%	25.4%	21.4%
100-149	8.3%	15.0%	8.4%
150-199	4.3%	8.0%	5.3%
200-249	2.8%	5.5%	2.6%
250 or more	7.4%	13.4%	10.4%
TOTAL	100.0%	100.0%	100.0%
SAMPLE SIZE (N)	**18,436**	**4,514**	**2,704**
Average number of bags or boxes of food distributed, among valid responses[c]	81	n.a.	n.a.
Median number of bags or boxes of food distributed, among valid responses[c]	32	n.a.	n.a.
Average number of meals served, among valid responses[c]	n.a.	137	77
Median number of meals served, among valid responses[c]	n.a.	76	42
SAMPLE SIZE (N)	**13,222**	**2,976**	**1,607**

SOURCE: This table was constructed based on usable responses to Question 6c of the agency survey.

NOTES: The percentages presented in this table are based only on usable responses, excluding missing, don't know, and refusal responses. All usable responses were weighted as described in Chapter 3 and in the Technical Appendix volume to represent all emergency food programs of the A2H National Network. The sample sizes (N) also include missing data.

Missing, don't know, and refusal responses combined are 31.3% for pantry programs, 35.4% for kitchen programs, and 42.5% for shelter programs.

TABLE 11.2.1 *(continued)*

_____

[a]For pantries and kitchens, responses greater than 1,000 bags or boxes distributed or meals served were recoded as 1,000 bags or boxes distributed or meals served. For shelters, responses greater than 300 meals served were recoded as 300 meals served.

[b]It should be noted that, particularly for pantries, amounts distributed per day can vary substantially over the month, so responses may depend on when the survey was filled out.

[c]Zeros as responses were not included as valid responses for calculating the average and the median.

n.a. = not applicable.

Emergency food programs vary greatly in size. Some programs served several people and others several hundred people when they were last open. On average, the pantry programs distributed 81 boxes/bags (median: 32) of food when they were last open. The kitchen programs distributed 137 meals (median: 76) and the shelter programs distributed 77 meals (median: 42). Details follow:

- 19.7% of the pantries and 17.6% of the shelters distributed 1 to 9 boxes or bags on the day they were last open.

- 57.4% of the pantries and 55.7% of the shelters distributed 10 to 99 boxes or bags on the day they were last open.

- 10.3% of the pantries and 12.9% of the shelters distributed 200 or more boxes or bags on the day they were last open.

- 14.2% of the kitchens served more than 200 people on the day they were last open.

12. AGENCIES AND FOOD PROGRAMS: ABILITY TO MEET CLIENT NEEDS

The study has also examined the capacity of the agencies and food programs to meet client needs. Below, we consider the stability of the programs, the main problems they face, and the degree to which they have had to stretch resources or turn away clients. Reasons why some agencies have had to turn away clients are also discussed.

12.1 STABILITY OF EXISTING FOOD PROGRAMS

Agencies were asked whether their food programs are stable or facing problems that threaten their food programs' continued operation and, if so, which of several listed factors were the causes of the threat. Agencies were asked to check more than one reason, if more than one was appropriate. Table 12.1.1 shows the percentage of food programs affected by each of the factors cited. However, the data in this table are not directly comparable to similar data in the 2001 study. In the 2001 study, a prior question was asked concerning *whether* the selected program was threatened by any serious problems threatening their continued operations. Only those respondents indicating "yes" to this prior question were tracked into the questions about the nature of the threatening problem. In the 2005 study, the prior question was dropped, and respondents were tracked directly into a question about which, if any, of the problems listed were threats to stability. The result appears to have been a significant increase in reported perceptions of threats to stability in the programs.

TABLE 12.1.1

STABILITY OF EXISTING FOOD PROGRAMS

	Pantry Programs	Kitchen Programs	Shelter Programs
Nature of the problem[a]			
Problems related to funding	42.3%	50.3%	65.7%
Problems related to food supplies	30.7%	23.3%	12.5%
Problems related to paid staff or personnel	7.1%	14.0%	19.9%
Problems related to volunteers	18.0%	17.7%	9.9%
Community resistance	1.9%	3.6%	5.8%
Other problems	4.6%	4.0%	3.3%
Programs not facing problems that threaten their continued operation	38.1%	35.0%	27.9%
SAMPLE SIZE (N)	**18,436**	**4,514**	**2,704**

SOURCE: This table was constructed based on usable responses to Question 17 of the agency survey.

NOTES: All usable responses were weighted as described in Chapter 3 and in the Technical Appendix volume to represent all emergency food programs of the A2H National Network. The sample sizes (N) also include missing data.

Missing, don't know, and refusal responses combined are 8.3% for pantry programs, 15.0% for kitchen programs, and 13.2% for shelter programs.

[a]Multiple responses were accepted.

As Table 12.1.1 shows, 61.9% of the pantries, 65.0% of the kitchens, and 72.1% of the shelters believe they are facing one or more problems that threaten their continued operation:

- Of the programs facing threats, 42.3% of the pantries, 50.3% of the kitchens, and 65.7% of the shelters referred to funding issues as a threat; 30.7% of the pantries, 23.3% of the kitchens, and 12.5% of the shelters indicated food supplies as a threat to their continued operation.

- 14.0% of the threatened kitchens and 19.9% of the threatened shelters identified issues related to paid staff or personnel as a threat; 18.0% of the pantries and 17.7% of the kitchens stated that volunteer-related problems posed a threat.

Chart 12.1.1 shows the percentage of programs that have at least one problem threatening their operation while Chart 12.1.1P shows the problems affecting pantry programs.

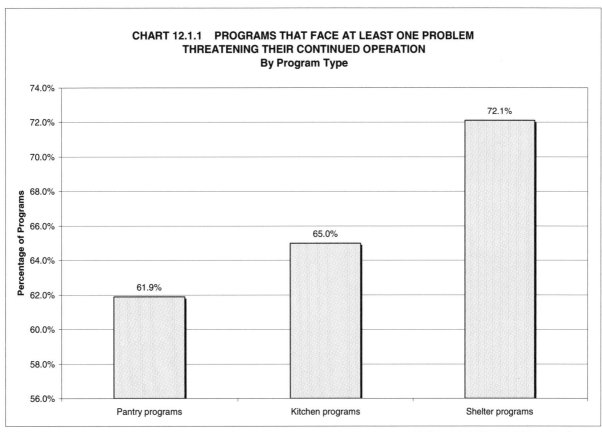

CHART 12.1.1   PROGRAMS THAT FACE AT LEAST ONE PROBLEM THREATENING THEIR CONTINUED OPERATION
By Program Type

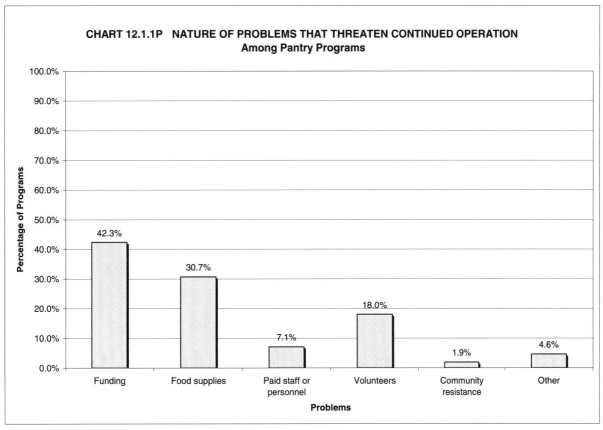

CHART 12.1.1P   NATURE OF PROBLEMS THAT THREATEN CONTINUED OPERATION
Among Pantry Programs

CH 12. AGENCIES AND FOOD PROGRAMS: ABILITY TO MEET CLIENT NEEDS

12.2   FREQUENCY OF STRETCHING FOOD RESOURCES

Agencies were asked whether their programs ever had to ration or limit food in order to provide some food to all clients and, if so, how often. Table 12.2.1 and Chart 12.2.1 show the varying degrees of frequency with which the food programs stretched food resources.

TABLE 12.2.1

FREQUENCY OF STRETCHING FOOD RESOURCES

During 2005, How Often Did the Program Have to Reduce Meal Portions or Reduce the Quantity of Food in Food Packages Because of a Lack of Food	Pantry Programs	Kitchen Programs	Shelter Programs
Never	39.4%	65.1%	73.2%
Rarely	42.5%	25.6%	20.5%
SUBTOTAL	81.9%	90.6%	93.8%
Sometimes	17.0%	8.7%	5.7%
Always	1.1%	0.7%	0.5%
SUBTOTAL	18.1%	9.4%	6.2%
TOTAL	100.0%	100.0%	100.0%
SAMPLE SIZE (N)	**18,436**	**4,514**	**2,704**

SOURCE: This table was constructed based on usable responses to Question 13 of the agency survey.

NOTES: The percentages presented in this table are based only on usable responses, excluding missing, don't know, and refusal responses. All usable responses were weighted as described in Chapter 3 and in the Technical Appendix volume to represent all emergency food programs of the A2H National Network. The sample sizes (N) also include missing data.

Missing, don't know, and refusal responses combined are 5.7% for pantry programs, 12.4% for kitchen programs, and 13.4% for shelter programs.

During the year 2005, 39.4% of pantries, 65.1% of kitchens, and 73.2% of shelters never experienced the need to stretch food resources (reduce meal portions or reduce the quantity of food in food packages).

- Nevertheless, 18.1% of the pantries, 9.4% of the kitchens, and 6.2% of the shelters indicated that they sometimes or always had to stretch food resources.

The data presented above indicate that substantial numbers of programs found it necessary, either sometimes or always, to reduce meal portions or reduce the quantity of food in food packages due to lack of food (Table 12.2.1N).

TABLE 12.2.1N

ESTIMATED NUMBER OF PROGRAMS HAVING TO STRETCH FOOD RESOURCES

During 2005, How Often the Program Had to Reduce Meal Portions or Reduce the Quantity of Food in Food Packages Because of a Lack of Food	Pantry Programs	Kitchen Programs	Shelter Programs
Never	11,681	3,646	3,033
Rarely	12,600	1,434	849
SUBTOTAL	24,281	5,080	3,882
Sometimes	5,040	487	236
Always	326	39	21
SUBTOTAL	5,366	526	257
ESTIMATED TOTAL NUMBER OF PROGRAMS[a]	**29,647**	**5,601**	**4,143**

[a]See Chapter 4 for details.

Key findings include:

- An estimated 5,366 pantries, 526 kitchens, and 257 shelters reported having to take steps to stretch the available food.

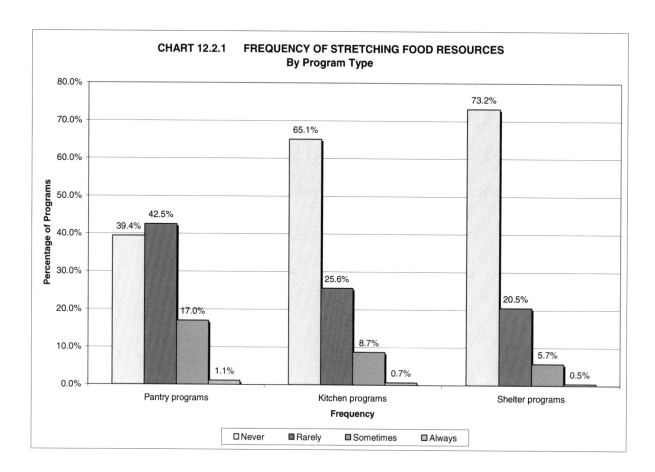

CHART 12.2.1   FREQUENCY OF STRETCHING FOOD RESOURCES
By Program Type

CH 12. AGENCIES AND FOOD PROGRAMS: ABILITY TO MEET CLIENT NEEDS

12.3   PROGRAMS THAT TURNED AWAY CLIENTS

Agencies were asked whether clients had been turned away within the past year and, if so, how many and for what reasons. Agencies were asked to use either their records or their best estimates to supply this information. Tables 12.3.1 and 12.3.2 show the results. Chart 12.3.1P shows results for pantry programs.

TABLE 12.3.1

PROGRAMS THAT TURNED AWAY CLIENTS

	Pantry Programs	Kitchen Programs	Shelter Programs
Did the program turn away clients during the past year?[a]			
Yes	32.9%	12.8%	51.6%
No	67.1%	87.2%	48.4%
TOTAL	100.0%	100.0%	100.0%
SAMPLE SIZE (N)	**18,436**	**4,514**	**2,704**
Average number of clients turned away in the past year among those that turned away at least one client	66	108	191
Median number of clients turned away in the past year among those that turned away at least one client	12	10	38
SAMPLE SIZE (N) – Programs providing a valid number of clients who were turned away	**3,226**	**306**	**627**
Reasons for turning away clients[b]			
Lack of food resources	34.4%	32.1%	14.5%
Services needed not provided by the program	22.3%	16.5%	44.7%
Clients were ineligible or could not prove eligibility	36.3%	14.6%	37.5%
Clients abused program/came too often	50.9%	8.4%	14.2%
Clients exhibited drug, alcohol, or behavior problem	18.2%	54.4%	55.1%
Clients lived outside service area	40.2%	6.6%	7.2%
Clients had no proper identification	25.7%	4.7%	9.9%
Client's income exceeded the guidelines	20.7%	2.2%	1.7%
Other	7.9%	19.4%	39.9%
SAMPLE SIZE (N) – Programs that turned away clients	**5,713**	**490**	**1,186**

SOURCE: This table was constructed based on usable responses to questions 9, 10, and 12 of the agency survey.

NOTES: All usable responses were weighted as described in Chapter 3 and in the Technical Appendix volume to represent all emergency food programs of the A2H National Network. The sample sizes (N) also include missing data.

CH 12. AGENCIES AND FOOD PROGRAMS: ABILITY TO MEET CLIENT NEEDS

TABLE 12.3.1 *(continued)*

For programs that turned away clients, missing, don't know, and refusal responses combined are 7.1% for pantry programs, 14.7% for kitchen programs, and 15.5% for shelter programs.

For reasons for turning away clients, missing, don't know, and refusal responses combined are 1.4% for pantry programs, 3.8% for kitchen programs, and 1.6% for shelter programs.

[a]For pantries, responses greater than 3,000 clients turned away were recoded as 3,000 clients. For kitchens and shelters, responses greater than 2,500 clients turned away were recoded as 2,500 clients.

[b]Multiple responses were accepted.

As Table 12.3.1 shows, 32.9% of the pantries, 12.8% of the kitchens, and 51.6% of the shelters responded that they turned away clients during the past year. Reasons for turning away clients follow:

- Among programs turning away clients, 34.4% of the pantries, 32.1% of the kitchens, and 14.5% of the shelters turned away clients at least once due to lack of food resources.

- Among programs turning away clients, 22.3% of the pantries, 16.5% of the kitchens, and 44.7% of the shelters turned away clients at least once because the services needed were not provided by the program.

- Among programs turning away clients, 36.3% of the pantries, 14.6% of the kitchens, and 37.5% of the shelters turned away clients at least once because the clients were ineligible or could not prove eligibility.

- Among programs turning away clients, 50.9% of the pantries, 8.4% of the kitchens, and 14.2% of the shelters turned away clients at least once because the clients abused the program or because they came too often.

CH 12. AGENCIES AND FOOD PROGRAMS: ABILITY TO MEET CLIENT NEEDS

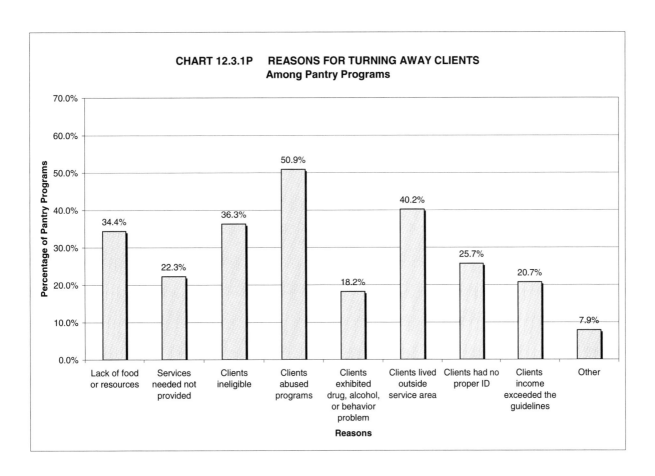

CHART 12.3.1P   REASONS FOR TURNING AWAY CLIENTS
Among Pantry Programs

CH 12. AGENCIES AND FOOD PROGRAMS: ABILITY TO MEET CLIENT NEEDS

TABLE 12.3.2

MOST FREQUENT REASONS THE PROGRAM TURNED AWAY CLIENTS

	Pantry Programs	Kitchen Programs	Shelter Programs
Most frequent reason			
Lack of food or resources	23.2%	23.3%	10.0%
Services needed not provided by the program	7.0%	5.2%	13.1%
Clients were ineligible or could not prove eligibility	9.6%	7.6%	14.6%
Clients abused program/came too often	23.4%	4.4%	3.1%
Clients exhibited drug, alcohol, or behavior problem	3.3%	41.7%	21.0%
Clients lived outside service area	18.0%	3.4%	0.9%
Clients had no proper identification	6.0%	1.4%	1.3%
Client's income exceeded the guidelines	5.0%	0.2%	0.1%
Other	4.5%	12.8%	35.8%
TOTAL	100.0%	100.0%	100.0%
Second most frequent reason			
Lack of food or resources	8.9%	17.5%	3.8%
Services needed not provided by the program	11.3%	16.6%	24.8%
Clients were ineligible or could not prove eligibility	13.4%	11.6%	17.3%
Clients abused program/came too often	22.2%	4.5%	7.4%
Clients exhibited drug, alcohol, or behavior problem	5.6%	25.6%	31.3%
Clients lived outside service area	16.1%	6.7%	3.3%
Clients had no proper identification	11.8%	2.9%	5.0%
Client's income exceeded the guidelines	8.1%	1.9%	0.6%
Other	2.7%	12.7%	6.5%
TOTAL	100.0%	100.0%	100.0%
SAMPLE SIZE (N) – Programs that turned away clients	**5,713**	**490**	**1,186**

SOURCE: This table was constructed based on usable responses to Question 11 of the agency survey.

NOTES: The percentages presented in this table are based only on usable responses, excluding missing, don't know, and refusal responses. All usable responses were weighted as described in Chapter 3 and in the Technical Appendix volume to represent all emergency food programs of the A2H National Network. The sample sizes (N) also include missing data.

For most frequent reason, missing, don't know, and refusal responses combined are 5.6% for pantry programs, 8.4% for kitchen programs, and 6.6% for shelter programs.

For second most frequent reason, missing, don't know, and refusal responses combined are 29.7% for pantry programs, 59.1% for kitchen programs, and 29.4% for shelter programs.

CH 12. AGENCIES AND FOOD PROGRAMS: ABILITY TO MEET CLIENT NEEDS

12.4   ADDITIONAL FOOD RESOURCES NEEDED PER WEEK

Agencies were asked how much additional food is needed during a typical week to adequately meet the demand for food. Results are summarized in Table 12.4.1 and Chart 12.4.1.

TABLE 12.4.1

ADDITIONAL FOOD RESOURCES NEEDED PER WEEK

	Pantry Programs	Kitchen Programs	Shelter Programs
No additional meals or meal equivalents needed[a]	55.0%	69.4%	76.9%
1 to 10 additional meals or meal equivalents needed	1.8%	3.4%	3.6%
11 to 49 additional meals or meal equivalents needed	7.0%	6.5%	6.2%
50 to 149 additional meals or meal equivalents needed	10.2%	10.5%	6.3%
150 or more additional meals or meal equivalents needed	26.1%	10.1%	6.9%
TOTAL	100.0%	100.0%	100.0%
SAMPLE SIZE (N)	**18,436**	**4,514**	**2,704**
Average number of additional meal equivalents needed among valid answers[b]	404	216	215
Median number of additional meal equivalents needed among valid answers[b]	154	80	50
Average amount of additional food needed (pounds)[b]	525	281	280
Median amount of additional food needed (pounds)[b]	200	104	65
SAMPLE SIZE (N) – Programs that need more food resources	**5,847**	**878**	**386**

SOURCE: This table was constructed based on usable responses to Question 14 of the agency survey.

NOTES: The percentages presented in this table are based only on usable responses, excluding missing, don't know, and refusal responses. All usable responses were weighted as described in Chapter 3 and in the Technical Appendix volume to represent all emergency food programs of the A2H National Network. The sample sizes (N) also include missing data.

Missing, don't know, and refusal responses combined are 29.5% for pantry programs, 35.3% for kitchen programs, and 36.2% for shelter programs.

[a]This variable was constructed from two variables, one asking food poundage and the other number of meals. Poundage was converted to meals by dividing the poundage by 1.3. Then, the resulting number of meals and the other variable of actual number of meals were summed to produce the number of meals reported here. The 1.3 pounds per meal factor is based on tabulations from U.S. Department of Agriculture: "Food Consumption and Dietary Levels of Households in the United States, 1987-88." Washington, DC: U.S. Government Printing Office, 1994.

[b]Zeros as responses were not included as valid responses for calculating the average and the median. For pantries, responses greater than 2,500 lb. (1,923 meals) were recoded as 2,500 lb. (1,923 meals). For kitchens, responses greater than 1,690 lb. (1,300 meals) were recoded as 1,690 lb. (1,300 meals). For shelters, responses greater than 2,080 lb. (1,600 meals) were recoded as 2,080 lb. (1,600 meals).

CH 12. AGENCIES AND FOOD PROGRAMS: ABILITY TO MEET CLIENT NEEDS

The percentage of programs that answered that they did not need additional food for distribution is 55.0% for pantries, 69.4% for kitchens, and 76.9% for shelters. Results among the programs in need of additional food follow:

- The median pantry needed more than 200 additional pounds of food per week.

- The median kitchen needed more than 80 additional meal equivalents per week.

- The median shelters needed more than 50 additional meal equivalents per week.

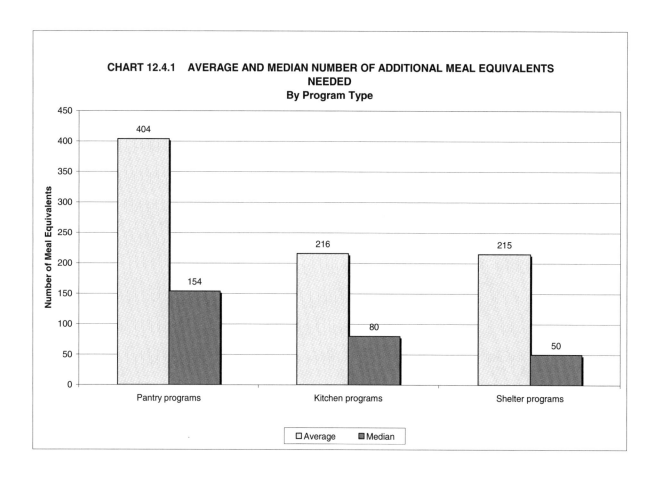

CHART 12.4.1 AVERAGE AND MEDIAN NUMBER OF ADDITIONAL MEAL EQUIVALENTS NEEDED
By Program Type

CH 12. AGENCIES AND FOOD PROGRAMS: ABILITY TO MEET CLIENT NEEDS

13. AGENCIES AND FOOD PROGRAMS: RESOURCES

Substantial resources are required to operate emergency food programs effectively, including food, staffing, and physical space. This chapter reports the types and sources of the resources used by providers of the A2H National Network. We begin by examining the sources of food reported by the providers. The use of paid and unpaid staff is then examined, with a focus on the great importance of volunteers to the system.

13.1   SOURCES OF FOOD DISTRIBUTED BY PROGRAMS

The survey asked how much of the food distributed through the emergency food programs comes from food banks, versus other sources. In particular, agencies were asked to state the percentage of food received from each of the sources shown in Table 13.1.1.

TABLE 13.1.1

SOURCES OF FOOD DISTRIBUTED BY PROGRAMS

Sources of Food	Pantry Programs	Kitchen Programs	Shelter Programs
Average percentage of food received from food bank(s)	74.2%	49.0%	41.5%
Percentage of programs receiving food from[a]:			
TEFAP or CSFP	68.7%	49.4%	45.9%
Church or religious congregations	76.2%	58.7%	56.2%
Local merchant or farmer donations	40.8%	45.8%	45.0%
Local food drives (e.g., Boy Scouts)	49.9%	27.2%	40.3%
Food purchased by agency	53.9%	74.9%	81.4%
Other[b]	22.4%	19.3%	24.6%
SAMPLE SIZE (N)	**18,436**	**4,514**	**2,704**

SOURCE: This table was constructed based on usable responses to questions 8, 8a, and 8b of the agency survey.

NOTES: The percentages presented in this table are based only on usable responses, excluding missing, don't know, and refusal responses. All usable responses were weighted as described in Chapter 3 and in the Technical Appendix volume to represent all emergency food programs of the A2H National Network. The sample sizes (N) also include missing data.

TABLE 13.1.1 *(continued)*

_____

For average percentage of food received from food bank, missing, don't know, and refusal responses combined are 5.2% for pantry programs, 9.9% for kitchen programs, and 13.4% for shelter programs.

For percentage of programs that distribute government or USDA commodities (TEFAP or CSFP) received from food bank(s) or a state agency, missing, don't know, and refusal responses combined are 11.4% for pantry programs, 18.5% for kitchen programs, and 21.8% for shelter programs.

For percentage of food from the other listed sources, missing, don't know, and refusal responses combined are 15.9% for pantry programs, 13.7% for kitchen programs, and 13.9% for shelter programs.

[a]Multiple responses were accepted.

[b]This includes individual donations, organization gardens, and donations from other volunteer or civic groups.

Food banks are a major source of food. 74.2% of the food the pantries distribute, 49.0% of the food the kitchens serve, and 41.5% of the food the shelters serve are provided by their food banks. Programs also receive food from other sources:

- 68.7% of pantries, 49.4% of kitchens, and 45.9% of shelters receive food from federal food or commodity programs, such as TEFAP or CSFP.

- 76.2% of pantries, 58.7% of kitchens, and 56.2% of shelters receive food from churches or religious congregations.

- 40.8% of pantries, 45.8% of kitchens, and 45.0% of shelters receive food from local merchants or farmer donations.

- 49.9% of pantries, 27.2% of kitchens, and 40.3% of shelters receive food from local food drives.

13.2 STAFF AND VOLUNTEER RESOURCES DURING PREVIOUS WEEK

Agencies were asked how many paid staff and volunteers they had and how many volunteer hours they had received during the previous week. Table 13.2.1 and Chart 13.2.1 present the results.

TABLE 13.2.1

STAFF AND VOLUNTEER RESOURCES DURING PREVIOUS WEEK

Staff and Volunteer Resources	Pantry Programs	Kitchen Programs	Shelter Programs	Other Programs
Number of paid staff[a]				
None	66.2%	40.5%	10.8%	n.a.
1	15.6%	17.9%	6.6%	n.a.
2	7.7%	12.4%	6.4%	n.a.
3	3.5%	7.7%	5.9%	n.a.
4	1.9%	4.9%	5.4%	n.a.
5	1.2%	3.3%	4.9%	n.a.
6-10	2.4%	7.1%	23.6%	n.a.
More than 10	1.4%	6.2%	36.4%	n.a.
TOTAL	100.0%	100.0%	100.0%	n.a.
Average number of paid staff among valid responses	1	3	11	n.a.
Median number of paid staff among valid responses	0	1	7	n.a.
Number of volunteers[b]				
None	10.1%	13.6%	28.6%	27.4%
1	6.1%	3.5%	6.5%	5.5%
2-3	19.1%	12.5%	18.6%	13.7%
4-6	23.0%	18.6%	15.3%	15.1%
7-10	18.0%	16.7%	11.9%	11.5%
11-20	15.5%	16.9%	8.2%	12.8%
21-50	6.8%	12.4%	8.2%	9.1%
More than 50	1.4%	5.8%	2.8%	4.9%
TOTAL	100.0%	100.0%	100.0%	100.0%
Average number of volunteers among valid responses	9	15	9	19
Median number of volunteers among valid responses	5	7	3	4
Estimated total number of network volunteers[c]	113,381	38,866	9,978	141,745

TABLE 13.2.1 *(continued)*

Staff and Volunteer Resources	Pantry Programs	Kitchen Programs	Shelter Programs	Other Programs
Number of volunteer hours[d]				
None	10.1%	13.6%	28.6%	27.4%
1-5	21.4%	12.6%	9.3%	8.6%
6-10	16.4%	13.6%	11.1%	9.3%
11-25	20.7%	18.4%	16.0%	16.0%
26-50	14.8%	16.6%	13.6%	13.9%
51-100	9.9%	12.0%	9.4%	10.2%
More than 100	6.8%	13.5%	12.2%	14.8%
TOTAL	100.0%	100.0%	100.0%	100.0%
Average number of volunteer hours among valid responses (hours)	35	58	51	35
Median number of volunteer hours among valid responses (hours)	35	58	51	4
SAMPLE SIZE (N)	**18,436**	**4,514**	**2,704**	**28,810**

SOURCE: This table was constructed based on usable responses to questions 15, 16, and 27 of the agency survey.

NOTES: The percentages presented in this table are based only on usable responses, excluding missing, don't know, and refusal responses. All usable responses were weighted as described in Chapter 3 and in the Technical Appendix volume to represent all emergency food programs of the A2H National Network. The sample sizes (N) also include missing data.

For number of paid staff, missing, don't know, and refusal responses combined are 10.9% for pantry programs, 14.6% for kitchen programs, and 11.7% for shelter programs.

For number of volunteers, missing, don't know, and refusal responses combined are 6.9% for pantry programs, 12.6% for kitchen programs, 14.3% for shelter programs, and 59.8% for other programs.

For number of volunteer hours, missing, don't know, and refusal responses combined are 6.9% for pantry programs, 12.6% for kitchen programs, 14.3% for shelter programs, and 59.8% for other programs.

[a]For pantries and kitchens, responses greater than 50 paid staff members were recoded as 50 paid staff members. For shelters, responses greater than 75 paid staff members were recoded as 75 paid staff members.

[b]For pantries, kitchens, and shelters, responses greater than 200 volunteers were recoded as 200 volunteers. For other programs, responses greater than 3,500 volunteers were recoded as 3,500 volunteers.

[c]The number of volunteers in a week were estimated by multiplying the number of programs of each type times the median number of volunteers for agencies in the program types. (We used the median rather than the mean out of concern that the higher averages may reflect incorrect high "outlier" observations.) Then, to account for nonparticipating Network members, we multiply by a factor of 1.23.

[d]For pantries, kitchens, and shelters, responses greater than 1,000 volunteer hours were recoded as 1,000 volunteer hours. For other programs, responses greater than 7,000 volunteer hours were recoded as 7,000 volunteer hours.

As Table 13.2.1 shows, 66.2% of the pantries, 40.5% of the kitchens, and 10.8% of the

shelters had no paid staff in their workforce during the week prior to this study. The median

number of paid staff was 0 for the pantries, 1 for the kitchens, and 7 for the shelters. More

results include:

- The median number of volunteers in a week was 5 for the pantries, 7 for the kitchens, and 3 for the shelters, and 4 for the other programs.

- The median number of volunteer hours during the previous week of this study was 35 for the pantries, 58 for the kitchens, and 51 for the shelters, and 4 for the other programs.

- 10.1% of the pantries, 13.6% of the kitchens, and 28.6% of the shelters, and 27.4% of the other programs had no volunteers in their workforce during the previous week of this study.

- The midpoint ($7.90) of the current minimum wage ($5.15) and the average hourly earning from service occupations ($10.65) can be used to obtain a dollar value of volunteer hours.[42] This factor is used in the next table.

---

[42] U.S. Department of Labor, Bureau of Labor Statistics. "National Compensation Survey: Occupational Wages in the United States, 2004." August 2005, Table 1, p. 3.

As shown in Table 13.2.1N, from a monetary standpoint, the contributions made by volunteers staff to the A2H system are very extensive.

TABLE 13.2.1N

ESTIMATED NUMBER OF VOLUNTEERS AND VOLUNTEER HOURS DURING PREVIOUS WEEK

	Pantry Programs	Kitchen Programs	Shelter Programs
Average number of volunteers hours	35	58	51
Number of programs	29,647	5,601	4,143
Total number of volunteer hours during previous week	1,037,645	324,858	211,293
Total dollar value of volunteer hours during previous week ($7.90/hour)[a]	$8,197,396	$2,566,378	$1,669,215

[a]The hourly wage used here ($7.90) is the midpoint of the current minimum wage ($5.15) and the average hourly earning from service occupations ($10.65). The latter was obtained from U.S. Department of Labor, Bureau of Labor Statistics: "National Compensation Survey: Occupational Wages in the United States, 2004." August 2005, Table 1, p. 3.

Key findings are:

- The value of volunteer time in pantry programs in a typical week is nearly $8.2 million.

- Comparable estimates for kitchen and shelter programs are $2.6 million and $1.7 million, respectively.

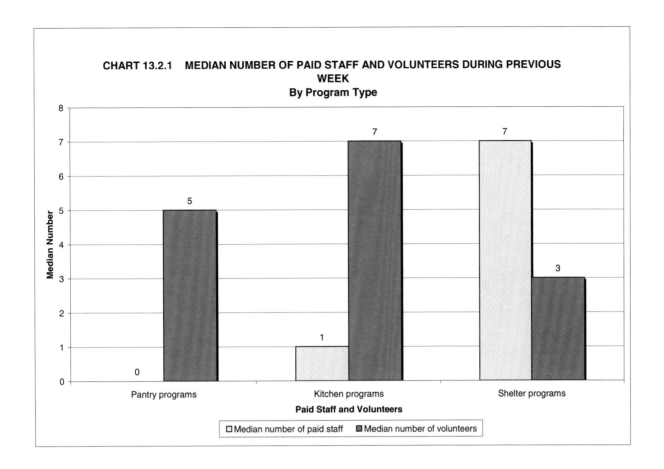

CHART 13.2.1 MEDIAN NUMBER OF PAID STAFF AND VOLUNTEERS DURING PREVIOUS WEEK
By Program Type

CH 13. AGENCIES AND FOOD PROGRAMS: RESOURCES

13.3   PRODUCTS PURCHASED FROM SOURCES OTHER THAN FOOD BANKS

Agencies were asked to indicate the categories of products that their programs purchased with cash from sources other than their food bank resources. Results based on agency responses are summarized in Table 13.3.1.

TABLE 13.3.1

PRODUCTS PURCHASED FROM SOURCES OTHER THAN FOOD BANK

Categories of Products Programs Purchased with Cash from Sources Other than the Agency's Food Bank[a]	Pantry Programs	Kitchen Programs	Shelter Programs
Bread, cereal, rice, and pasta	37.7%	53.4%	59.1%
Fresh fruits and vegetables	21.6%	59.0%	67.8%
Canned or frozen fruits and vegetables	29.6%	43.1%	44.3%
Meat, poultry, fish, beans, eggs, and nuts	40.2%	69.0%	75.2%
Milk, yogurt, and cheese	20.3%	58.7%	73.9%
Fats, oils, condiments, and sweets	16.1%	51.0%	53.6%
Cleaning or personal hygiene products, diapers, and toilet paper	36.0%	53.6%	81.4%
Other[b]	7.9%	11.6%	11.2%
No outside purchases	31.5%	7.4%	5.0%
SAMPLE SIZE (N)	**18,436**	**4,514**	**2,704**

SOURCE: This table was constructed based on usable responses to Question 23 of the agency survey.

NOTES: All usable responses were weighted as described in Chapter 3 and in the Technical Appendix volume to represent all emergency food programs of the A2H National Network. The sample sizes (N) also include missing data.

Missing, don't know, and refusal responses combined are 7.5% for pantry programs, 10.1% for kitchen programs, and 11.6% for shelter programs.

[a]Multiple responses were accepted.

[b]This includes beverages, such as coffee, tea, and juice; paper products, such as plastic utensils, paper plates, and garbage bags; and laundry products.

As Table 13.3.1 shows, 31.5% of the pantries, 7.4% of the kitchens, and 5.0% of the shelters did not purchase products from sources other than their food banks. However, most emergency food programs purchased products they needed from sources other than their food

banks. More details follow:

- 37.7% of the pantries, 53.4% of the kitchens, and 59.1% of the shelters purchased bread, cereal, rice, and pasta.

- 21.6% of the pantries, 59.0% of the kitchens, and 67.8% of the shelters purchased fresh fruits and vegetables.

- 29.6% of the pantries, 43.1% of the kitchens, and 44.3% of the shelters purchased canned or frozen fruits and vegetables.

- 40.2% of the pantries, 69.0% of the kitchens, and 75.2% of the shelters purchased meat, poultry, fish, beans, eggs, and nuts.

- 20.3% of the pantries, 58.7% of the kitchens, and 73.9% of the shelters purchased milk, yogurt, and cheese.

- 16.1% of the pantries, 51.0% of the kitchens, and 53.6% of the shelters purchased fats, oils, condiments, and sweets.

- 36.0% of the pantries, 53.6% of the kitchens, and 81.4% of the shelters purchased cleaning or personal hygiene products, diapers, and toilet paper.

14. AGENCIES AND FOOD PROGRAMS: IMPORTANCE OF FOOD BANKS

At the national level, food banks are by far the single largest source of food to A2H providers. This chapter examines the providers' relationship to the food banks in more detail. We first present tabulations of what products the providers would like to be able to obtain in greater quantity from their food banks. Subsequent sections explore the overall importance of the food banks to the operations of the providers and additional types of services the providers would like to obtain from the food banks.

14.1 PRODUCTS NEEDED FROM FOOD BANKS

Agencies were also asked to identify the categories of products they need more of from their food bank. Table 14.1.1 and Charts 14.1.1P, 14.1.1K, and 14.1.1S present the findings.

TABLE 14.1.1

PRODUCTS NEEDED FROM FOOD BANKS

Categories of Food and Nonfood Products Programs Need or Need More of from Their Food Bank[a]	Pantry Programs	Kitchen Programs	Shelter Programs
Bread, cereal, rice, and pasta	42.1%	30.8%	33.1%
Fresh fruits and vegetables	35.0%	49.2%	51.4%
Canned or frozen fruits and vegetables	33.1%	33.1%	25.7%
Meat, poultry, fish, beans, eggs, and nuts	60.9%	63.0%	62.4%
Milk, yogurt, and cheese	37.6%	43.0%	51.1%
Fats, oils, condiments, and sweets	19.9%	27.5%	27.1%
Cleaning or personal hygiene products, diapers, and toilet paper	53.7%	37.2%	63.1%
Other[b]	8.7%	9.5%	11.3%
SAMPLE SIZE (N)	**18,436**	**4,514**	**2,704**

SOURCE: This table was constructed based on usable responses to Question 24 of the agency survey.

NOTES: All usable responses were weighted as described in Chapter 3 and in the Technical Appendix volume to represent all emergency food programs of the A2H National Network. The sample sizes (N) also include missing data.

TABLE 14.1.1 *(continued)*

Missing, don't know, and refusal responses combined are 5.2% for pantry programs, 14.1% for kitchen programs, and 14.1% for shelter programs.

[a]Multiple responses were accepted.

[b]This includes paper products, such as plastic utensils, paper plates, and garbage bags; beverages, such as juice, coffee, and tea; and dietary supplements, such as vitamins and Ensure.

As presented in Table 14.1.1, many agencies wish to receive more of certain products from their food banks. Specifics are as follows:

- 42.1% of the pantries, 30.8% of the kitchens, and 33.1% of the shelters need more bread, cereal, rice, and pasta.

- 35.0% of the pantries, 49.2% of the kitchens, and 51.4% of the shelters need more fresh fruits and vegetables.

- 33.1% of the pantries, 33.1% of the kitchens, and 25.7% of the shelters need more canned or frozen fruits and vegetables.

- 60.9% of the pantries, 63.0% of the kitchens, and 62.4% of the shelters need more meat, poultry, fish, beans, eggs, and nuts.

- 37.6% of the pantries, 43.0% of the kitchens, and 51.1% of the shelters need more milk, yogurt, and cheese.

- 19.9% of the pantries, 27.5% of the kitchens, and 27.1% of the shelters need more fats, oils, condiments, and sweets.

- 53.7% of the pantries, 37.2% of the kitchens, and 63.1% of the shelters need more products in the category of cleaning or personal hygiene products, diapers, and toilet paper.

CH 14. AGENCIES AND FOOD PROGRAMS: IMPORTANCE OF FOOD BANKS

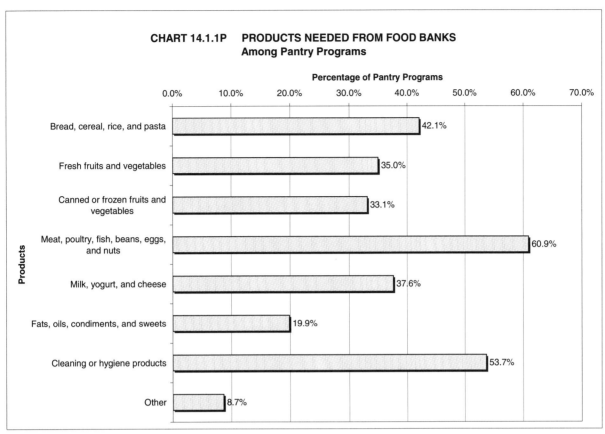

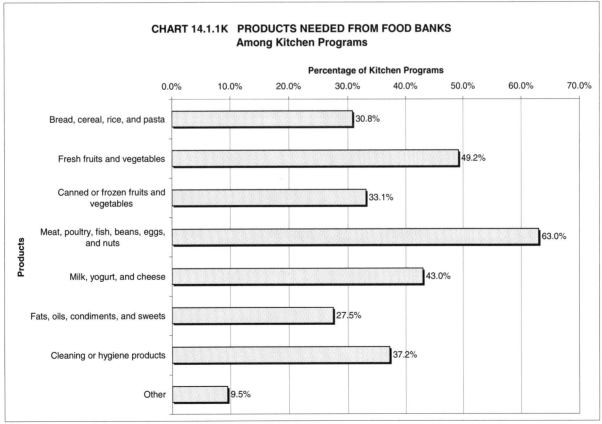

CH 14. AGENCIES AND FOOD PROGRAMS: IMPORTANCE OF FOOD BANKS

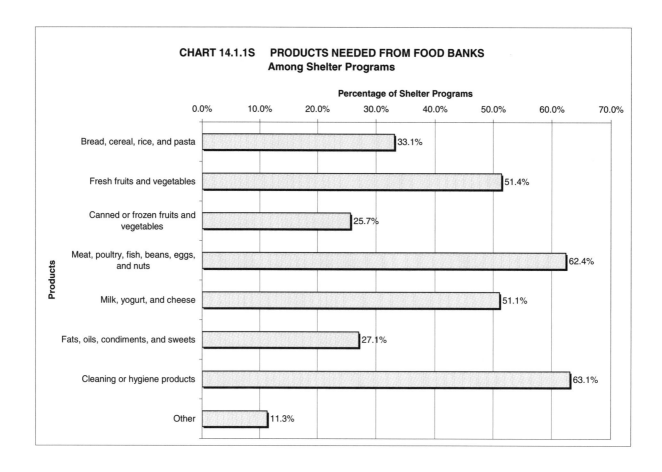

CHART 14.1.1S   PRODUCTS NEEDED FROM FOOD BANKS
Among Shelter Programs

Percentage of Shelter Programs

Product	Percentage
Bread, cereal, rice, and pasta	33.1%
Fresh fruits and vegetables	51.4%
Canned or frozen fruits and vegetables	25.7%
Meat, poultry, fish, beans, eggs, and nuts	62.4%
Milk, yogurt, and cheese	51.1%
Fats, oils, condiments, and sweets	27.1%
Cleaning or hygiene products	63.1%
Other	11.3%

CH 14. AGENCIES AND FOOD PROGRAMS: IMPORTANCE OF FOOD BANKS

14.2 IMPACT OF ELIMINATION OF FOOD BANK

Agencies were asked how much of an impact the elimination of their food bank would have on their programs. Table 14.2.1 and Chart 14.2.1 show the results.

TABLE 14.2.1

IMPACT OF ELIMINATION OF FOOD BANK

If the Food Supply You (i.e., Agency) Receive from Your Food Bank Was Eliminated, How Much of an Impact Would This Have on Your Program?	Pantry Programs	Kitchen Programs	Shelter Programs
No impact at all	1.6%	4.8%	5.2%
Minimal impact	6.8%	15.1%	16.6%
Significant impact	29.3%	37.0%	43.9%
Devastating impact	59.6%	40.4%	31.1%
Unsure	2.7%	2.7%	3.3%
TOTAL	100.0%	100.0%	100.0%
SAMPLE SIZE (N)	**18,436**	**4,514**	**2,704**

SOURCE: This table was constructed based on usable responses to Question 25 of the agency survey.

NOTES: The percentages presented in this table are based only on usable responses, excluding missing, don't know, and refusal responses. All usable responses were weighted as described in Chapter 3 and in the Technical Appendix volume to represent all emergency food programs of the A2H National Network. The sample sizes (N) also include missing data.

Missing, don't know, and refusal responses combined are 4.8% for pantry programs, 9.3% for kitchen programs, and 10.9% for shelter programs.

88.9% of the pantries, 77.4% of the kitchens, and 75.0% of the shelters said that the elimination of support from their food banks would have a significant or devastating impact on their operation. Details include:

- 59.6% of the pantries, 40.4% of the kitchens, and 31.1% of the shelters believed that the elimination of the food bank would have a devastating impact on their programs.

- Another 29.3% of the pantries, 37.0% of the kitchens, and 43.9% of the shelters believed that the elimination of the food bank would have a significant impact on their programs.

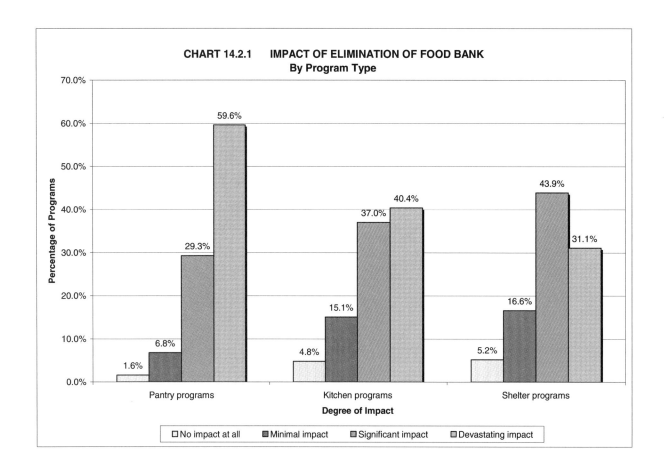

CH 14. AGENCIES AND FOOD PROGRAMS: IMPORTANCE OF FOOD BANKS

14.3   AREAS OF ADDITIONAL ASSISTANCE DESIRED

Agencies were asked what kinds of additional assistance, in addition to food, they need to meet their clients' needs. Findings are presented in Table 14.3.1 and Charts 14.3.1P, 14.3.1K, and 14.3.1S.

TABLE 14.3.1

AREAS OF ADDITIONAL ASSISTANCE DESIRED

Programs That Need Additional Assistance in Any of the Following Areas[a]	Pantry Programs	Kitchen Programs	Shelter Programs
Nutrition education	28.6%	31.6%	39.9%
Training in food handling	16.1%	28.6%	34.8%
Accessing local resources	41.8%	36.2%	33.8%
Advocacy training	16.3%	15.8%	19.1%
Other[b]	3.5%	2.4%	2.9%
SAMPLE SIZE (N)	**18,436**	**4,514**	**2,704**

SOURCE: This table was constructed based on usable responses to Question 26 of the agency survey.

NOTE: All usable responses were weighted as described in Chapter 3 and in the Technical Appendix volume to represent all emergency food programs of the A2H National Network.

[a]Multiple responses were accepted.

[b]This includes funding and addiction programs.

Some programs wished to receive further assistance from their food banks in one or more of the areas specified in Table 14.3.1. Details include:

- 28.6% of the pantries, 31.6% of the kitchens, and 39.9% of the shelters said that they needed additional assistance in nutrition education.

- 16.1% of the pantries, 28.6% of the kitchens, and 34.8% of the shelters said that they needed additional assistance in training in food handling.

- 41.8% of the pantries, 36.2% of the kitchens, and 33.8% of the shelters said that they needed additional assistance in accessing local resources.

- 16.3% of the pantries, 15.8% of the kitchens, and 19.1% of the shelters said that they needed additional assistance in advocacy training.

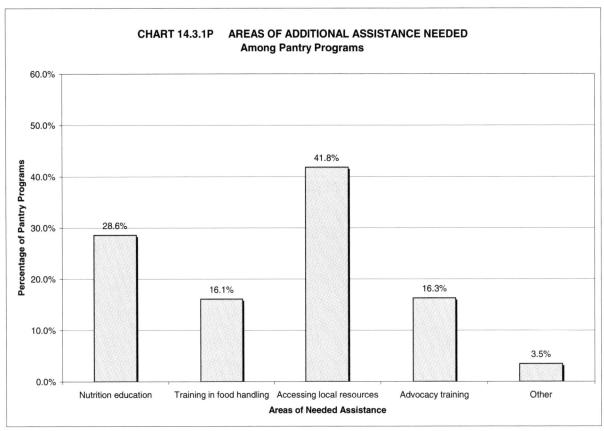

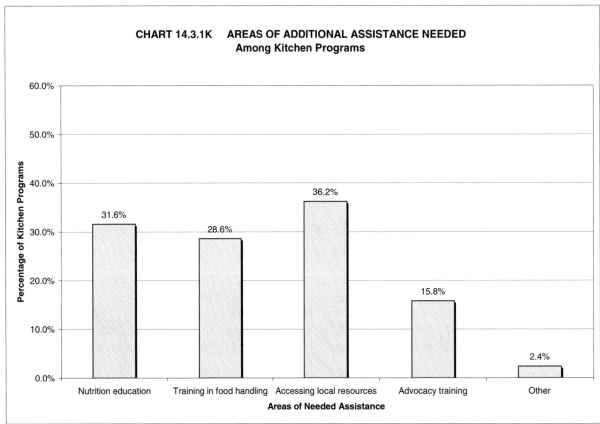

CH 14. AGENCIES AND FOOD PROGRAMS: IMPORTANCE OF FOOD BANKS

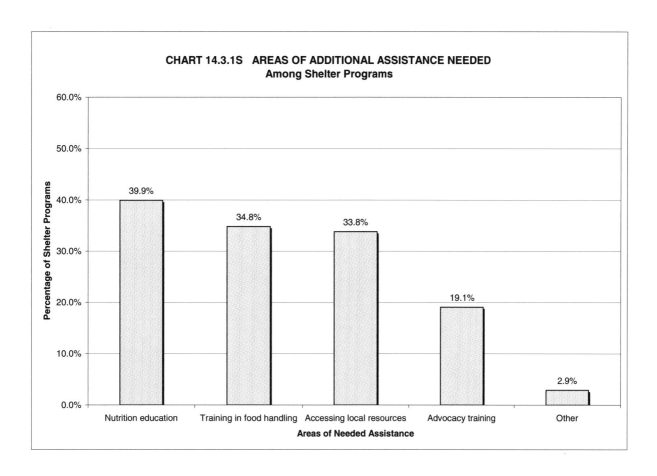

15. SELECTED CROSS-TABULAR ANALYSIS

15.1   INTRODUCTION

The analysis in this report is largely descriptive, presenting tabulations of key client and agency characteristics for the three types of programs included in the study. In addition to supporting this descriptive work, the data assembled for this study provide extensive opportunities to gain additional insight into the relationships between key variables through cross-tabular analysis of the survey results. Such analysis can be conducted internally within each of two basic data sets (the client data and the agency data), and it can also be performed *across* the two types of data, using a merged client/agency file.

Time considerations precluded our undertaking extensive cross-tabular work in the initial round of analysis, since the basic descriptive tabulations had to be made available as quickly as possible. However, to illustrate some of the types of cross-tabular work that can be undertaken, this section presents the results of a limited number of lines of cross-tabular analysis. The specific cross-tabulations that have been conducted in this work were chosen by A2H staff, with input from the Technical Advisory Group for the project. Except where otherwise noted, the tabulations in this section are aggregated across the three types of agencies that were studied— pantries, emergency kitchens, and shelters. Percentage figures in the tables are based on weighted data, while the sample sizes indicated are the number of usable responses for related variables.[43]

---

[43] For details about the weights, see Chapter 3 of this report or the Technical Appendix volume, available separately.

15.2   OBSERVED LEVELS OF FOOD SECURITY FOR SELECTED SUBGROUPS OF EMERGENCY FOOD CLIENTS

The data presented in Chapter 6 showed that the emergency food clients in the A2H Network experience high levels of food insecurity and hunger. To gain additional insight into this and into exactly what groups are most vulnerable, it is useful to cross-tabulate levels of food security by various client characteristics. These data are presented in this subsection.

Food Security and Income. Table 15.2.1 examines the relationship between income and food security.

TABLE 15.2.1

INCOME IN 2004 AND FOOD SECURITY

	All Client Households	Income in 2004	
		0% to 130% of Federal Poverty Level	131% or Higher of Federal Poverty Level
Food secure	28.5%	25.9%	42.7%
Food insecure without hunger	37.1%	38.2%	30.7%
Food insecure with hunger	34.4%	35.8%	26.6%
TOTAL	100.0%	100.0%	100.0%
SAMPLE SIZE (N)	**47,878**	**40,908**	**6,970**

NOTES: In calculating percentages and sample sizes, we excluded item nonresponses to all variables involved.

Statistically significant based on chi-square test (d.f. = 2) at the 1% level.

As shown in the table, within the overall group of A2H clients, lower-income households are much more vulnerable than higher-income households to food insecurity.

- Among the households with incomes less than or equal to 130% of the federal poverty level in year 2004, only 25.9% are food secure, while 42.7% of the households with incomes more than 130% of the federal poverty level are food secure.

- On the other hand, as many as 35.8% of the client households with income less than or equal to 130% of the federal poverty level are food insecure with hunger. The comparable figure is 26.6% for the households with income more than 130% of the federal poverty level.

Food Security and Health. Table 15.2.2 presents similar information regarding health status.

TABLE 15.2.2

HEALTH AND FOOD SECURITY

| | All Households | Households with or Without Members in Poor Health | |
		With Members in Poor Health	Without Members in Poor Health
Food secure	29.7%	21.4%	33.1%
Food insecure without hunger	36.9%	39.4%	35.9%
Food insecure with hunger	33.4%	39.3%	31.0%
TOTAL	100.0%	100.0%	100.0%
SAMPLE SIZE (N)	**52,016**	**15,747**	**36,269**

NOTES: In calculating percentages and sample sizes, we excluded item nonresponses to all variables involved.

Statistically significant based on chi-square test (d.f. = 2) at the 1% level.

The findings seem to show a significant negative correlation between food security and health status:

- Among the client households with at least one member in poor health, 21.4% are food secure; 39.4% are food insecure without hunger; and 39.3% are food insecure with hunger.

- Among the client households with no one in poor health, 33.1% are food secure; 35.9% are food insecure without hunger; and 31.0% are food insecure with hunger.

- That is, a much higher percentage of the households with members in poor health are food insecure compared with the households with no one in poor health.

Food Security and Food Stamp Receipt. Associations between food security and food stamp receipt are of interest for at least two reasons. On the one hand, it is important that the households who are least food secure have effective access to the major government nutrition assistance programs, such as food stamps. On the other hand, it is of interest to examine whether food stamp receipt appears to increase food security, recognizing, however, that causality may be difficult to establish in a cross-sectional study such as this one.

The relevant tabulations are shown in Table 15.2.3.

TABLE 15.2.3

FOOD STAMP RECEIPT AND FOOD SECURITY

		Food Stamp Receipt Status of Households		
	All Client Households	Receiving Food Stamps	Eligible, Not Receiving[a]	Ineligible Because of Income, Not Receiving[a]
Food secure	28.7%	25.3%	27.6%	47.6%
Food insecure without hunger	37.0%	38.4%	37.3%	30.0%
Food insecure with hunger	34.3%	36.3%	35.1%	22.4%
TOTAL	100.0%	100.0%	100.0%	100.0%
SAMPLE SIZE (N)	**48,852**	**19,107**	**24,975**	**4,770**

NOTES: In calculating percentages and sample sizes, we excluded item nonresponses to all variables involved.

Statistically significant based on chi-square test (d.f. = 4) at the 1% level.

[a]Eligibility was estimated based on the previous month's income alone.

Households receiving food stamps are about as likely to be experiencing food insecurity and hunger as households that appear to be eligible for food stamps but are not participating. On the other hand, households apparently ineligible for food stamps are substantially less likely to be food insecure. To at least some degree, these findings reflect the positive correlation, noted earlier in this subsection, between food security and income.

Note that the fact that substantial numbers of client households are classified as hungry despite receiving food stamps does not by itself mean that the Food Stamp Program is not providing useful assistance. Indeed, many of these households might be much worse off without food stamps. However, the data do suggest that, for many households in the A2H Network, the Food Stamp Program's benefits may not be sufficient to prevent hunger.

Specific findings in this analysis include:

- 25.3% of A2H client households receiving food stamps are food secure; and 36.3% are experiencing hunger. Similar figures apply to nonparticipants who are apparently eligible for food stamps.

- By contrast, 47.6% of A2H households who appear not to be eligible for food stamps are food secure; and 22.4% are experiencing hunger.

Associations Between Food Security and Having Children. Food insecurity may cause particular hardships in households with children. In this subsection, we explore associations between food security and the presence of children younger than 18.

Almost three-quarters of households with children under 18 are food insecure with or without hunger, while the percentage among childless households is somewhat lower at 68.9% (Table 15.2.4). Similar findings emerge, although to a lesser degree, when only households with young children ages 0 to 5 are considered (Table 15.2.5).

TABLE 15.2.4

HAVING CHILDREN AND HOUSEHOLD FOOD SECURITY

| | All Client Households | Households with or Without a Child Younger than 18 | |
		With Children Younger than 18	Without Children Younger than 18
Food secure	29.7%	26.8%	31.1%
Food insecure without hunger	36.9%	41.8%	34.3%
Food insecure with hunger	33.4%	31.3%	34.5%
TOTAL	100.0%	100.0%	100.0%
SAMPLE SIZE (N)	**52,041**	**17,538**	**34,503**

NOTES: In calculating percentages and sample sizes, we excluded item nonresponses to all variables involved.

Statistically significant based on chi-square test (d.f. = 2) at the 1% level.

TABLE 15.2.5

HAVING YOUNG CHILDREN AND FOOD SECURITY

| | All Client Households | Households with or Without a Children Ages 0-5 | |
		With Children Ages 0-5	Without Children Ages 0-5
Food secure	29.7%	27.9%	30.0%
Food insecure without hunger	36.9%	42.6%	35.8%
Food insecure with hunger	33.4%	29.4%	34.2%
TOTAL	100.0%	100.0%	100.0%
SAMPLE SIZE (N)	**52,041**	**8,135**	**43,906**

NOTES: In calculating percentages and sample sizes, we excluded item nonresponses to all variables involved.

Statistically significant based on chi-square test (d.f. = 2) at the 1% level.

Specific findings include:

- 31.3% of A2H client households with children under 18 and 29.4% with children ages 0 to 5 are classified as experiencing hunger.

- 41.8% of A2H client households with children under 18 and 42.6% of those with children ages 0 to 5 are experiencing food insecurity but no hunger.

Associations Among the Presence of Senior Household Members, the Presence of Children, and Food Security. To explore further the relationship between household composition and food security, Table 15.2.6 breaks down household composition in terms of both the presence of children younger than 18 and the presence of seniors age 65 or older. There are four panels in the table, the top panel showing the tabulations for the entire A2H client data and the subsequent three disaggregating the analysis by type of A2H program.

TABLE 15.2.6

HAVING SENIORS OR CHILDREN AND FOOD SECURITY

	All Households	Households with Seniors	Households with Children, No Seniors	One-Person Households with Neither Children nor Seniors	Households with Two or More People but with Neither Children nor Seniors
For All Three Programs					
Food secure	29.7%	48.0%	26.2%	23.2%	24.7%
Food insecure without hunger	36.9%	35.8%	41.5%	32.5%	38.2%
Food insecure with hunger	33.4%	16.2%	32.4%	44.2%	37.1%
TOTAL	100.0%	100.0%	100.0%	100.0%	100.0%
SAMPLE SIZE (N) – ALL	**52,041**	**11,536**	**15,987**	**16,598**	**7,920**
For Pantry Programs					
Food secure	29.6%	46.7%	24.8%	23.4%	23.1%
Food insecure without hunger	39.2%	36.9%	42.1%	35.9%	40.5%
Food insecure with hunger	31.2%	16.4%	33.1%	40.7%	36.4%
TOTAL	100.0%	100.0%	100.0%	100.0%	100.0%
SAMPLE SIZE (N) – PANTRIES	**36,109**	**9,136**	**13,517**	**7,521**	**5,935**

CH 15. SELECTED CROSS-TABULAR ANALYSIS

TABLE 15.2.6 *(continued)*

	All Households	Households with Seniors	Households with Children, No Seniors	One-Person Households with Neither Children nor Seniors	Households with Two or More People but with Neither Children nor Seniors
For Kitchen Programs					
Food secure	30.6%	53.5%	33.2%	23.8%	32.1%
Food insecure without hunger	29.9%	31.0%	37.5%	28.0%	28.8%
Food insecure with hunger	39.5%	15.4%	29.3%	48.2%	39.1%
TOTAL	100.0%	100.0%	100.0%	100.0%	100.0%
SAMPLE SIZE (N) – KITCHENS	**10,297**	**1,966**	**1,262**	**5,527**	**1,542**
For Shelter Programs					
Food secure	25.0%	63.2%	40.9%	22.9%	20.3%
Food insecure without hunger	29.9%	17.4%	27.4%	30.5%	28.9%
Food insecure with hunger	45.1%	19.4%	31.7%	46.6%	50.7%
TOTAL	100.0%	100.0%	100.0%	100.0%	100.0%
SAMPLE SIZE (N) – SHELTERS	**4,001**	**68**	**663**	**3,076**	**194**

NOTES: In calculating percentages and sample sizes, we excluded item nonresponses to all variables involved.

Statistically significant based on chi-square test (d.f. = 8) at the 1% level.

In general, households with elderly members are much less likely than households with children to experience food insecurity or hunger. Also, for the overall sample, rates of hunger tend to be highest among single-person households with neither elderly nor child members. Among shelter clients, however, households with two or more people but without elderly members or children are most likely to experience hunger. Specific findings include:

- For the overall sample, 32.4% of households that include children but no seniors are estimated to be experiencing hunger, compared with 44.2% of single-person households with neither children nor seniors.

- For pantry and kitchen programs, the highest rates of hunger are for one-person households with neither children nor elderly members; these rates are 40.7% and 48.2%, respectively.

- For shelters, the highest rate, 50.7%, is for two-person households with neither seniors nor children.

Citizenship Status and Food Security. In light of recent policy discussions as to whether people who are not U.S. citizens should be able to receive benefits from the Food Stamp Program, it is also of interest to examine associations between citizenship status and food security among A2H client households. Table 15.2.7 presents the relevant data.

TABLE 15.2.7

CITIZENSHIP STATUS AND HOUSEHOLD FOOD SECURITY

		Citizenship Status of Clients at A2H Program Sites	
	All Client Households	Households Represented by Citizen Clients[a]	Households Represented by Noncitizen Clients
Food secure	29.7%	30.2%	23.6%
Food insecure without hunger	36.9%	36.4%	43.0%
Food insecure with hunger	33.4%	33.4%	33.4%
TOTAL	100.0%	100.0%	100.0%
SAMPLE SIZE (N)	**51,839**	**48,771**	**3,068**

NOTES: In calculating percentages and sample sizes, we excluded item nonresponses to all variables involved.

Statistically significant based on chi-square test (d.f. = 2) at the 1% level.

[a]Households represented by respondents who are U.S. citizens.

As shown in the table, rates of food security are greater among households represented by citizens than among those represented by noncitizens. In particular,

- 43.0% of the noncitizen households are food insecure without hunger, compared with 36.4% of the citizen households.

- The comparable rates for hunger are similar at around 33%.

Table 15.2.8 combines elements of the two previous tables, contrasting, within noncitizen households, food security rates for households that have and do not have young children.

TABLE 15.2.8

HAVING YOUNG CHILDREN AND FOOD SECURITY AMONG HOUSEHOLDS
CONTAINING AT LEAST ONE NONCITIZEN

| | All Client Households Having at Least One Noncitizen Member | Noncitizen Households with or Without a Child Ages 0-5 | |
		With Children Ages 0-5	Without Children Ages 0-5
Food secure	25.2%	21.1%	27.5%
Food insecure without hunger	42.1%	47.4%	39.2%
Food insecure with hunger	32.7%	31.5%	33.3%
TOTAL	100.0%	100.0%	100.0%
SAMPLE SIZE (N)	**3,745**	**1,436**	**2,309**

NOTES: In calculating percentages and sample sizes, we excluded item nonresponses to all variables involved.

Statistically significant based on chi-square test (d.f. = 2) at the 1% level.

Noncitizen households with young children are far more likely to be food insecure and experiencing hunger: only 21.1% of the households with young children, compared with 27.5% of those without them, are classified as food secure. This is of great policy concern as malnutrition during childhood is likely to have negative effects on physical and cognitive development.

15.3 ASSOCIATIONS BETWEEN INCOME AND OTHER KEY VARIABLES AMONG A2H CLIENTS

Income plays a central role in determining the opportunities and constraints faced by households below or near the poverty line. Thus it is of considerable interest to examine how household income levels are related to other aspects of the lives of households in the A2H client population. We do this below, based on annual income for the year 2004 as reported by respondents (see Table 15.3.1).

Income and Housing Status. A comparison with other households in the population shows, as might be expected, that a significantly higher percentage of clients who reported being homeless had no income. Interestingly, the percentage with income above 130% of the federal poverty line is slightly higher among clients who have no place to live than among those who do.

TABLE 15.3.1

HOUSING STATUS AND INCOME IN 2004

Income in 2004 as Percentage of Federal Poverty Level	All Clients	Housing Status	
		Clients with a Place to Live	Clients Without a Place to Live
0% (no income)	7.8%	5.1%	25.4%
1%-50%	27.2%	26.7%	30.4%
51%-75%	22.9%	24.2%	13.8%
76%-100%	15.6%	17.0%	6.3%
101%-130%	11.2%	11.7%	7.4%
SUBTOTAL	84.6%	84.8%	83.4%
131%-150%	4.5%	4.8%	2.4%
151%-185%	4.0%	4.0%	3.7%
186% or Higher	6.9%	6.4%	10.4%
SUBTOTAL	15.4%	15.2%	16.6%
TOTAL	100.0%	100.0%	100.0%
SAMPLE SIZE (N)	**47,960**	**41,064**	**6,896**

NOTES: In calculating percentages and sample sizes, we excluded item nonresponses to all variables involved.

Statistically significant based on chi-square test (d.f. = 7) at the 1% level.

235

Key findings include:

- Over a quarter (25.4%) of the clients who are homeless had no income in 2004, compared with only 5.1% of the clients who have a place to live.

- In 2004, among the clients who had a place to live, 84.8% had an income less than or equal to 130% of the federal poverty level, while 15.2% had an income above 130% of the federal poverty level.

- In 2004, among the clients who were homeless, 83.4% had an income less than or equal to 130% of the federal poverty level, while 16.6% had an income above 130% of the federal poverty level.

Among clients with a place to live, there is a positive association between income and home ownership (Table 15.3.2).

TABLE 15.3.2

HOME OWNERSHIP AND INCOME IN 2004

Income in 2004 as Percentage of Federal Poverty Level	All Clients with a Place to Live	Clients Who Own a Place	Clients Who Rent a Place	Clients Who Live with Someone for Free	Other
0% (no income)	5.2%	2.0%	4.6%	20.6%	14.8%
1%-50%	26.5%	16.6%	29.0%	36.9%	32.8%
51%-75%	24.3%	24.1%	25.4%	15.3%	17.1%
76%-100%	17.0%	19.0%	17.1%	9.0%	16.5%
101%-130%	11.8%	16.6%	10.6%	6.6%	8.9%
SUBTOTAL	84.8%	78.2%	86.7%	88.4%	90.1%
131%-150%	4.9%	6.7%	4.4%	3.9%	1.4%
151%-185%	3.9%	5.6%	3.3%	4.1%	3.5%
186% or higher	6.4%	9.5%	5.6%	3.6%	5.0%
SUBTOTAL	15.2%	21.8%	13.3%	11.6%	9.9%
TOTAL	100.0%	100.0%	100.0%	100.0%	100.0%
SAMPLE SIZE (N)	**40,605**	**11,590**	**25,686**	**2,216**	**1,113**

NOTES: In calculating percentages and sample sizes, we excluded item nonresponses to all variables involved.

Statistically significant based on chi-square test (d.f. = 21) at the 1% level.

Among the findings illustrated by the table are:

- 2.0% of the clients who own a place to live, 4.6% of the clients who rent, and 20.6% of the clients who live with someone else for free had no income in 2000.

- 78.2% of the clients who own a place to live, 86.7% of the clients who rent, and 88.4% of the clients who live with someone else for free had either no income or an income at or below 130% of the federal poverty level.

- On the other hand, 21.8% of the clients who own a place to live, 13.3% of the clients who rent, and 11.6% of the clients who live with someone else for free had an income over 130% of the federal poverty level.

Income and Education Status. Not surprisingly, education status is also highly correlated with income (Table 15.3.3).

TABLE 15.3.3

EDUCATION AND INCOME IN 2004

Income in 2004 as Percentage of Federal Poverty Level	All Clients	Highest Education Level Achieved				
		Less than High School	Completed High School	Completed Noncollege/ Business/ Technical School	Some College/ Two-Year Degree	Completed College
0% (no income)	7.8%	8.2%	7.9%	4.8%	7.8%	7.5%
1%-50%	27.2%	30.5%	27.9%	23.7%	22.0%	18.5%
51%-75%	22.8%	26.5%	21.8%	18.4%	20.5%	14.4%
76%-100%	15.6%	16.2%	15.3%	18.3%	14.9%	14.1%
101%-130%	11.2%	10.0%	11.8%	14.4%	11.5%	11.7%
SUBTOTAL	84.6%	91.4%	84.7%	79.5%	76.6%	66.1%
131%-150%	4.5%	3.3%	4.3%	7.4%	6.1%	7.0%
151%-185%	3.9%	2.5%	3.8%	5.3%	5.4%	9.4%
186% or higher	7.0%	2.8%	7.3%	7.8%	11.9%	17.4%
SUBTOTAL	15.4%	8.6%	15.3%	20.5%	23.4%	33.9%
TOTAL	100.0%	100.0%	100.0%	100.0%	100.0%	100.0%
SAMPLE SIZE (N)	**47,620**	**17,792**	**17,271**	**1,806**	**8,290**	**2,461**

NOTES: In calculating percentages and sample sizes, we excluded item nonresponses to all variables involved.

Statistically significant based on chi-square test (d.f. = 28) at the 1% level.

Findings presented in Table 15.3.3 include:

- In 2004, 91.4% of the clients who had not completed high school and 84.7% of the clients who had completed up to high school had either no income or an income less than 130% of the federal poverty level. On the other hand, only 66.1% of the clients who had completed college had either no income or an income less than 130% of the federal poverty level.

- The percentage of the clients who had an income more than 130% of the federal poverty level in 2000 is only 8.6% among the clients who had not completed high school. It is as high as 33.9% among the clients who had completed college.

Income and Food Security Status. Households that were food insecure with or without hunger tended to have lower incomes than households that were food secure (Table 15.3.4). For instance, among households that were food insecure with hunger, 42.6% had either no income or an income below 50% of poverty, compared with only 27.9% of food secure households.

TABLE 15.3.4

FOOD SECURITY STATUS AND INCOME IN YEAR 2004

Income in 2004 as Percentage of Federal Poverty Level	All Client Households	Food Security Status at Client Households		
		Food Secure	Food Insecure Without Hunger	Food Insecure with Hunger
0% (no income)	7.7%	6.3%	6.2%	10.5%
1%-50%	27.1%	21.6%	26.7%	32.1%
51%-75%	22.9%	17.8%	25.4%	24.6%
76%-100%	15.7%	17.2%	17.1%	12.8%
101%-130%	11.2%	14.1%	11.9%	8.2%
SUBTOTAL	84.6%	77.0%	87.2%	88.1%
131%-150%	4.5%	6.3%	4.0%	3.6%
151%-185%	3.9%	5.8%	3.4%	2.9%
186% or higher	6.9%	10.9%	5.3%	5.3%
SUBTOTAL	15.4%	23.0%	12.8%	11.9%
TOTAL	100.0%	100.0%	100.0%	100.0%
SAMPLE SIZE (N)	**47,836**	**13,734**	**17,819**	**16,283**

NOTES: In calculating percentages and sample sizes, we excluded item nonresponses to all variables involved.

Statistically significant based on chi-square test (d.f. = 14) at the 1% level.

Other findings include:

- In 2004, 88.1% of the client households characterized as food insecure with hunger, 87.2% of those characterized as food insecure without hunger, and 77.0% of those characterized as food secure had income less than or equal to 130% of the federal poverty level.

- In 2004, 11.9% of the client households characterized as food insecure with hunger, 12.8% of those characterized as food insecure without hunger, and 23.0% of those characterized as food secure had income more than 130% of the federal poverty level.

Income and Household Structure. As shown in Table 15.3.5, there are moderate differences in income between households with various s household structures.

TABLE 15.3.5

HAVING SENIORS OR CHILDREN AND INCOME IN 2004

Income in 2004 as Percentage of Federal Poverty Level	All Households	Households with Seniors	Households with Children, No Seniors	One-Person Households with Neither Children nor Seniors	Households with Two or More People but with Neither Children nor Seniors
0% (no income)	7.8%	2.2%	4.3%	16.1%	5.5%
1%-50%	27.2%	15.2%	38.8%	23.0%	28.3%
51%-75%	22.8%	24.5%	23.7%	20.2%	24.4%
76%-100%	15.6%	23.0%	12.8%	15.2%	12.3%
101%-130%	11.2%	18.4%	9.0%	9.1%	9.9%
SUBTOTAL[a]	84.6%	83.3%	88.7%	83.5%	80.4%
131%-150%	4.5%	6.7%	4.0%	3.1%	5.5%
151%-185%	3.9%	4.7%	3.4%	4.0%	3.8%
186% or higher	6.9%	5.3%	4.0%	9.3%	10.3%
SUBTOTAL	15.4%	16.7%	11.3%	16.5%	19.6%
TOTAL	100.0%	100.0%	100.0%	100.0%	100.0%
SAMPLE SIZE (N)	**52,041**	**11,536**	**15,987**	**16,598**	**7,920**

NOTES: In calculating percentages and sample sizes, we excluded item nonresponses to all variables involved.

Statistically significant based on chi-square test (d.f. = 28) at the 1% level.

Key findings include:

- Households with children and no seniors are considerably more likely than households with seniors to be at or below 50% of the poverty level (43.2% compared with 17.4%).

- A higher percentage of households with two or more people but without seniors or children (19.6%) have incomes above 130% of the federal poverty level, compared with 15.4% of all households in the population.

Income and Medicaid Receipt. Households that receive Medicaid benefits are much more likely than households not receiving Medicaid to be below the poverty level (Table 15.3.6).

TABLE 15.3.6

MEDICAID AND INCOME IN 2004

Income in 2004 as Percentage of Federal Poverty Level	All Clients	Client Households Receiving Medicaid Benefits	
		Yes	No
0% (no income)	7.9%	4.6%	10.6%
1%-50%	27.3%	31.5%	23.7%
51%-75%	22.9%	29.8%	17.1%
76%-100%	15.6%	16.8%	14.6%
101%-130%	11.1%	8.3%	13.4%
SUBTOTAL	84.8%	91.0%	79.5%
131%-150%	4.5%	3.2%	5.5%
151%-185%	3.9%	2.6%	4.9%
186% or higher	6.9%	3.1%	10.1%
SUBTOTAL	15.2%	9.0%	20.5%
TOTAL	100.0%	100.0%	100.0%
SAMPLE SIZE (N)	**46,445**	**21,202**	**25,243**

NOTE: In calculating percentages and sample sizes, we excluded item nonresponses to all variables involved.

Statistically significant based on chi-square test (d.f. = 7) at the 1% level.

Findings presented in Table 15.3.6 include:

- Among the client households receiving Medicaid benefits, 91.0% had income at or below 130% of the federal poverty level in 2004. In comparison, only 79.5% of the clients not receiving Medicaid benefits had income at or below that level.

15.4 ASSOCIATIONS BETWEEN METROPOLITAN STATUS AND OTHER KEY VARIABLES

Households in nonmetropolitan areas as compared with metropolitan areas may have different opportunities to ensure adequate nutrition for their members. For instance, nonmetropolitan households may face considerable transportation barriers in shopping for food. On the other hand, they may have greater access to food that is grown at home or on nearby farms. Here we examine how metropolitan status is associated with other variables of interest for the A2H client sample.

Households were classified by center city, non-center city metro, or nonmetropolitan status based on their zip codes using the Metropolitan Area Central City Indicator (MACCI) information from the U.S. Census Bureau. The three types of areas are:

- *Center city or urban area central places* that function as the dominant center of urban areas. The U.S. Census Bureau identifies one or more central places for each urbanized area (UA) or urban cluster (UC).

- *Metropolitan areas* that include all areas designated by the U.S. Census Bureau within UA or UC boundaries encompassing densely settled areas.

- *Nonmetropolitan areas* that consist of all areas located outside of UAs and UCs.

Metropolitan Status and Food Security. Table 15.4.1 tabulates answers to three child-related food security questions by metropolitan status. For all three questions, the answer placed first in the table is the one that indicates a lower status on the food security scale.

Overall, there is a consistent tendency in this population for children in non-metropolitan areas to be moderately less food secure than households in either of the two metropolitan categories.

TABLE 15.4.1

URBAN/METROPOLITAN STATUS AND CHILD FOOD SECURITY QUESTIONS

	All Client Households with One or More Children Younger than 18	Urban/Metropolitan Status		
		Center City	Metro, not Center City	Nonmetro
Child did not eat enough because not enough money[a]				
Often true	5.4%	3.5%	5.3%	6.1%
Sometimes true	21.7%	19.6%	21.6%	22.4%
Never true	72.9%	76.9%	73.1%	71.5%
TOTAL	100.0%	100.0%	100.0%	100.0%
SAMPLE SIZE (N)	**16,923**	**3,809**	**5,416**	**7,698**
Child skipped meals because there was not enough money[b]				
Yes	13.7%	10.8%	13.6%	14.7%
No	86.3%	89.2%	86.4%	85.3%
TOTAL	100.0%	100.0%	100.0%	100.0%
SAMPLE SIZE (N)	**16,914**	**3,799**	**5,409**	**7,706**
Child went hungry because there was not enough money[b]				
Yes	16.5%	14.0%	17.6%	16.7%
No	83.5%	86.0%	82.4%	83.3%
TOTAL	100.0%	100.0%	100.0%	100.0%
SAMPLE SIZE (N)	**16,854**	**3,783**	**5,398**	**7,673**

NOTE: In calculating percentages and sample sizes, we excluded item nonresponses to all variables involved.

[a]Statistically significant based on chi-square test (d.f. = 4) at the 1% level.

[b]Statistically significant based on chi-square test (d.f. = 2) at the 1% level.

Findings presented in Table 15.4.1 include:

- 23.1% of the households served in center city areas, 26.9% of the households served in suburban areas (metropolitan areas outside center cities), and 28.5% of the households served in nonmetropolitan areas answered that their children often or sometimes did not eat enough during the past year because there was not enough money to buy more food.

- 10.8% of the households served in center city areas, 13.6% of those served in suburban areas (metropolitan areas outside center cities), and 14.7% of those served in nonmetropolitan areas provided an affirmative answer to whether their children skipped a meal during the past year because there was not enough money to buy more food.

- 14.0% of the households served in center city areas, 17.6% of those served in suburban areas (metropolitan areas outside center cities), and 16.7% of those served in nonmetropolitan areas answered that their children went hungry during the past year because there was not enough money to buy more food.

The above results are supported in Table 15.4.2 by an analysis of the numbers of affirmative answers given in the three questions.

TABLE 15.4.2

URBAN/METROPOLITAN STATUS AND RESPONSES TO THREE CHILD FOOD SECURITY QUESTIONS

	All Client Households with One or More Children Younger than 18	Urban/Metropolitan Status		
		Center City	Metro, not Center City	Nonmetro
No affirmative answers	69.2%	74.2%	68.7%	67.8%
One affirmative answer	13.6%	12.4%	13.2%	14.3%
Two affirmative answers	8.4%	5.3%	9.9%	8.6%
Three affirmative answers	8.8%	8.1%	8.2%	9.3%
TOTAL	100.0%	100.0%	100.0%	100.0%
SAMPLE SIZE (N)	**17,029**	**3,831**	**5,449**	**7,749**

NOTES: In calculating percentages and sample sizes, we excluded item nonresponses to all variables involved.

Statistically significant based on chi-square test (d.f. = 6) at the 1% level.

Findings presented in Table 15.4.2 include:

- Among the client households served at the programs at center cities, 74.2% provided no affirmative answers to questions indicating food insecurity of the children in the household. The corresponding figures for the ones served at suburban areas (metropolitan areas outside center cities) and those served at nonmetropolitan areas are 68.7% and 67.8%, respectively.

Metropolitan Status and the Presence of Elderly Members in the Household.

Providers located in center cities tended to serve a higher percentage of elderly people. This is true both for clients actually at the sites and for their broader households (Table 15.4.3).

TABLE 15.4.3

URBAN/METROPOLITAN STATUS AND ELDERLY CLIENTS

| | All Clients | Urban/Metropolitan Status | | |
		Center City	Metro, not Center City	Nonmetro
Clients at program sites				
Elderly Clients	17.3%	23.2%	20.3%	14.2%
Nonelderly clients	82.7%	76.8%	79.7%	85.8%
TOTAL	100.0%	100.0%	100.0%	100.0%
SAMPLE SIZE (N)	**52,147**	**11,595**	**14,458**	**26,094**
Client households				
Elderly person in household	21.4%	27.4%	25.0%	18.1%
No elderly person in household	78.6%	72.6%	75.0%	81.9%
TOTAL	100.0%	100.0%	100.0%	100.0%
SAMPLE SIZE (N)	**52,723**	**11,708**	**14,607**	**26,408**

NOTES: In calculating percentages and sample sizes, we excluded item nonresponses to all variables involved.

Statistically significant based on chi-square test (d.f. = 2) at the 1% level.

Findings presented in Table 15.4.3 include:

- 23.2% of the clients at the programs located in center cities, 20.3% of the clients at the programs located in suburban areas (metropolitan areas outside center cities), and 14.2% at the programs located in nonmetropolitan areas are age 65 or over.

- As for the client *households* with at least one senior member (including household members not present at the A2H sites), 27.4% of the client households served at the programs located in center cities, 25.0% served at the programs located in suburban areas, and 18.1% served at the programs located in nonmetropolitan areas have at least one senior member.

Metropolitan Status and Food Stamp Receipt. Suburban households are the least likely to receive food stamps (Table 15.4.4).

TABLE 15.4.4

URBAN/METROPOLITAN STATUS AND FOOD STAMP RECEIPT/ELIGIBILITY STATUS BASED ON PREVIOUS MONTH'S INCOME

| | All Clients | Urban/Metropolitan Status | | |
		Center City	Metro, not Center City	Nonmetro
Receiving food stamps	38.7%	42.3%	33.3%	40.2%
Probably eligible but not receiving[a]	51.3%	47.5%	54.9%	50.7%
Probably not eligible because of income[a]	10.0%	10.2%	11.8%	9.1%
TOTAL	100.0%	100.0%	100.0%	100.0%
SAMPLE SIZE (N)	**49,033**	**10,966**	**13,508**	**24,559**

NOTES: In calculating percentages and sample sizes, we excluded item nonresponses to all variables involved.

Statistically significant based on chi-square test (d.f. = 4) at the 1% level.

[a]Eligibility was estimated based on the previous month's income alone.

Findings presented in Table 15.4.4 include:

- 42.3% of the clients served at the programs located in center cities, 33.3% of those served at the programs located in suburban areas (metropolitan areas outside center cities), and 40.2% of those served at the programs located in nonmetropolitan areas are currently receiving food stamps.

- 47.5% of the clients served at the programs located in center cities, 54.9% of those served at the programs located in suburban areas (metropolitan areas outside center cities), and 50.7% of those served at the programs located in nonmetropolitan areas appear to be eligible based on their previous month's income but are not currently receiving food stamps.

- 10.2% of the clients served at the programs located in center cities, 11.8% of those served at the programs located in suburban areas (metropolitan areas outside center cities), and 9.1% of those served at the programs located in nonmetropolitan areas appear to be income-ineligible for food stamps.

15.5   ASSOCIATIONS BETWEEN CHOICES HOUSEHOLDS FACE AND SELECTED OUTCOME VARIABLES

The survey asked households whether, during the previous year, they had had to make choices between buying food and spending money on other necessities, such as medical care or rent. The responses to this question provide another indicator of the constraints that households face, and it is therefore of interest to examine how these responses are correlated with selected measures of household well-being.

Household Trade-offs and Food Security.   Facing direct trade-offs among necessities is a strong indicator of food insecurity (Table 15.5.1).

As shown in Table 15.5.1, regardless of the kind of trade-offs, households that are food insecure with hunger are much more likely to indicate that they face the trade-off than are the food secure households. Specific results include:

- 10.5% of the households categorized as food secure, 31.4% of those categorized as food insecure without hunger, and 51.0% of those categorized as food insecure with hunger had to choose between food and medical care during the past year.

- 13.8% of the households categorized as food secure, 44.3% of those categorized as food insecure without hunger, and 63.1% of those categorized as food insecure with hunger had to choose between food and utilities (or heating fuel) during the past year.

- 9.8% of the households categorized as food secure, 35.0% of those categorized as food insecure without hunger, and 57.4% of those categorized as food insecure with hunger had to choose between food and rent (or mortgage) during the past year.

CH 15. SELECTED CROSS-TABULAR ANALYSIS

TABLE 15.5.1

FOOD SECURITY STATUS AND HOUSEHOLD TRADE-OFFS

	All Client Households	Food Security Status of Client Households		
		Food Secure	Food Insecure Without Hunger	Food Insecure with Hunger
Choose between food and medical care				
Yes	31.7%	10.5%	31.4%	51.0%
No	68.3%	89.5%	68.6%	49.0%
TOTAL	100.0%	100.0%	100.0%	100.0%
SAMPLE SIZE (N)	**51,402**	**15,206**	**19,103**	**17,093**
Choose between food and utilities or heating fuel				
Yes	41.5%	13.8%	44.3%	63.1%
No	58.5%	86.2%	55.7%	36.9%
TOTAL	100.0%	100.0%	100.0%	100.0%
SAMPLE SIZE (N)	**51,390**	**15,200**	**19,084**	**17,106**
Choose between food and rent or mortgage				
Yes	35.0%	9.8%	35.0%	57.4%
No	65.0%	90.2%	65.0%	42.6%
TOTAL	100.0%	100.0%	100.0%	100.0%
SAMPLE SIZE (N)	**51,356**	**15,184**	**19,083**	**17,089**

NOTES: Item nonresponses to all variables involved were excluded in calculating percentages and sample sizes.

Statistically significant based on chi-square test (d.f. = 2) at the 1% level.

Household Trade-offs and Household Structure. There is also a notable association between household structure and reporting direct trade-offs between necessities (Table 15.5.2).

TABLE 15.5.2

HAVING SENIORS OR CHILDREN AND HOUSEHOLD TRADE-OFFS

	All Households	Households with Seniors	Households with Children, No Seniors	One-Person Households with Neither Children nor Seniors	Households with Two or More People but with Neither Children nor Seniors
Choose between food and medical care[a]					
Yes	31.6%	28.7%	34.3%	28.6%	36.4%
No	68.4%	71.3%	65.7%	71.4%	63.6%
TOTAL	100.0%	100.0%	100.0%	100.0%	100.0%
SAMPLE SIZE (N)	**51,496**	**11,423**	**15,856**	**16,422**	**7,795**
Choose between food and utilities or heating fuel[b]					
Yes	41.4%	30.8%	52.4%	34.8%	47.5%
No	58.6%	69.2%	47.6%	65.2%	52.5%
TOTAL	100.0%	100.0%	100.0%	100.0%	100.0%
SAMPLE SIZE (N)	**51,484**	**11,428**	**15,861**	**16,402**	**7,793**
Choose between food and rent or mortgage[c]					
Yes	34.9%	19.5%	42.6%	34.7%	41.2%
No	65.1%	80.5%	57.4%	65.3%	58.8%
TOTAL	100.0%	100.0%	100.0%	100.0%	100.0%
SAMPLE SIZE (N)	**51,445**	**11,401**	**15,855**	**16,398**	**7,791**

NOTES: In calculating percentages and sample sizes, we excluded item nonresponses to all variables involved.

Statistically significant based on chi-square test (d.f. = 4) at the 1% level.

Many of the results shown in Table 15.5.2 mimic correlations seen earlier between income and household structure. In general, households with children are more likely than others to report having to make a trade-off between food and other necessities.

- 28.7% of households with seniors and 34.3% of households with children and no seniors reported making trade-offs between food and medical care, compared with 31.6% for the whole population.

- The comparable percentages for trade-offs between food and utilities were 30.8% for households with seniors and 52.4% for households with children but no seniors, compared with 41.4% for the whole population.

- For the trade-off between food and rent (or mortgage payments), 42.6% of households with children but no seniors had to face the trade-off, compared with only 19.5% of households with seniors.

15.6   FACTORS ASSOCIATED WITH NOT RECEIVING FOOD STAMPS

Given the importance of understanding why some households that need food stamp assistance fail to get it, another set of illustrative cross-tabulation tables examines the relationship between household structure and factors associated with not receiving food stamps (Table 15.6.1 and Table 15.6.2).

As Table 15.6.1 shows, households with children and no seniors are more likely than others to indicate that they were not getting food stamps because they think they are ineligible.

In particular:

- 57.9% of households with children but no seniors mentioned one or more reasons related to eligibility, compared with 46.4% of households with seniors.

- Elderly clients and households with elderly members were more likely than others to mention factors associated with program access, operation, and needs.

TABLE 15.6.1

REASONS THAT RESPONDENTS OR THEIR HOUSEHOLDS DO NOT
CURRENTLY RECEIVE FOOD STAMPS

Reasons That Respondents or Their Households DO NOT Currently Receive Food Stamps, Among the Ones Who Have Applied for Food Stamps[a]	Elderly Clients at Program Sites	Households with Seniors	Households with Children Younger than 18	Households with Children Ages 0-5
Factors associated with eligibility				
Ineligible income level				
All	42.9%	43.1%	49.0%	43.2%
Income 130% of federal poverty level or lower	31.7%	33.3%	37.6%	34.0%
Income higher than 130% of federal poverty level	9.5%	8.0%	9.3%	7.8%
Unknown	1.7%	1.8%	2.1%	1.5%
Change of household makeup	1.7%	2.0%	4.3%	4.7%
Time limit receiving for the help ran out	1.4%	2.6%	5.1%	5.7%
Citizenship status	0.5%	0.5%	1.7%	3.3%
SUBTOTAL[b]	45.7%	46.4%	57.9%	55.0%
Factors associated with program access and operation				
Too much hassle	18.3%	16.7%	12.1%	10.2%
Hard to get to food stamp office	7.5%	6.1%	5.6%	5.4%
SUBTOTAL	22.8%	20.4%	15.0%	12.8%
Factors associated with need				
No need for benefits	6.4%	6.0%	5.9%	5.0%
Others need benefits more	2.2%	2.0%	2.5%	1.8%
Need is only temporary	2.8%	3.8%	3.6%	2.8%
SUBTOTAL	10.2%	10.5%	9.7%	8.0%
Other Factors				
Other reasons	21.1%	22.2%	23.0%	28.3%
SAMPLE SIZE (N) – Respondents who have applied for but are not currently receiving food stamps	**2,226**	**2,979**	**5,928**	**2,567**

NOTE: In calculating percentages and sample sizes, we excluded item nonresponses to all variables involved.

[a]Multiple responses were accepted.

[b]The subtotal indicates the percentage of people who provided one or more component items as their responses; thus, it may differ from the sum of component items.

CH 15. SELECTED CROSS-TABULAR ANALYSIS

Somewhat different patterns hold for the analysis of reasons for never applying among

clients who said they had never applied (Table 15.6.2):

TABLE 15.6.2

REASONS WHY CLIENTS NEVER APPLIED FOR FOOD STAMPS

Reasons Why Respondents or Their Households Never Applied for Food Stamps[a]	Elderly Clients at Program Sites	Households with Seniors	Households with Children Younger than 18	Households with Children Ages 0-5
Factors associated with eligibility				
Don't think eligible because of income or assets				
All	37.9%	38.4%	34.0%	29.9%
Income 130% of federal poverty level or lower	24.3%	24.8%	21.8%	21.3%
Income higher than 130% of federal poverty level	10.3%	9.9%	9.0%	6.4%
Unknown	3.3%	3.7%	3.1%	2.2%
Don't think eligible because of citizenship status	1.2%	1.7%	10.4%	12.7%
Eligible for only a low benefit amount	3.9%	4.4%	3.7%	3.3%
SUBTOTAL[b]	41.7%	43.1%	45.7%	43.6%
Factors associated with program access and operation				
Don't know where to go or whom to contact to apply	4.7%	4.9%	6.2%	10.0%
Hard to get to the food stamp office	4.7%	4.8%	3.6%	4.7%
Application process is too long and complicated	3.8%	4.7%	5.9%	4.2%
Questions are too personal	1.2%	1.2%	2.1%	1.8%
Food stamp office staff are disrespectful	0.6%	1.8%	2.7%	3.4%
Food stamp office is unpleasant or in unsafe area	0.2%	0.5%	1.0%	0.5%
SUBTOTAL	13.6%	15.4%	17.8%	22.0%
Factors associated with need				
No need for benefit	19.9%	18.6%	9.0%	9.8%
Others need benefits more	7.7%	7.3%	5.5%	4.0%
Need is only temporary	0.8%	1.4%	3.6%	3.3%
SUBTOTAL	26.9%	25.4%	16.6%	16.0%
Factors associated with social stigma				
Feel embarrassed applying for benefits	3.1%	3.2%	3.4%	4.8%

TABLE 15.6.2 *(continued)*

Reasons Why Respondents or Their Households Never Applied for Food Stamps[a]	Elderly Clients at Program Sites	Households with Seniors	Households with Children Younger than 18	Households with Children Ages 0-5
Family or friends do not approve of my receiving benefits	0.2%	0.2%	1.4%	2.3%
Dislike relying on the government for assistance	2.5%	2.7%	2.7%	3.6%
Feel embarrassed using benefits	2.8%	2.7%	2.8%	3.4%
SUBTOTAL	7.7%	7.6%	8.0%	10.3%
Other factors				
Planning to apply, but not yet	1.3%	1.6%	5.0%	4.3%
Other	13.2%	13.6%	16.5%	16.5%
SAMPLE SIZE (N) – Respondents or their households who never applied for food stamps	**4,992**	**5,681**	**4,051**	**1,786**

Note: In calculating percentages and sample sizes, we excluded item nonresponses to all variables involved.

[a]Multiple responses were accepted.

[b]The subtotal indicates the percentage of people who provided one or more component items as their responses; thus it may differ from the sum of component items. See Appendix C for food stamp eligibility criteria.

- 22.0% of households with young children cited factors associated with program operation for not applying, compared with 15.4% of households with seniors.

- 25.4% of households with seniors, compared with 16.0% of households with young children indicated a reason associated with their financial needs.

15.7   ASSOCIATIONS BETWEEN FOOD STAMP RECEIPT AND RESPONSES TO INDIVIDUAL QUESTIONS ABOUT FOOD SECURITY

There are a number of reasons why food stamp receipt and food security might be associated. On the one hand, food stamp receipt may increase food security, other things equal. On the other hand, food insecurity may influence households to apply for food stamps. Other types of associations caused by both food stamp participation and food security being determined by other factors are also possible.

Table 15.7.1 examines the associations between responses to the food security questions in the client survey and their food stamp participation.

TABLE 15.7.1

FOOD STAMP RECEIPT AND RESPONSES TO SIX HOUSEHOLD FOOD SECURITY QUESTIONS

		Food Stamp Receipt Status of Households		
	All Client Households	Receiving Food Stamps	Apparently Eligible, not Receiving	Apparently Ineligible Because of Income, not Receiving[a]
Food didn't last; no money to buy more[b]				
Often true	32.8%	36.8%	32.4%	19.9%
Sometimes true	42.8%	43.6%	43.5%	36.1%
Never true	24.3%	19.6%	24.0%	44.0%
TOTAL	100.0%	100.0%	100.0%	100.0%
SAMPLE SIZE (N)	**48,196**	**18,902**	**24,573**	**4,721**
Couldn't afford to eat balanced meals[b]				
Often true	25.4%	25.4%	26.9%	17.9%
Sometimes true	41.2%	42.6%	41.8%	33.0%
Never true	33.3%	32.0%	31.3%	49.0%
TOTAL	100.0%	100.0%	100.0%	100.0%
SAMPLE SIZE (N)	**48,170**	**18,866**	**24,595**	**4,709**
Cut size/skip meals because not enough food[c]				
Almost every month	25.3%	28.6%	25.0%	14.1%

CH 15. SELECTED CROSS-TABULAR ANALYSIS

TABLE 15.7.1 *(continued)*

	All Client Households	Food Stamp Receipt Status of Households		
		Receiving Food Stamps	Apparently Eligible, not Receiving	Apparently Ineligible Because of Income, not Receiving[a]
Some months but not every month	18.9%	18.7%	19.5%	16.9%
Only one or two months	6.9%	7.1%	7.1%	5.8%
Never	48.8%	45.6%	48.4%	63.0%
TOTAL	100.0%	100.0%	100.0%	100.0%
SAMPLE SIZE (N)	**47,753**	**18,683**	**24,384**	**4,686**
Ever ate less than should because no money[d]				
Yes	52.9%	55.7%	53.9%	37.2%
No	47.1%	44.3%	46.1%	62.8%
TOTAL	100.0%	100.0%	100.0%	100.0%
SAMPLE SIZE (N)	**48,389**	**18,942**	**24,723**	**4,724**
Ever hungry but didn't eat because no money[d]				
Yes	39.5%	41.4%	40.7%	25.8%
No	60.5%	58.6%	59.3%	74.2%
TOTAL	100.0%	100.0%	100.0%	100.0%
SAMPLE SIZE (N)	**48,433**	**18,933**	**24,768**	**4,732**
Ever not eat for whole day because no money[d]				
Yes	26.9%	28.6%	27.8%	15.8%
No	73.1%	71.4%	72.2%	84.2%
TOTAL	100.0%	100.0%	100.0%	100.0%
SAMPLE SIZE (N)	**48,516**	**18,981**	**24,794**	**4,741**

NOTE: In calculating percentages and sample sizes, we excluded item nonresponses to all variables involved.

[a]Eligibility was determined based on the previous month's income alone.

[b]Statistically significant based on chi-square test (d.f. = 4) at the 1% level.

[c]Statistically significant based on chi-square test (d.f. = 6) at the 1% level.

[d]Statistically significant based on chi-square test (d.f. = 2) at the 1% level.

Overall, households receiving food stamps and households that appear to be eligible but are not receiving food stamps have similar response patterns. Further, both these groups are substantially more likely to provide responses that indicate food insecurity than the households who appear to be ineligible for food stamps.

- 36.8% of food stamp recipients and 32.4% of apparently eligible nonparticipants said that it was "often true" that food didn't last and there was no money to buy more; the comparable percentage for apparently ineligible A2H clients was much lower (19.9%).

- 55.7% of food stamp recipients and 53.9% of apparently eligible nonparticipants said they eat less than they should because they lack money to buy food; the comparable figure for the apparently ineligible respondents was 37.2%.

- Similar patterns are observed for the responses to the other questions.

CH 15. SELECTED CROSS-TABULAR ANALYSIS

16. COMPARISON OF SELECTED VARIABLES ACROSS FOUR A2H STUDIES

In this chapter, we present a limited number of comparisons of selected descriptive variables collected across each of the four national studies sponsored by A2H: 1993, 1997, 2001, and the current study, 2005.

Because of differences in certain factors (including food bank coverage, survey questionnaire wording, survey response rates, sampling methods, application of sampling weights, and general variable definitions), data from 1993, 1997, 2001, and 2005 are not directly comparable. Nevertheless, as long as these limitations are kept in mind, it is of general interest to examine the trends over time for selected key variables as a preliminary step toward investigating what system changes may have occurred in the A2H National Network. Following is a comparison of a limited number of variables at the three points in time.

16.1   COMPARISON OF SELECTED CLIENT CHARACTERISTICS

Table 16.1.1 presents selected characteristics of clients served by the A2H National Network for the 1993, 1997, 2001, and 2005 A2H national research studies: the percentages of clients who are currently employed, clients who are currently receiving food stamps, and clients without a place to live.

The percentage of food pantry clients currently working has gradually increased between 1993 and 2001, but declined between 2001 and 2005. In 2005, 22% of the pantry clients interviewed at the A2H-affiliated emergency food programs were employed, which is about three percentage points lower than in 2001. A similar trend was found among the kitchen clients, but the percentage employed in 2005 is higher at 25% than among pantry clients. There was little change in the percentage employed among shelter clients between 1993 and 2005 studies.

TABLE 16.1.1

SELECTED CLIENT CHARACTERISTICS IN NATIONAL DATA:
1993, 1997, 2001, AND 2005

	1993	1997	2001	2005
Percentage of clients interviewed employed[a]				
Pantries	17.9%	20.7%	24.7%	21.9%
Kitchens	16.6%	18.9%	27.7%	25.3%
Shelters	22.2%	23.0%	22.0%	22.4%
Percentage receiving food stamps				
Pantries	48.3%	41.7%	31.0%	35.8%
Kitchens	37.9%	36.3%	23.6%	35.0%
Shelters	49.2%	42.4%	25.6%	31.7%
Percentage homeless				
Pantries	4.8%	4.1%	2.8%	3.2%
Kitchens	27.9%	26.4%	26.3%	26.1%
Shelters	77.2%	75.8%	75.7%	80.3%

NOTE: Data for 1993, 1997, and 2001 are taken from previous Second Harvest reports. Data for 2005 are taken from tables presented in earlier chapters of this report.

[a]Based on clients directly interviewed. Percentages do not include other members of the household.

Estimates of food stamp participation among A2H clients showed a considerable decrease during periods between previous studies, but this trend is reversed in 2005: among the pantry clients, 36% are receiving food stamps, compared with 31% in 2001. A similar pattern holds across client groups served by different program types and mirrors national trends.[44]

The trends in the percentage of clients without a place to live vary by the program type. Small percentages (less than 5%) of pantry clients were found to be homeless in all four studies. This small number is not surprising, since pantry clients typically need a place to store and prepare food. The percentage of homeless clients at kitchen sites is much higher than at pantries

---

[44] Llobrera, Joseph. *Food Stamp Caseloads Are Rising*. Washington, DC: Center on Budget and Policy Priorities, August 16, 2004.

and shows little change across four points in time, in the range of 26% to 28%. On the other hand, as many as over 80% of shelter clients are homeless in 2005, up from 76% to 77% during the years of previous studies.

16.2 COMPARISON OF SELECTED PROGRAM CHARACTERISTICS

Table 16.2.1 presents selected characteristics of the emergency food programs in the A2H National Network. To examine possible trends in those variables, we present results from the 1993, 1997, 2001, and 2005 A2H national research studies together in the table.

The percentage of the programs run by faith-based or religion-affiliated organizations appears to have gradually increased through 2001, but it dropped somewhat in 2005. The upward trend during the previous study periods is most notable among the shelter programs. Compared with 1993, when only 28% of the shelters were run by faith-based agencies, as many as 43% were run by faith-based agencies in 2001 and 2005, an increase of 15 percentage points. Although not as dramatic, there was a steady increase of about 5 points in the percentage of pantry programs operated by faith-based agencies between 1997 and 2001, followed by a small decrease in 2005. The percentage of kitchen programs in this category was stable, at 71% until 2005, when it declined to 66%.

As for the percentage of the programs that have been in operation for 10 or more years, the pantries and the kitchens show consistent upward trends from 1993 to 2005. These figures indicate a stable network of emergency food programs in A2H. The share of shelters at least 10 years old, on the other hand, decreased between 1993 and 1997 (from 43% to 36%), then grew dramatically to 65% in 2001, which suggests that many shelters opened between 1987 and 1991. The percentage is maintained at a similar level (66%) in 2005.

TABLE 16.2.1

SELECTED AGENCY CHARACTERISTICS IN 1993, 1997, 2001, AND 2005

	1993	1997	2001	2005
Percentage faith-based				
Pantries	71.1%	72.0%	75.7%	74.3%
Kitchens	70.8%	70.9%	71.4%	65.5%
Shelters	28.0%	29.5%	43.0%	42.9%
Percentage more than 10 years old				
Pantries	41.5%	44.0%	48.5%	49.8%
Kitchens	34.7%	40.4%	52.2%	55.8%
Shelters	42.8%	35.7%	64.7%	65.9%
Percentage of food received from food bank				
Pantries	60.6%	61.4%	58.5%	74.0%
Kitchens	40.9%	45.4%	43.1%	48.8%
Shelters	37.6%	38.3%	35.8%	41.2%

NOTE: Data for 1993, 1997, and 2001 are taken from two previous Second Harvest reports. Data for 2005 are taken from tables presented in earlier chapters of this report.

The percentage of the food received from the affiliated food banks had been fairly stable over the three earlier time periods for all three program types. However, in 2005, this share moved up notably for all program types. The average percentage of food received from food banks increased by 16 points, to 74%, for pantries; by 6 percentage points, to 49%, for kitchens; and by 5 percentage points, to 41%, for shelters.

CH 16. COMPARISON OF SELECTED VARIABLES ACROSS FOUR A2H STUDIES

APPENDIX A

SIMULATING 2005 METHODS ON 2001 DATA

To evaluate further the effects of changes in methodology between the 2001 and 2005 studies, we have, to the extent possible, applied 2005 methods to the 2001 data to examine what results would have been found in 2001 if the new methods had been used. This appendix summarizes the results.

To conduct the analysis, we began with the 2001 participant estimates as presented in the 2001 report and then simulated what would have happened to these estimates if certain of the 2005 methods had been employed. For instance, to simulate the tighter ineligibility screening applied to providers in 2005, we increased the assumed rates of provider ineligibility in the 2001 data to bring these rates up to the observed 2005 levels.

Four components of the methodological changes were simulated:

1. Increased provider eligibility screening (which decreases the 2001 estimates)

2. Consideration of the fact that some 2001 providers were open longer than the on-site interviewing period (which increases the 2001 estimates)

3. Recognition of the fact that some providers are open less than once a week (which decreases the 2001 estimates)

4. Improvement in the analytic treatment of multiple interviewing days at the same provider (which decreases the 2001 estimate)

Note that in some instances the 2001 data were not sufficiently detailed to simulate the changed methodology fully. It is also possible that not all changes have been recognized and included in the simulation. For these reasons, the simulations should be regarded as likely underestimates of the full effects of the changes made in 2005. They do, however, provide some indication of their approximate magnitude.

In simulating the changes, to facilitate estimating sampling variation, we have focused on the sampling units as they were defined in the studies in both years. There are households for pantry users and adults using the provider's services for both kitchens and pantries.

The results are shown in Table A.1.

The top panel of the table (the first three rows of numbers) shows how results just for participating food banks. The bottom panel shows results after using the 1.5 and 1.23 "expansion factors" to convert to all A2H food banks in 2001 and 2005, respectively.

In general, after the simulations, the 2001 numbers remain higher than the 2005 estimates. This is due, at least in part, to the difficulties of fully carrying out the simulation, as noted earlier. However, in no instance is there a statistically significant difference between the adjusted 2001 estimate and the 2005 estimate. In general, these results are supportive of the belief that the differences between the 2001 and the 2005 data are due largely to the methodological changes that were made.

TABLE A.1

SIMULATING 2005 METHODS ON 2001 DATA

	Original 2001 Estimates	2001 Estimates Adjusted for 2005 Methods	2005 Estimates
Participating food banks only			
Pantry clients (households)	1,425,000	1,183,000	1,237,000
Kitchen clients (adults)	494,000	416,000	455,000
Pantry clients (adults)	190,000	151,000	181.000
All A2H food banks			
Pantry clients (households)	2,138,000	1,774,000 (s.e. = 124,000)	1,525,000 (se = 48,000)
Kitchen clients (adults)	741,000	624,000 (s.e. = 75,000)	547,000 (s.e. = 30,000)
Pantry clients (adults)	285,000	226,000 (s.e. = 52,000)	223,000 (s.e. = 12,000)

APPENDIX B

**DETAILS OF CALCULATION OF THE NUMBER OF PEOPLE
SERVED IN SUBGROUPS OF A2H CLIENTS**

Much of the body of this report examines the percentage distribution of A2H clients by various characteristics and categories. In certain instances, however, *absolute numbers* of clients are also reported.[45] For easy reference, all absolute number tables are numbered with an added suffix "N" (for example, Table 5.3.2N).

We calculated estimates of absolute numbers of clients by applying percentage distributions to a table containing counts of total households and persons, disaggregated by A2H provider type and by whether the people are adults or children. This appendix provides details of how this underlying table, shown as Table B.1, was derived.

The first row for pantry clients, 8.6 million, is the estimated total number of A2H adult clients at program sites, based on the midpoint of estimates presented in Chapter 4 of this report. Since the client base of pantries includes all members of households, this figure itself is of limited use, except that the number of households served by A2H affiliated pantries is equal to this number. This is because the sampling frame for pantry clients was constructed to use the household rather than the individual as the unit by interviewing only one adult from each sampled household. This explains why the first row of the pantry adult column is equal to the third row of the pantry total column. Using this total number of households and percentage information contained in this report, we calculated the number of households with specific characteristics, such as households with at least one child younger than age 18 or households currently receiving food stamps.

The second row of the pantry total column, 23.2 million, is a midpoint of the estimated total number of persons served by A2H programs. The details of its derivation are discussed in

---

[45] Numbers presented in Table B.1 and tables with a suffix "N" are based on the midpoint of estimated ranges of numbers of different clients or households served in any given year. Readers should consider standard errors and confidence intervals associated with these estimates, which are presented in Appendix A.

Chapter 4 and Appendix A of this report. Using the age distribution presented in Table 5.3.2 among pantry clients, we broke down the total number into the number of adults (66%) and that of children (34%).

TABLE B.1

ESTIMATED NUMBER OF DIFFERENT PEOPLE AND HOUSEHOLDS SERVED IN A GIVEN YEAR

	Adults	Children	Total
Pantry Clients			
Number of clients at program sites	8,600,000	n.a.	8,600,000
Number of all members of client households	15,300,000	7,900,000	23,200,000
Number of client households	n.a.	n.a.	8,600,000
Kitchen Clients			
Number of clients at program sites	1,000,000	300,000	1,300,000
Number of all members of client households	1,500,000	400,000	1,900,000
Number of client households	n.a.	n.a.	1,000,000
Shelter Clients			
Number of clients at program sites	670,000	130,000	800,000
Number of all members of client households	820,000	120,000	940,000
Number of client households	n.a.	n.a.	670,000

NOTE: Number of pantry programs: 29,647
        Number of kitchen programs: 5,601
        Number of shelter programs: 4,143

n.a. = not applicable.

As for kitchens and shelters, the client base was defined to be the persons who were present at program sites. The midpoint of the estimated total number of clients is 1.3 million for the kitchens, and 0.8 million for the shelters. These estimates also include children who come to kitchens and shelters accompanied by adults. As discussed in Chapter 4, we estimate that there are, on average, 3 children per 10 adults at kitchen programs and 2 children per 10 adults at shelter programs. The breakdowns of adults and children in the first row for the kitchens and shelters were based on those estimates.

We obtained the totals in the second row for the kitchen and the shelter columns by multiplying the number of adult clients in the first row by the average household sizes (1.9 for kitchen clients and 1.4 for shelter clients). Then, the age distribution in Table 5.3.2 was used to break the total into adults and children. For the third row, we used the number of adults at the program sites to approximate the number of client households both for the kitchens and for the shelters.[46]

---

[46] It is an approximation because more than one adult from the same household could have been interviewed at kitchen and shelter sites.

APPENDIX C

FOOD STAMP ELIGIBILITY CRITERIA

FOOD STAMP ELIGIBILITY CRITERIA

Source: http://www.fns.usda.gov/fsp/applicant_recipients/resources.htm

For 2005, the following food stamp eligibility rules applied to households in the 48 contiguous states and the District of Columbia.

A. RESOURCES (RULES ON RESOURCE LIMITS)

Households may have $2,000 in countable resources, such as a bank account, or $3,000 in countable resources if at least one person is age 60 or older or is disabled. However, certain resources are *not* counted, such as a home and lot, the resources of people who receive Supplemental Security Income (SSI), the resources of people who receive Temporary Assistance for Needy Families (TANF) (formerly AFDC), and most retirement (pension) plans.

A licensed vehicle is *not* counted if:

- It is used for income-producing purposes
- It is annually producing income consistent with its fair market value
- It is needed for long distance travel for work (other than daily commute)
- It is used as the home
- It is needed to transport a physically disabled household member
- It is needed to carry most of the household's fuel or water
- The household has little equity in the vehicle (because of money owed on the vehicle, it would bring no more than $1,500 if sold)

For the following licensed vehicles, the fair market value over $4,650 is counted:

- One per adult household member
- Any other vehicle a household member under 18 drives to work, school, job training, or to look for work

For all other vehicles, the fair market value over $4,650 or the equity value, whichever is more, is counted as a resource.

B. INCOME (RULES ON INCOME LIMITS)

Households must meet income tests *unless* all members are receiving Title IV (TANF), SSI, or, in some places, general assistance.

Most households must meet both the gross and net income tests, but a household with an elderly person or a person who is receiving certain types of disability payments only has to meet the net income test. Gross income means a household's total, nonexcluded income, before any deductions have been made. Net income means gross income minus allowable deductions.

Households, except those noted, that have income over the amounts listed below cannot get food stamps.

People in Household	Gross Monthly Income Limits	Net Monthly Income Limits
1	$1,037	$798
2	$1,390	$1,070
3	$1,744	$1,341
4	$2,097	$1,613
5	$2,450	$1,885
6	$2,803	$2,156
7	$3,156	$2,428
8	$3,509	$2,700
Each additional person	+$354	+$272

Note: Updated October 2005, effective through September 2006.

C. DEDUCTIONS (RULES ON ALLOWABLE DEDUCTIONS FROM INCOME)

Gross income means a household's total, nonexcluded income, before any deductions have been made. Net income means gross income minus allowable deductions.[47]

---

[47] As of October 2005, effective through September 2006.

- A 20% deduction from earned income

- A standard deduction of $134 for most households (higher for larger households, and in Alaska, Hawaii, and Guam)

- A dependent care deduction when needed for work, training, or education—but not more than $200 for each child under age 2 and not more than $175 for each other dependent

- Medical expenses for elderly or disabled members which are more than $35 for the month if they are not paid by insurance or someone else

- Legally owed child support payments

- Excess shelter costs that are more than half the household's income after the other deductions. Allowable costs include the cost of fuel to heat and cook with, electricity, water, the basic fee for one telephone, rent or mortgage payments, and taxes on the home. The amount of the shelter deduction cannot be more than $400 unless one person in the household is elderly or disabled. (The limit is higher in Alaska, Hawaii, and Guam.)

D. WORK AND ALIENS (RULES ON WORK, AND LEGAL IMMIGRANTS)

With some exceptions, able-bodied adults between 16 and 60 must register for work, accept suitable employment, and take part in an employment and training program to which they are referred by the food stamp office. Failure to comply with these requirements can result in disqualification from the program. In addition, able-bodied adults between 18 and 50 who do not have any dependent children can get food stamps for only 3 months in a 36-month period if they do not work or participate in a workfare or employment and training program other than job search. This requirement is waived in some locations.

E. IMMIGRANT ELIGIBILITY REQUIREMENTS

The 2002 Farm bill restores food stamp eligibility to most legal immigrants that:

- Have lived in the country five years

- Are receiving disability-related assistance or benefits, regardless of entry date

- Starting October 1, 2003, are children regardless of entry date

Certain non-citizens, such as those admitted for humanitarian reasons and those admitted for permanent residence, are also eligible for the program. Eligible household members can get food stamps even if there are other members of the household that are not eligible.

Non-citizens that are in the United States temporarily, such as students, are not eligible.

A number of states have their own programs to provide benefits to immigrants who do not meet the regular Food Stamp Program eligibility requirements.

APPENDIX D

**SOURCES OF INFORMATION SHOWN IN THE CHARTS AND TABLES IN
CHAPTERS 5 THROUGH 14**

Table	Client Question	Agency Question
5.1.1	Client data	
5.2.1	2. Sex 3. Age 4. Relationship 6. Employment 7. Are there any children age 0-5 years in household? 11. Are you Spanish, Latino, or of Hispanic descent or origin? 11a. Would that be Mexican, Puerto Rican, Cuban, some other Spanish, Hispanic, or Latino group? 12. What is your race?	
5.3.1	2. Sex 3. Age 5. Citizen	
5.3.2	2. Sex 3. Age 5. Citizen 6a. Are there more than 10 people in the household? 6b. How many of those people are children less than 18 years old?	
5.4.1	9. Are you married, living with someone as married, widowed, divorced, separated, or have you never been married?	
5.5.1	10. What is the highest level of education you completed?	
5.6.1	11. Are you Spanish, Latino, or of Hispanic descent or origin? 11a. Would that be Mexican, Puerto Rican, Cuban, some other Spanish, Hispanic, or Latino group? 12. What is your race?	
5.7.1	3. Age 6. Employment	

Table	Client Question	Agency Question
5.7.2	6. Employment 12a. Is respondent working? 13. You mentioned that you are not working now. How long has it been since you worked? 14a. Is this job a managerial or professional job? 15. Are you participating in any gov't sponsored job training or work experience programs, such as Welfare to Work or the food stamp employment training program?	
5.8.1	Federal Poverty Level Table	
5.8.2.1	29. What was your total income last month before taxes? 29a. What was your household's total income for last month?	
5.8.3.1	29. What was your total income last month before taxes? 30. What was your household's main source of income last month?	
5.8.3.2	6. Employment 25. Did you get money in the last month from any of the following….? 29. What was your total income last month before taxes?	
5.8.4.1	29. What was your total income last month before taxes? 31. What was your household's total income before taxes and other deductions last year from all sources, including Social Security and other gov't programs?	
5.9.1.1	16. Please tell me the kind of place where you now live. 17. Do you own, rent, live free with someone else? 18. Were you late paying your last month's rent or mortgage? 81. Does your household receive Section 8 or Public Housing Assistance?	
5.9.2.1	19. Do you have access to a place to prepare a meal, a working telephone, and a car that runs?	

Table	Client Question	Agency Question
6.1.1	42. "The food I/we bought just didn't last, and I/we didn't have money to get more." (Often, sometimes, never true) 43. "I/We couldn't afford to eat balanced meals." (Often, sometimes, never true) 44. In the last 12 months, did you ever cut the size of your meals or skip meals because there wasn't enough money for food? 44a. How often did this happen? 45. In the last 12 months, did you ever eat less than you felt you should because there wasn't enough money to buy food? 46. In the last 12 months, were you ever hungry but didn't eat because you couldn't afford enough food?	
6.1.2	42. "The food I/we bought just didn't last, and I/we didn't have money to get more." (Often, sometimes, never true) 43. "I/We couldn't afford to eat balanced meals." (Often, sometimes, never true) 44. In the last 12 months, did you ever cut the size of your meals or skip meals because there wasn't enough money for food? 44a. How often did this happen? 45. In the last 12 months, did you ever eat less than you felt you should because there wasn't enough money to buy food? 46. In the last 12 months, were you ever hungry but didn't eat because you couldn't afford enough food?	
6.2.1	42. "The food I/we bought just didn't last, and I/we didn't have money to get more." (Often, sometimes, never true) 43. "I/We couldn't afford to eat balanced meals." (Often, sometimes, never true)	

Table	Client Question	Agency Question
6.3.1	44a. How often did this happen? 45. In the last 12 months, did you ever eat less than you felt you should because there wasn't enough money to buy food? 46. In the last 12 months, were you ever hungry but didn't eat because you couldn't afford enough food? 47. In the last 12 months, did you ever not eat for a whole day because there wasn't enough money for food?	
6.4.1	3. Age 6b. How many of the other people in your household are children less than 18 years old? 49. "My child was not eating enough because I/we just couldn't afford enough food." (Often, sometimes, never true) 50. In the last 12 months, did your child ever skip meals because there wasn't enough money for food? 51. In the last 12 months, was your child ever hungry but you just couldn't afford more food?	
6.5.1	52. In the past 12 months, have you or anyone in your household every had to choose between: paying for food and paying for medicine or medical care; paying for food and paying for utilities or heating fuel; paying for food and paying for rent or mortgage?	
7.1.1	32. Have you ever applied for Food Stamps? 33. Are you receiving Food Stamps now? 34. Did you receive Food Stamps in the past 12 months? 36. How long have you been receiving Food Stamps? 37. How many weeks do your Food Stamps usually last?	
7.2.1	38. Why haven't you applied for the Food Stamp Program?	
7.3.1	35. Why don't you receive Food Stamps now?	

Table	Client Question	Agency Question
7.4.1	7a. Do any of your younger-than-school-age children go to day care? 8. Does the government pay part of the cost of day care? 41. In which, if any, of the following programs do you currently participate?	
7.5.1	26. Did you receive general assistance, welfare, or TANF at any time in the past two years? 27. Was that assistance ever stopped during the past two years? 28. Why was your assistance stopped?	
7.6.1	40. Where do you do most of your grocery shopping?	
8.1.1	20. Would you say your own health is excellent, very good, good, fair, or poor? 21. Is anyone in your household in poor health?	
8.2.1	22a-f. Do you have any of the following kinds of health insurance? 23. Do you have unpaid medical or hospital bills? 24. In the past 12 months, have you been refused medical care because you could not pay or because you had a Medicaid or Medical Assistance card?	
9.1.1	56. How many different food pantries gave you food in the past month? 57. How many different soup kitchens gave you meals in the past month?	
9.2.1	53. Please rate how satisfied you are with the food that you and others in your household receive here. 54. When you come here, how often are you treated with respect by the staff who distribute food?	
9.3.1	55. If this agency weren't here to help you with food, what would you do?	
10.1.1		Agency data
10.2.1		1. Record the total number of emergency shelters, pantries, kitchens, and other programs you currently operate.
10.3.1		1. Record the total number of emergency shelters, pantries, kitchens, and other programs you currently operate.

Table	Client Question	Agency Question
10.4.1		3b. In what year did each selected program open?
10.5.1		4. For each selected program, please indicate which of the following services, if any, are currently being provided.
10.5.2		4. For each selected program, please indicate which of the following services, if any, are currently being provided.
10.5.3		27. Does your agency operate any of the following types of facilities?
10.6.1		28. Type of agency.
10.7.1		18. Do the selected programs currently serve any of the following groups?
10.8.1		7. Compared to 3 years ago, that is, 2001, is this program providing food to more, fewer, same number of clients?
10.9.1		19. In which of the following ways does the client mix change during the year for any of the selected programs?
11.1.1		6. During a typical week, approximately how many meals are served and/or bags or boxes of food distributed by each of the selected programs? 6a. How much does a typical bag or box usually weigh?
11.2.1		6c. How many different persons or households did you serve on the last day you were open? And how many meals were served and/or bags or boxes of food distributed by each of the selected programs on that day?
12.1.1		17. Is the continued operation of the selected programs threatened by one or more serious problems?
12.2.1		13. During the past year, about how often did each of the selected programs have to reduce meal portions or reduce the quantity of food in food packages because of a lack of food?

Table	Client Question	Agency Question
12.3.1		9. During the past year, did the selected programs turn away any clients for <u>any</u> reason? 10. For which of the following reasons did each selected program turn clients away? 12. During the past year, approximately how many clients did each selected program turn away?
12.3.2		11. What were each selected program's two most frequent reasons for turning away clients?
12.4.1		14. In your opinion, during a *typical week,* how much *more* food, if any, does each of the selected programs need in order to adequately meet their demand for food? Your best estimate is fine.
13.1.1		8. For each selected program, approximately what percent of the distributed food comes from the food bank? 8a. Do the selected programs distribute government or USDA commodities? 8b. Approximately what percent of the distributed food comes from other sources?
13.2.1		15. Currently, how many <u>paid</u> staff are employed by each of the selected programs? 16. During the past week, how many volunteers assisted and the number of volunteer hours for each selected program.
13.3.1		23. Please indicate for each selected program, which of the following categories of products are <u>purchased</u> with cash from sources other than your food bank?
14.1.1		24. What categories of food and non-food products do you <u>need</u> that you are not getting now, or need more of from your food bank to meet your clients' needs?
14.2.1		25. If the food supply you receive from your food bank were eliminated, how much of an impact would this have on your program?
14.3.1		26. Does your program need additional assistance in any of the following areas?